THE STRANGE GENIUS OF IGNATIUS DONNELLY

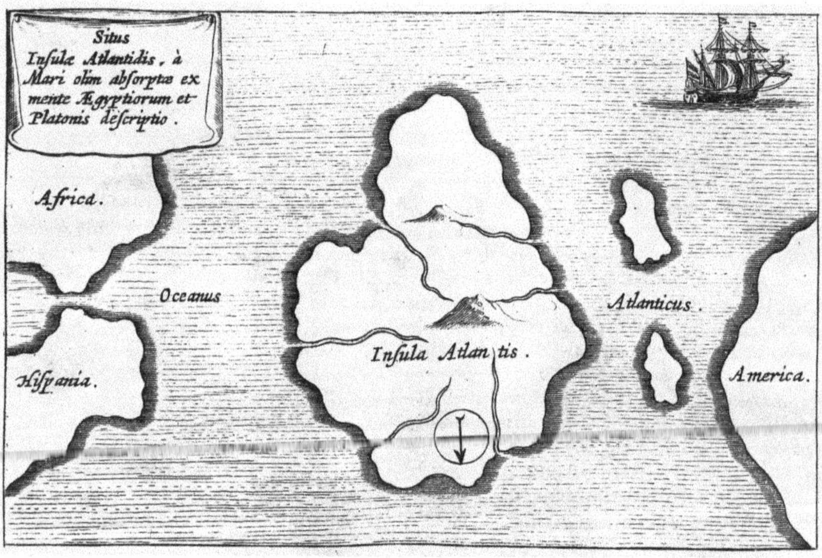

FIGURE 1. Illustration of the island kingdom of Atlantis, from *Mundus Subterraneus*, by Athanasius Kircher (1678).

THE STRANGE GENIUS OF IGNATIUS DONNELLY

THE POPULIST WHO DEBUNKED SHAKESPEARE AND FOUND ATLANTIS

ZACHARY MICHAEL JACK

NORTHERN ILLINOIS UNIVERSITY PRESS
An imprint of
CORNELL UNIVERSITY PRESS
Ithaca and London

First published 2024 by Cornell University Press

Printed in the United States of America

Library of Congress Cataloging-in-Publication Data

Names: Jack, Zachary Michael, 1973- author.
Title: The strange genius of Ignatius Donnelly : the populist who debunked Shakespeare and found Atlantis / Zachary Michael Jack.
Description: Ithaca : Northern Illinois University Press, an imprint of Cornell University Press, 2024. | Includes bibliographical references and index.
Identifiers: LCCN 2024008299 (print) | LCCN 2024008300 (ebook) | ISBN 9781501776939 (hardcover) | ISBN 9781501776946 (epub) | ISBN 9781501776953 (pdf)
Subjects: LCSH: Donnelly, Ignatius, 1831–1901. | Donnelly, Ignatius, 1831–1901—Political and social views.
Classification: LCC PS1545.D55 Z73 2024 (print) | LCC PS1545.D55 (ebook) | DDC 813/.4—dc23/eng/20240304
LC record available at https://lccn.loc.gov/2024008299
LC ebook record available at https://lccn.loc.gov/2024008300

For Ignatius Donnelly, in memoriam,
and for the many
who dare to dream of a better,
more equitable tomorrow

Contents

Acknowledgments *ix*

Author's Note *xi*

Introduction: On the Trail of the Sage of Nininger 1

1. The Making of a Midwestern Sage 7
2. *Atlantis: The Antediluvian World* 27
3. *Ragnarok: The Age of Fire and Gravel* 50
4. The Shakespearean Cipher 65
5. *The Great Cryptogram* 85
6. *Caesar's Column* 114
7. *Doctor Huguet* 135
8. *The Golden Bottle* 154
9. *Donnelliana* and *The American People's Money* 164
10. *The Cipher in the Plays, and on the Tombstone* 191

Notes *205*

Selected Bibliography *225*

Index *229*

Acknowledgments

Special thanks to the Faculty Development and Recognition Committee (FDRC) at North Central College for the research and writing grant that enabled the completion of this book, and to the Minnesota Historical Society for the exhibits and editions that proved indispensable to it, including the journal *Minnesota History* and the Minnesota Digital Newspaper Hub.

Author's Note

To enhance the readability of this book, efforts have been made, where practical, to guard against the proliferation of numbered endnotes, especially in paragraphs that draw multiple contiguous references from a single cited source, in the manner traditionally indicated by "Ibid." Except where noted, all materials from the Donnelly Manuscript Collection appearing herein are cited from Martin Ridge's foundational work, *Ignatius Donnelly: The Portrait of a Politician* (Chicago: University of Chicago Press, 1962).

THE STRANGE GENIUS OF IGNATIUS DONNELLY

Introduction

On the Trail of the Sage of Nininger

Ignatius Donnelly—three-term US congressman, lieutenant governor of Minnesota, popular author of bestselling dystopian and speculative fiction, father of American populism, popularizer of the Shakespeare authorship controversy, pioneering enigmatologist, proponent of the theory of Atlantis, People's Party candidate for vice president of the United States, Sage of Nininger, Minnesota—defies categorization. In the preface to *Donnelliana*, his first biographer, Everett Fish, observes that "Donnelly's career had been so active, he had lived through so many and such important events, and had taken such an active part in them all, that I felt it would require years of time, and a volume of hundreds of pages, to do justice to his life and acts."[1]

Though he was ridiculed by his detractors as a "crank," many of Donnelly's most compelling theories have proven prescient since his death on January 1, 1901. His controversial belief in a vast island continent submerged by cataclysm beneath the Atlantic Ocean has gained credence in a number of peer-reviewed twenty-first-century studies, most recently in the work of the geologist Douwe van Hinsbergen of Utrecht University in the Netherlands, whose research suggests a lost continent buried beneath Italy and Greece. Donnelly's notion of a catastrophic comet strike on earth, dismissed by many as ludicrous when he first described it in his 1882 nonfiction book

Ragnarok, likewise finds resonance in the resurgent study of near-earth objects (NEOs).

Donnelly's iconoclastic hypothesis that Shakespeare did not author the plays that made him famous has found new converts in a digital age. While twenty-first-century lexical analysis has not yet confirmed Francis Bacon as the clandestine pen behind the most influential works in Western literature, it has established to the satisfaction of many scholars the hand of multiple authors in the Bard's literary canon. As recently as 2019, the Bacon theory gained new momentum, too, with the publication by Routledge of *Francis Bacon's Contribution to Shakespeare: A New Attribution Method*, by Barry R. Clarke. Using computerized textual analysis, including searches of fifty thousand texts published prior to 1700, Clarke concludes that Bacon contributed significantly to *The Tempest* and *Love's Labour's Lost.* His findings have convinced Sir Mark Rylance, the first artistic director of Shakespeare's Globe in London, of the fundamental soundness of the Baconian theory that Donnelly popularized in the 1880s. Sounding very much like a twenty-first-century Donnelly, Rylance writes in the foreword to Clarke's volume, "Thirty years on, I continue to be regularly and passionately attacked . . . for my doubt about the attribution of the works of Shakespeare to the uneducated man from Stratford-on-Avon."[2] The esteemed editors of the *New Oxford Shakespeare* agree, finding the lexical evidence compelling enough to credit Bacon's contemporary Christopher Marlowe as coauthor of the three *Henry VI* plays.

In politics, Donnelly's cautionary tales illustrating the dangers of income inequality, racial discrimination, and violent domestic unrest in the United States have proven prophetic. His dire warnings against American dictators and their makeshift armies of violent supporters, first expressed in his book-length speculative fiction *Caesar's Column*, ring as true today as they did in the Gilded Age. Donnelly's singular prescience on the page no doubt accounts for his novel's phenomenal sales, estimated at nearly three quarters of a million copies as of 2003.[3] In the preface to the 2017 edition of his book *The Populist Persuasion*, the historian Michael Kazin asserts that "nearly everyone who wrote about the fate of the United States and Europe seemed to agree that 'populism' was on the rise" in the period between the great recession of 2007 and Donald Trump's inauguration in 2017. In Kazin's book, Donnelly is one of the most emblematic examples of the prototypical and perhaps purest type of American populism, the brand that "directs its ire exclusively upward at corporate elites and their enablers in government who have allegedly betrayed the interests of the men and women who do the nation's essential work."[4] Such populists, the author points out, do vital work, then as now, holding the country to its original promise, muckraking where necessary for the common good, performing a vital service to the nation. Unsurprisingly, Donnelly figures prominently in Kazin's account of the movement's formative years, both as pioneering charismatic crusader against the American plutocracy and as author of the famed Omaha Platform of 1892, the definitive statement Kazin calls the most widely circulated populist credo of all time.

In the century-plus since *Donnelliana* was published, relatively few biographers have embarked on the difficult task that so daunted Everett Fish. In 1962's *Ignatius Donnelly: The Portrait of a Politician*, Martin Ridge undertakes what is widely considered the first serious scholarly biography of Donnelly as a political figure. While *Ignatius Donnelly* surely sets the gold standard, its author chooses to focus on Donnelly the public servant and statesman rather than on Donnelly the author and sage, as he traces Donnelly's political evolution from his early days as a lawyer in Philadelphia to his failed vice presidential campaign on the People's Party ticket of 1900. In this book I focus instead on the subject as author, populist visionary, and "crank," beginning with his breakthrough nonfiction book, *Atlantis: The Antediluvian World* (1882), and concluding with his last published work, *The Cipher in the Plays, and on the Tombstone* (1899). I opt to begin *in medias res* with Donnelly's midlife transformation from frustrated (and some said "has-been") politician to world-renowned Sage of Nininger—a career shift that stands as perhaps the most complete professional transformation of any American politician ever to hold high office. While there have been cases of successful American actors and entertainers who later became prominent politicians (Ronald Reagan and Donald Trump spring to mind), the reverse is far more rare: the nationally prominent public servant who, later in life, publishes multiple bestselling works of fiction and nonfiction. It is Donnelly the author-politician that I seek to illuminate here, and to that end I devote significant time to each of the books he published while campaigning for his political reform agenda. It is by virtue of these books, after all, that he became a household name not just in the United States but also in Europe and the United Kingdom, where *Atlantis* and *The Great Cryptogram* earned him fame and infamy.

In the closing chapter of his biography, Ridge makes the provocative claim that the Sage of Nininger nearly qualifies as an American folk hero. True to the folk hero archetype, Donnelly eagerly matched wits with the elite and the entitled as a complicated character whose sundry and often shifting alliances forever kept his critics guessing and grumbling. Allied with a bevy of antithetical political parties throughout his long life, he is perhaps the only prominent American politician to have been at one time or another a "radical" (read: progressive) Republican, Democrat, Granger, Anti-Monopolist, and Mid-Road Populist. Meanwhile, his virtuoso talents helped him achieve prominence in a remarkably diverse panoply of professions, ranging from farmer to newspaper editor to public servant.

Perhaps because Donnelly was regarded as a national rather than a merely regional figure, his deep ties to the upper Midwest have been consistently overlooked. But his historical significance cannot be properly understood without an exploration of the ways in which the upper Midwest during the late eighteenth century served as a petri dish for the protean, pluralistic, often populist politics that came to define his inimitable brand. To be competitive in the region's political landscape, one had to speak to the interests of uniquely diverse and often ethnically distinct groups of immigrants, farmers, factory workers, and day laborers, many of whom spoke their own native languages and received their news from sources tailored to their specific cultural and linguistic heritage. That Donnelly, born to an Irish-Catholic family in Philadelphia, could gain an enduring electoral foothold in agrarian Minnesota, whose politics were dominated by Scandinavian Republican farmers, attests to his rare ability to transcend race, class, and creed. As an agricultural and industrial frontier, Minnesota brought robber barons directly to Donnelly's doorstep. For most politicians prior to Theodore Roosevelt, resolving to fight the graft, corruption, bribery, voter intimidation, and influence peddling of all-powerful monopolistic rings amounted to political suicide, and contemporary historians still wonder to what heights Donnelly might have soared had he not wounded his prospects in repeated confrontations with the corporatist Goliaths he decried as plutocrats. Still, it was precisely this dauntless spirit that prepared him to challenge the intellectual, historical, and cultural orthodoxies he targets in his remarkable multigenre literary oeuvre.

Inevitably, literary historians ask why Donnelly's fiction and nonfiction are not better remembered. Beyond the usual historical amnesia, the most frequently given answer is that, as with Teddy Roosevelt, distinctions earned in politics overshadowed Donnelly's literary achievements, in effect fossilizing a complex career into the too-easy formulation that Ignatius Donnelly equals podium-thumping, pro-labor populist politician. Risk-averse publishers in the Gilded Age United States exacerbated this pigeonholing by encouraging the use of noms de plume if and when a well-known author strayed too far from his core professional calling card. This partly explains why Donnelly initially published what would be his most successful novel, *Caesar's Column*, under the pen name of Edmund Boisgilbert.

A second factor in the lack of attention given the Donnelly oeuvre is his curious comingling of popular pulp style with serious didactic literature. Though *Caesar's Column* is a social reform novel at heart, for example, just as *Doctor Huguet* is a rigorous examination of racial injustice in the United States, the important social critiques these novels offer come disguised in the trappings of melodrama, featuring the kind of overtly romantic subplots and sensational plot devices deemed cringeworthy by highbrow critics. While the fantastical aspects of these novels of ideas may diminish their legacy among some literati, these same reader-friendly elements made the novels popular successes in their time. Indeed, Donnelly was the first to admit that his books were often written quickly on the campaign trail or during intervals between legislative sessions, an admission that served the simultaneous purpose of excusing their lack of refinement while subtly reinforcing his prodigious intellectual and imaginative gifts: Donnelly could produce literary works in months that would take lesser minds years to complete.

Finally, the highly politicized nature of Donnelly's literary writing may partly explain its neglect by scholars. Several of the novels, including *Caesar's Column*, *The Golden Bottle*, and *The Bryan Campaign for the American People's Money*, served as vehicles for the author's spirited advocacy of People's Party platforms and functioned as de facto campaign tracts. While their adoption for partisan purposes surely boosted the books' profiles during the populist heyday of the late nineteenth century, their ideological impetus now overshadows their literary merit.

In this book, I explore this complicated literary legacy, documenting the reception Donnelly's books received in newspapers and periodicals of the time, as well as among the public. I follow a chronological path, seeking convergences between events in Donnelly's political and personal life and his literary projects while resisting the temptation to treat the political as primary and the literary as secondary. A slip of Donnelly's many and sundry calling cards is suggested by his numerous sobriquets, which include not just the Sage of Nininger but also the Little Giant, the Prince of Cranks, and the Apostle of Protest.[5]

Donnelly believed strongly that the spirits of past poets, philosophers, and politicians find new human hosts in subsequent generations, all but ensuring, for example, that the greatness of a Francis Bacon might be found again, under a different name in a different human form, centuries hence. If so, and if such gifts of soul and intellect could be a kind of heirloom lost, found, and recovered across the decades, in what twentieth-century figures might we find a slip of Donnelly's strange genius? Precious few of the would-be analogs achieved true distinction in both politics and literature. Among fellow midwesterners, Robert "Fighting Bob" La Follette, reform-minded member of Congress, governor of Wisconsin, and third-party presidential candidate, offers perhaps the most compelling analog for Donnelly as a political figure and force, though La Follette's two books, written strictly on political topics, lacked the breadth and learnedness of a Donnelly oeuvre that spanned topics as diverse as Atlantis, comet impacts, Shakespearean ciphers, and monetary policy. In midwestern arts and letters, Donnelly's contemporary Mark Twain—newspaperman, publisher, local-color novelist, satirist, and fatalist—offers a compelling enough comparison, as the two shared a gift for biting social commentary and bathos capable of leveling the high and mighty. But Twain, who claimed to have been nominated to run for governor of New York on the Independent ticket, was never elected to high office. In the twenty-first century, Newt Gingrich—former Speaker of the House, presidential candidate, and author of more than a dozen works of fiction and nonfiction—channels something of Donnelly's virtuoso intellect and political prowess, though Gingrich, a mainstream Republican and consummate Washington, DC, insider, utterly lacks Donnelly's third-party independence of mind, motive, and action.

Congressman, cryptologist, conspiracy theorist, crank, champion of the common man. After a thorough review of the record, one is left with a certain conclusion: Ignatius Donnelly is as close to a true American original as one may ever hope to find.

Chapter 1

The Making of a Midwestern Sage

On November 3, 1881, Ignatius Loyola Donnelly, former Minnesota lieutenant governor and three-term US representative, stared down the barrel of middle age at his home in Nininger City on the banks of the Mississippi River. "*This my 50th birthday*," he wrote in his diary. Outside, wintry weather descended on the small town Donnelly had helped found twenty-five years earlier. "This machine has been running on the face *of the earth a half century today*. It is said to grow old and yet one must grow old or die; and if statistics are correct, one half of all who started in the race of life with me, in 1831, are today, nothing."[1]

The birthday reflections mingled frontier sobriety with a kind of coy self-congratulation that bespoke Donnelly's genius for survival. In his journal that evening he paused for self-inventory—yes, he had gained a few too many pounds in the twelve years since he had last occupied national political office, and yet he had avoided the other slings and arrows of advancing age, gray hair, and lassitude. He still possessed his trademark vigor and hopefulness for a better future. Likewise he could notch in the positive column the health and happiness of his wife, Katharine, and their three adult children: Ignatius Carroll Donnelly, who, at twenty-five, had left to study medicine in Donnelly's birthplace of Philadelphia; Mary, recently engaged to the engineer George Giltinan; and his younger son, Stanislaus, who was showing a keen interest in law and would soon begin law school. And Kate had adapted reasonably well to the rigors of frontier life after moving to Minnesota from Philadelphia. "She is a dear, good, woman," he opined, "honest and true through all; a better and purer woman never lived."

On the political front, however, Donnelly's prospects had never been more dire than they were on his fiftieth birthday. His halcyon days as Minnesota's wunderkind lieutenant governor and member of Congress were now nearly two decades behind him. The intervening years had brought a series of bruising political battles that tested even his famous fighting spirit. Pitched battles over Black suffrage and civil rights, child labor laws, and antimonopoly legislation, all of which Donnelly enthusiastically supported, had become contentious, most recently costing him the seat in the state legislature he had held until 1879. The man known as the Sage of Nininger had watched his once limitless political stock drop, he noted ruefully, to zero.[2] A succession of electoral defeats such as he had endured, not to mention a grim set of personal finances, would, he felt certain, "destroy the prestige of Julius Caesar."[3]

And yet for Donnelly's obvious gift for overstatement, he had achieved much in the intervening five decades, including a lengthy stint as acting governor of Minnesota, a brief but significant tenure that afforded his supporters the right to legitimately call him "Governor Donnelly" thereafter. While Alexander Ramsey chased vice presidential aspirations in the East, Donnelly as acting governor had answered the call of Abraham Lincoln by signing executive orders mustering troops for the Union cause in an hour of "terrible necessity" for Minnesota and the rest of the country.[4] At the time of Donnelly's patriotic call to arms, his state was reported to have had just two hundred troops and a single cannon.[5] In 1860, at twenty-nine years of age, he had assumed office as the youngest lieutenant governor ever elected in the United States.[6]

Donnelly may have lacked the political prestige he had enjoyed during his days as acting governor, lieutenant governor, and three-term US representative, but on the evening of his fiftieth birthday he possessed an abundance of time to begin a new, second life born of the hard lessons of defeat. No longer required to make the long journey to the state or national capital for the fraught business of lawmaking in the Gilded Age, he could settle into his extensive library at Nininger and catch up on his reading in archaeology, ancient civilizations, and Shakespeare. Without a political machine to feed or political boss to answer to, he had rededicated himself to satisfying his own intellectual curiosity and growing his knowledge of the light of humanity that lay beyond the dark recesses of the political mind.

Importantly, Donnelly had something else to look forward to as his fifty-first year commenced, a particular seed planted the prior winter that he earnestly hoped would bear fruit. The seed was a book of nonfiction on a lost civilization, which he had sold to Harper & Brothers in March and which was due for release early in the coming winter, if his many political enemies didn't first succeed in suppressing its publication. Donnelly had trafficked in the rough-and-tumble world of lawmaking long enough to know that craven politicians would stop at nothing to stop a rival. His own meteoric rise had been fueled by self-righteous indignation at their graft, greed, and corruption. And as he had made a public fool of many pompous elected officials with his gift for leveling humor and biting rhetoric, the paranoiac in him grimly accepted the chance that his political enemies might cancel the publication of his daring, some said apocryphal, history.[7]

Donnelly didn't know it yet, but the nonfiction manuscript that waited in press that early November of 1881—*Atlantis: The Antediluvian World*—would in the months that followed become an international sensation, successful enough to generate a series of nonfiction spin-offs in which the politician turned man of letters would introduce the masses to daring theories about ancient civilizations lost beneath the waters of the Atlantic, to the existence of world-ending comets, and to great cryptograms purported to reveal the true authorship of Shakespeare's plays. In an uncanny reversal of the usual midcareer doldrums, the latter half of Donnelly's remarkable tenure on Earth would generate more fame and infamy than had his former life as a combative congressman and lieutenant governor. The publication of his visionary treatises caused the haters to hate Donnelly all the more, dismissing him as an American crank, crackpot, and pseudoscientist, while legions of true believers declared him a certified genius. In the 1870s, few outside his adopted home state of Minnesota used the sobriquet "Sage of Nininger," but with the publication of visionary book after visionary book, the man grew into his moniker, and by the late 1880s, he was known by that name in newspapers across the Great Plains and beyond. The prescient tomes he researched at home in Nininger City, and at bookstores and libraries throughout the upper Midwest, would, in this remarkable second act, earn him the adoration of readers and voters across the nation and a nomination for vice president, while establishing his reputation as a public intellectual par excellence.

Donnelly's four works of visionary nonfiction—*Atlantis: The Antediluvian World*, *Ragnarok: The Age of Fire and Gravel*, *The Great Cryptogram*, and *The Cipher in the Plays, and on the Tombstone*—in addition to his dystopian novel *Caesar's Column*, would make him a figure of national notoriety for the first time since his feud with his fellow congressman Elihu Washburne made headlines in 1868. The personal rancor between Donnelly and his powerful accuser from Illinois would go down in the annals of Congress as one of the most contentious of all time. It would establish Donnelly as David in the David-and-Goliath power struggles of the Gilded Age United States, and it would prove him utterly unafraid of authority, seniority, or the censure of his colleagues—a man willing to speak truth to power, consequences be damned.

In a historical era characterized by patronage and insider politics, Donnelly appeared to play by an altogether different playbook, one whose scruples consistently limited his otherwise limitless political potential while growing his reputation as a sort of mad genius whose impulses often proved correct, if only in retrospect. Unlike the stereotype of the distanced ivory tower intellectual or genius in the garret, however, Donnelly was very much a man of the people, as delighted to debate the issues of the day in sweat-drenched capitol buildings and sunburned county fairs as to retreat to the cooler, more cerebral confines of his home study. His unlikely combination of charismatic, character-driven populism and a penchant for contrarianism and conspiracy theory informed by intellectual inquiry caused some to call him a crank, while others delighted in calling him a prophet.

The political controversy that first introduced him to the nation began quietly enough, when Congressman Donnelly penned what he believed to be a private letter to the newspaper editor Charles Folsom in Taylor Falls, Minnesota, a small town sixty miles upriver from Donnelly's Nininger City. In the missive he offered what amounted to an apology to Folsom for failing to secure a riverfront improvement bill, along with the explanation that a single congressman, Washburne of Illinois, appeared hell-bent on thwarting his attempts to do good for his constituents. Candid to a fault, he had merely stated the obvious, but both Folsom's newspaper and the anti-Donnelly *St. Paul Press* made his private letter public fodder. Washburne's retaliation was swift and punitive: he accused his would-be rival of a series of unsubstantiated transgressions, ranging from a supposedly checkered past in his childhood hometown of Philadelphia, to accusations that Donnelly was a closet Catholic, to a more serious charge in the agrarian Midwest that the so-called Sage of Nininger was in fact an "office-beggar"—someone who sought public office for personal fame rather than service to the people.[8]

Warned by advisers that his ardent campaigns against corruption and patronage had generated far too many personal enemies, Donnelly nevertheless registered disbelief at the unfounded attack against his character, bemoaning in his diary the Machiavellian nature of the enterprise he had entered. "Who have I injured. . .. What men have I attacked?" he wondered, incredulous at the fate that had befallen him. He vowed to defend his good reputation with vigor, even if it meant waging "eternal war with all assassins of reputation."[9] Donnelly backers used the politics-as-war metaphor to warn their man of the growing animosity against him by established politicians entrenched in the patronage system he decried. One supporter advised him to "prepare for death or victory," as the upstart Minnesota politician readied for the fight of his political life.[10] As Donnelly exposed the alleged patronage schemes of established politicians, he burned bridges, sacrificing quid-pro-quo relationships with those who, in a different world, might have served as valuable allies.

Washburne, who came from a powerful family, believed Donnelly to be a future threat to win a Senate seat, and he resolved to check the young man's populist appeal before it jeopardized the political prospects of the Minnesota branch of his family, including his brother William D. Washburn. Former Minnesota governor Alexander Ramsey, Washburne, and other upper Midwest Republicans believed Donnelly's presumed "rule or ruin" modus operandi would weaken their grip on the state party's constituents and, if left to run its course, put power in the hands of the crowds drawn to his charisma and reform-minded ideals.

The Donnelly-Washburne battle royale played out on the floor of the House of Representatives, when the thirty-seven-year-old wunderkind unleashed a rebuttal whose mercilessness both shocked and pleased the many members of Congress who disliked Elihu Washburne personally. Donnelly defended himself by impugning his fellow representative for nearly two hours, characterizing the Washburnes as ruling elites determined to maintain their privilege at any cost. Though it would rapidly degenerate into pure bile, Donnelly's rebuke of Washburne began with a modicum of civility: "Mr. Speaker, the charge comes from such a quarter that I cannot fail to notice it. Why sir, the gentleman's family are 'chronic office-beggars,'" he began, formally restating the case made against him, before twisting the knife. "They are for nothing if not in office. Out of office they are miserable, wretched, God-forsaken—as uncomfortable as the famous stump-tailed bull in fly-time."[11]

The Speaker of the House called the upstart politician to order several times during the hours-long rant that followed, but to no avail. Donnelly continued undaunted:

> I stand here reiterating the declaration I then made, that if anywhere on God's earth, down in the mire of filth and nastiness, the gentleman can pluck up anything that touches my honor, let it come. I have analyzed the contents of the gentleman's foul stomach. I have dipped my hands into its gall; I have examined the half-digested fragments that I found floating in the gastric juices, but if it is possible for the peristaltic actions of the gentleman from Illinois to bring up anything more loathsome, more disgusting than he has vomited over me . . . in God's name, let it come.

And still Donnelly wasn't done. He segued from defending his good name to attacking Washburne's character: "And if there is in our midst one low, sordid, vulgar soul; one barren, mediocre intelligence; one heart callous to every kindly sentiment; one mouth which like unto a den of foul beast giving forth deadly odors; if there be one character which, while blotched and spotted all over, yet raves and rants and blackguards like a prostitute; if there be here one bold, bad, empty, bellowing demagogue, it is the gentleman from Illinois."[12]

A colleague from Indiana, Representative George W. Julian, later recalled that the majority of Congress applauded the young man's audacious jibes and laughed approvingly as his barrage of insults hit their well-deserving target.[13] Still, reaction in the national press was not so favorable: it denounced the brash representative's vulgar metaphors and profane language. Back home, Washburne allies at the *Pioneer* slammed Minnesota's former lieutenant governor as "the nastiest and most foul-mouthed wretch who ever had a seat in the American Congress."[14] Other metropolitan newspapers, however, rushed to Donnelly's aid, including the *St. Paul Dispatch*, where editor Harlan P. Hall wrote his friend a cautionary note admitting that while Donnelly's supporters would remain true, his enemies would never forgive or forget the incident. Years later, Hall would look back on Donnelly's speech in Congress as a fork in the road that might, had the political prodigy exercised greater restraint, have propelled the Minnesotan to untold political heights—perhaps even the presidency. "I have always felt," Hall opined, "that if merciful Providence had intervened and prevented his speaking longer [than his allotted time], his political future, and indeed all his life, would have been different."[15]

To wish Ignatius Donnelly to stand down in the face of perceived injustice, however, was to wish the impossible of a man prone to taking political slings personally. For his followers, his willingness to meet conflict head-on was both a blessing and a curse, as A. Brower wrote in a letter to Donnelly dated May 21, 1868: "We are frontier people," he explained, "and are inclined at all times to support those who dare protect themselves. We have a conundrum here. Why is Donnelly like . . . green tea—because you do not know his strength until you get him in hot water."[16] Donnelly's indefatigable backers swallowed the strong tea he poured, but not without pucker. Meanwhile, a House of Representatives investigation found no credibility in Washburne's slanderous charges against Donnelly. The accusations proved so dubious, in fact, that even Washburne refused to repeat them under oath. A committee headed by Representative Francis Thomas cleared Donnelly of any wrongdoing and declared the rumors Washburne had circulated to be utterly false, but damage had been done to Donnelly's rapidly rising national star and to his wider political ambitions.

On the home front, however, the clash between rival midwestern congressmen played out differently than it had in the national press. When Donnelly returned home to Minnesota later that July, he found his supporters vocal in their support of a dauntless maverick who seemed willing to duke it out against powerful interests. Standing-room-only crowds cheered him, shouting down any naysayers who tried to steal his thunder at the podium. The following day, even the anti-Donnelly *Pioneer* called the meeting the liveliest in the city's history and reported that it was at a loss for words to describe the raucous atmosphere.[17] Based on the zealous reception, Donnelly wrote his wife, Kate, that despite the controversy over his hours-long attack on Washburne on the floor of the House, he was cautiously optimistic that he would be nominated on the first ballot for a fourth congressional term.[18] But Donnelly's cocksureness, and his continual need to replay the controversy to whip up public support, alienated party bosses, who developed an "anyone but Donnelly" posture. Meanwhile, his high-spirited, fiercely loyal delegates were banned from the convention hall in St. Paul, and, in the end, he lost his reelection bid in 1869 by approximately two thousand votes to the Democrat Eugene Wilson. In the aftermath, Donnelly unsuccessfully sought his party's nomination for US Senate in a contest that would have pitted him against Alexander Ramsey, the governor of Minnesota during the years Donnelly served as his lieutenant governor.

After Donnelly's term ran up in the spring of 1869, he returned home for what amounted to a consolation tour. The *St. Paul Press* conceded, "For a young gentleman of energy and ability, such as Mr. Donnelly is conceded to possess, the world has always a sphere and a future. . .. He will be wanted, bye and bye."[19] Meanwhile the *Pioneer* warned that the onetime politician turned private citizen would be more attractive than ever to voters drawn to his underdog ethos. It predicted that "the prairies will be on fire for Donnelly before the harvest ripens."[20]

In the decade that followed his failed House reelection bid, Donnelly mixed farm management with lecture circuit stints to finance his simmering political ambitions. As he toured the county fairs from whose stages he delivered an endless series of bully pulpit speeches, he distanced himself further from the Republican Party under whose banner he had served three consecutive terms in Congress, criticizing it for its support of farm- and industry-destroying tariffs and its subservience to special interests. Donnelly viewed GOP support of tariffs as evidence of the party's telltale choice of capitalism over the health and welfare of common workers.

Recognizing Donnelly's talent as a communicator, Harlan Hall at the *St. Paul Dispatch* hired the now out-of-work politician as a Washington correspondent, hoping Donnelly would write the sort of leveling critiques of entitled elites that had made him a sought-after speaker on the campaign trail. But a dark Donnelly was instead of a mind to offer bitter diatribes against the Washington, DC, social scene, sharpening the contrast between monied elites and folks back home in the upper Midwest. His political dispatches dripped with barely contained disdain for the privilege, profligacy, and pomp he witnessed:

> A carpet extends from the curb to the door. You enter. Stairs, hall, room, are packed with moving, jostling, surging, struggling people. . .. In one of the rooms near the door stand the host and hostess, smiling away . . . like clock-work, and mechanically shaking with everybody in the pump handle style. . .. Then there are the weak men who haunt the punch room and . . . dart in, as if to

say, "really is this what you have here?" as if they had never been there before! And there the sensible men who nose out of the supper room and who, selecting some quiet corner, near the tables, guzzle and are silent. But the great clatter, jangle and chatter goes on, a thousand interests, wishes, vanities, mingle together in one stupendous buzz and burr, while the mechanical host and hostess stand smiling away and working their pump handles, and the struggle in and out of the door. . .. And this is a Washington party.[21]

His time in the capital during the ostentations of the Ulysses S. Grant administration pushed Donnelly further away from Grant's Republicanism and toward a tenuous new alliance with the Democrats. In effect, his willingness to leave the party of Lincoln meant that he had become a third-party politician, an independent free to act his conscience, electoral success be damned. In an address to would-be voters in Minnesota's Second Congressional District, he declared, "I am before you at the solicitation of my fellow citizens, and if a platform is demanded, I plant myself on the platform of Ignatius Donnelly."[22] Donnelly's lost-cause mentality and his willingness to compete against all odds as a man alone came to define his political brand after his service in the US House of Representatives. In his address to the citizens of the Second District, he encouraged the underdog persona, saying, "Thousands upon thousands of dollars will be spent to defeat me. I may not be sustained by a single newspaper. I have no money to spend; I can only appeal, to the people, and ask them, if they believe I am with them to sustain me." Calling the average Minnesotan voter his "only hope and reliance," he vowed to "go among them, like Peter the Hermit, and preach a crusade against the rich powerful and omnipresent combination. I expect to triumph. I may go down in the fight, but if I do, the next blast of the trumpet will see me on my feet again, ready for another contest."[23]

By 1870, Donnelly had years of experience on both sides of the partisan divide, having been raised an urban Democrat in Philadelphia before gravitating to Republican causes—most notably antislavery and temperance—after settling in Minnesota.[24] While many dyed-in-the-wool Democrats mistrusted Donnelly for his long association with the GOP, his popularity with independent voters gave the Democrats their best chance of competing in the solidly Republican state of Minnesota, even if a Donnelly win would be a long shot. Once again, his political barometer proved accurate, as the very handicaps he had earlier named—scarce campaign financing, scant political patronage, relatively few allies in high places—proved his undoing in the 1870 bid to recapture his lost congressional seat, this time as a Democrat. Still, against all odds he came within two thousand votes of defeating the Republican John T. Averill, a former colonel in the Minnesota Infantry during the Civil War. The epitome of an establishment figure, Averill had served on the Republican National Committee for nearly four years prior to facing off against Donnelly, and he took a hard line against the South. Donnelly, meanwhile, embraced a more conciliatory view unpopular in Minnesota, insisting that five years after its surrender to Grant, the South should no longer be treated as an enemy of the US government.[25] Averill could boast battlefield experience while Donnelly, who was engaged in public service as the lieutenant governor of his state when the Civil War broke out, had volunteered to lead a Minnesota regiment only to be denied a commission by then governor Alexander Ramsey.

In the aftermath of his narrow defeat in the 1870 race for Minnesota's Second District, Donnelly continued a pattern begun after previous political losses: retreating to Nininger to lick his wounds while contemplating his next move. When friends attempted to buoy his spirits by urging him to reoccupy his political bully pulpit, he demurred, saying, "As I feel now I will stick to my farm and my books, and let the dirty angels of corruption stir the nasty pool of politics to its depths."[26] Anyone elected in such a thoroughly despoiled age, he insisted, must be counted suspect, whether Republican or Democrat.

Paradoxically, Donnelly's bitter defeats, which sent him back to part-time farm superintending, only added to his mythos; after all, he could hardly be called an office-beggar or a career politician after suffering the indignity of successive losses. That such a shining political star could now be found slopping hogs delighted the homegrown press corps that followed him just as willingly into the barnyard as into the statehouse. In June 1871, the *Duluth Minnesotan* claimed that the former congressman had set himself above the fray of petty partisan politics, "the Sage of Nininger being more lately intent on growing wheat and vegetables" than on raising hell.[27] In a piece aptly titled "Farmer Donnelly," the *Grange Advance* confessed that it, too, had badly underestimated Donnelly's yeomanry. The editors noted that they "had seen so much ridicule made of the idea that he is a practical farmer" that they were shocked to witness the great man cleaning hogs on a recent visit. While the politician turned plowman privately lamented his fate, good-natured reports from an ever-fascinated press corps were helping to rebrand him not as a sore or perennial loser but as an underappreciated renaissance man with better and more noble lives to lead. With his "magnificent farm" and its "well-filled library," the *Advance* could not help but wonder why the Donnelly had ever been "tempted from the peaceful, rural shades, into the stormy and tempestuous sea of politics."[28]

Donnelly's dark defeatism troubled his longtime supporters, among them Dr. Thomas Foster, who worried in a letter to his younger protégé, "You may rage and bust the air, but in that line of conduct you are powerless except to hurt yourself." Foster urged Donnelly to publicly recant his recent affiliation with the Democratic Party and to participate in the state Republican convention instead. The defeated Donnelly resisted, but he ultimately accepted the wisdom of a man who fancied himself a political mentor. When it came time to address convention delegates on the delicate matter of his recent defection from their ranks, he defused the tensions in the hall with an agrarian metaphor, joking that he had returned to them like a "drowned gopher."[29] He took pains to explain that he hadn't accepted the Democrats' endorsement because he had abandoned the GOP but because the Republicans had co-opted his message, in effect "elbowing" him off the platform he had built.[30] "A good deal has been said about my returning to the Republican party. I do not feel as if I ever was out of that party," he told conventioners assembled to hear his acceptance speech. "I may have had one leg over the traces, but I was in the harness all the while."[31]

The Minneapolis and St. Paul press marveled at how easily Donnelly was welcomed back into the fold after such a bitter breakup with the party. The *Minneapolis News* declared that he had staged a political coup in convincing Minnesota Republicans to endorse lower tariffs, a graduated income tax, and a resolution in support of agriculture. In a master stroke, the newspaper observed, he had managed to bring the state's conservatives closer to the positions he favored than they had been at any time during the prior campaign, in which he had abandoned their ranks in protest: "It is a little remarkable that a political corpse, which they [his enemies] esteemed Donnelly to be, should suddenly come to life. . .. The day of miracles has not passed for Donnelly."[32] Incredibly, the pride of Nininger City was immediately pressed into service by the state central committee to campaign on behalf of struggling Republican candidates, mere months after he ran on the opposing party's ticket.

In delivering campaign speeches across the state on behalf of others, Donnelly had honed the speaking skills he now put to good use on the lecture circuit. He drew large crowds nearly everywhere he went, primarily platooning two speeches: one on his six years in Washington, DC, and the other on American humor. Audiences, he learned, were far more engaged by wit than they were interested in his reminiscences on political life in the nation's capital. Politicians came and went, after all, rising to fame and falling from fortune with regularity—but good jokes well told reached across partisan divides. A season on the speaking tour reminded him of the importance of avoiding "topics which may conflict with political or sectarian views."[33] Residents of small towns across the Great Plains perennially suffered bloviating politicians and fly-by-night salespersons while earnestly hoping for speakers like Donnelly, who could stimulate their intellects while tickling their funny bones. Even when Donnelly opted for political speechmaking, spectators came away impressed. No friend of his, the *St. Paul Pioneer* conceded that "not another man in Minnesota, and but few in America, could draw such an audience."[34]

During his time on the lecture circuit Donnelly witnessed with his own eyes a political sea change, as the nation moved away from valorizing Grant and his Republican party of mostly military and industrial men, toward a more liberal form of Republicanism closer to Donnelly's own brand of thinking. For years the he had decried the patronage system and the protection of monied elites in Washington, and now voters even in Grant's Midwest were coming to see the uneven results of years of Republican rule. Donnelly's one-time political mentor, Dr. Foster, sensed the moment ripe for yet another renaissance, but his protege pushed back, reminding Foster that he had ceased to be a party man and that he now considered himself a lecturer more than a politician. Foster, intimating the end of his friend as political force if he did not remain within the Republican fold, attempted to serve as a kind of candidate whisperer, warning Donnelly that if he abandoned Grant and mainstream Republicanism a second time, he would face "death and destruction without benefit of clergy." On another occasion a worried Foster wrote at greater length, hoping to convince the stubborn younger man that he knew him better than he knew himself. Foster opined: "From your very nature, sanguine, impressed with your own powers, pugnacious, disposed more to push enemies than to heed friends, you are not always the best judge of the course best for *yourself* to take. Let me be your mentor on this occasion." In his letter Foster went so far as to call himself Donnelly's "Political Godfather."[35]

Predictably, Donnelly chose to navigate by his own stars. Rather than take the advice of his well-meaning "godfather" and circle the wagons around Grant, he did just the opposite, choosing to address a convention of newspaper editors on the urgent necessity of political reform. Republicans, he cautioned, must stop promoting business interests at the expense of citizen welfare, and cease protecting businesses from fair trade via protectionist tariffs that hurt farmers and urban laborers alike. Sounding a Socialist note, he warned that any economic regime was destined to fail if it increased income inequality among people. When men and women came to see the government as an ally in their struggle for a living wage, they would be inclined to participate in democracy as never before. Writers and editors, he maintained, had the best chance of sorting through political obfuscations to reach them. "You are perpetually talking to them in their workshops and at their firesides," he remined them. "You are bringing to them, in fact, incident, argument, inspiration . . .. It is as possible to measure your influence for good or evil as to measure the effects of the sun's rays upon our planet. It is not too much to say that the newspapers of the United States hold the destinies of the people of the United States in their hands."[36]

Donnelly had been a journalist of sorts in his early days on the midwestern frontier, serving as editor of a newspaper published in Philadelphia and later Nininger, Minnesota, the utopian "paper town" he helped found with several business partners before it went bust.[37] He had called his early journalistic venture the *Emigrant Aid Journal of Minnesota*, viewing it as a vehicle by which he might promote the cause of Nininger among immigrants who might help the new city grow and prosper. Coediting the inaugural issue with his friend Phillip Rohr, he was forthright about its aims, stating, "A newspaper in the West is the voice by which the new town makes its merits and claims known to the surrounding world. It is the voice by which those afar off are attracted towards it."[38] *Emigrant Aid Journal*'s run had proved short lived, however, with its thirty-second and final edition arriving in May 1858, just as an agricultural depression struck Nininger City and the rest of the region, causing Donnelly to move away from town founding and newspaper editing and toward a career in politics.

Now, more than twenty years after producing the *Emigrant Aid Journal*, Donnelly's disaffection with establishment Republicans led him to support the presidential campaign of his fellow newspaperman

Horace Greeley, who shared many of Donnelly's beliefs about the responsibility of a vigilant press to hold politicians to account, as well as his long-standing opposition to slavery and his support of African American voting rights. The vast majority of Republicans at the time still supported the midwesterner Grant, and Donnelly was expected to fall in line, but after much soul searching, he refused, eager to move the party in a more liberal direction. The pro-Grant *Northfield Standard* in Northfield, Minnesota, was much vexed by his abandonment of traditional Republican principles, declaring, "Too much ambition [has] made him mad."[39] In nearby Hastings, Minnesota, just down the road from Nininger City, the *Gazette* was more cautious in chastising the local maverick, offering its criticism in the form of a decidedly backhanded compliment: "Mr. Donnelly's political course for the past five years has been a series of blunders any one of which would have proved fatal to a man of less genius." This time, however, the newspaper felt sure that the strange genius had gone too far. "The present disaster will be found a Waterloo," it promised, adding, "No one regrets this more than ourselves."[40]

The *Gazette*'s lamentations put a fine point on an increasingly common characterization of Donnelly as a man who seemed to court defeat and who appeared to self-sabotage efforts that would bring him success in favor of making doomed ethical stands in support of lost causes. While the visionary Donnelly worked to build path-making coalitions between conservative Democrats and liberal Republicans, mainline Republicans praised Grant's war record while railing against the depravity of the defeated South. Meanwhile, conventional Democrats feared that Donnelly would be nominated on their ticket again, though this time he vowed to seek reform in lieu of elected office. Recognizing that the case made by a conservative Democrat and progressive Republican coalition was likely to fall on deaf ears in pro-Grant, pro-Republican Minnesota, Donnelly accepted invitations to speak to more progressive Republicans elsewhere in the Midwest, where, in addition to advocating free trade, he decried Grant's despotic rule while arguing for more humane, less humiliating treatment of the defeated South. Donnelly's speeches and rallies in Chicago, Madison, and Milwaukee drew high praise, with the Milwaukee *News* naming his the "Best Speech of the Campaign."[41] He was particularly pleased with his own performance, writing to Kate, "What a joy it is to find such a hall and such an audience—where one's words fall like showers of electric sparks kindling a blaze where they touch."[42]

While Greeley lost the election that November of 1872, Donnelly found a new identity as an independent-minded reformer determined to serve people over party. Neither exclusively Democrat nor Republican, he would choose the most promising causes offered by each and argue for those causes a la carte, putting together a meal he hoped would satisfy voters hungering for substance. The inherent difficulties of building common-sense coalitions in a two-party system led him inexorably toward a humanistic political philosophy resolved to transcend divisions of race, class, and ethnicity so often exploited by mainliners in both parties. While farmers in Minnesota traditionally voted Republican, which in effect meant voting for the railroad monopolies that skimmed many of their profits and lowered the prices paid for their crops at the grain elevators, Donnelly hoped that rural farmers and urban laborers would in time acknowledge their shared enemy: corporate greed.

Securing economic rights for the people entailed a spirited struggle against entrenched monopolies. Donnelly's success as an antimonopolist speaker and writer, and his ongoing fascination with newspapers as the ideal vehicle by which to take his case directly to the people, led him in 1874 to establish a newspaper, the *Anti-monopolist*, which refused allegiances to both Democratic metropolitan newspapers and Republican farm journals. Instead he aimed to combine the best of both sides under his own banner. The state's established newspapers welcomed the upstart entrant with a mix of trepidation and curiosity, with the diehard Republican editor Frank Daggett at the *Litchfield News-Ledger* in Meeker County, Minnesota, claiming that the journalistic startup was "as unlike other journals as Donnelly is unlike other men. . .. It is brimming of fight and fun, and bristles all over with invective . . . and is as dangerous a plaything as a porcupine. It is always erudite, humorous, sarcastic, and generally logical." Designed to appeal primarily to his home state's independent-minded agrarians, commonly known as Grangers for their membership in the fraternal organization known as the National Grange of the Order of Patrons of Husbandry, the singular paper demonstrated its editor's belief in public writing drafted to appeal to both high intellect and down-to-earth horse sense, and, when necessary, to engage in fisticuffs with the party in power. "In almost every column," Daggett noted, "you can read the determination of Mr. Donnelly to overthrow and ruin the Republican party, no matter what may come after. It breathes hostility to every Republican measure."[43] The *Anti-monopolist*'s growing readership gladly rewarded Donnelly for his willingness to speak truth to power, helping return him to the Minnesota State Senate from 1874 to 1878.

The idea that the mercurial, intellectually restless Donnelly had at various times in the preceding decade claimed membership in the Republican, Democrat, Greenback, and Anti-Monopoly parties troubled the editors of several Twin Cities newspapers, who refused to allow him to forget his past controversies, including the Washburne debacle. The *Minneapolis Daily Tribune* taunted the politician with four lines of verse penned by Ben Wilde, under the title "Pugnacious Explains": "Ignatius, the martyr as he usually is / Is in water so hot it fairly doth 'siz' / But he swears you can't prove it; I got not a cent / From the railroad to which my influence is lent."[44] The *Pioneer Press* in St. Paul likewise chided him for appearing to be on all sides of all issues, capturing the quality of his speech as "a rodomontade, full of empty bluster and boasting, of passionate adjurations, of morbid sentimentality, and of rhetorical pyrotechnics."[45] In an age of P. T. Barnum, critics pigeonholed the restless politician and his evolving views as something akin to a traveling circus of ever-shifting vistas, views, and sleights of hand meant to deceive, or at least distract, a gullible public. Such a politician, they said, was little better than the new word coined, circa 1849, to describe the sort of gifted hucksters who swindled the unsuspecting by first gaining their trust: confidence man.[46]

Donnelly maintained that the newspapers themselves were, in fact, the frauds and the charlatans, unable to evolve or alter their positions because their editorial visions were bought and paid for. Rather than deny his particular brand of political pantheism, Donnelly conceded as much to readers in the pages of his own newspaper, acknowledging, "We know it is charged that we are vacillating;—that we pass readily from party to party." Ever the rhetorician, he preferred to spin past political inconsistencies as a measure of independent thinking and an admirable autonomy from party rule. "No party owns us," he reminded readers. "We propose to make our life a protest against the slavish rule of caucuses and rings which now afflicts this country. We are well aware that this is not the pathway that leads to political honors and emoluments. We do not seek them." Donnelly's colorful description of how he and his fellow antimonopolists seized their independence revealed a self-dramatizing streak, as he described leaving the Republican Party "in the day of its power and greatness . . . and we enlisted with the guerillas, where there was neither pay nor plunder."[47]

Even as he distanced himself from partisanship, however, Donnelly was busy enacting progressive political reforms in the Minnesota State Senate, supported, paradoxically, by a party of nonparty people. He helped pass a number of important progressive reforms, including a bill curbing the power of creditors to charge exorbitant interest or to foreclose on property without sufficient notice. In a May 10 edition of the *Anti-monopolist*, under a headline that read simply "Ourselves," he inventoried at length the positive results of the advocacy already undertaken by his fledgling periodical, reaching a crescendo of righteousness in a final paragraph that read, "And now, with gratitude to our friends and defiance to our enemies . . . we spread our banner to the breeze, with Tom Jefferson's noble motto inscribed upon it, 'Eternal hostility to every form of oppression of the bodies and souls of men.' "[48]

By 1878, Donnelly reveled in his reputation as a political guerrilla—one who rejected partisanship when it proved an impediment to the common good. He would entertain prospective political nominations and appointments only if through them he could serve as an instrument of the people. In November 1878 he would turn forty-eight years old, and already it seemed to many political observers that he had lived nine political lives. At a time when many midcareer politicians looked to secure their future by doubling down on existing loyalties, Donnelly looked to pry himself loose from the grip of political orthodoxy. If he was asked to run against an establishment figure, he would consider it, but he preferred to pursue the people's reforms outside the statehouse or the halls of Congress. While he vehemently rejected the corporate cronyism of the Republicans, he regarded the Democrats as little better, chastising the party for its inability to be "reformers, revolutionists, friends of the people." Rather than fight the good fight for the good of the people, the Democrats had surrendered to Republicans, adopting a milquetoast platform reminiscent of "a mermaid . . . which viewed from one end is a woman, and viewed from the other is a cod-fish; and they try to slip in between the Republican Party and Wall Street, and by abusements and gyrations win the support of the capitalists who are perfectly satisfied with the Republicans."[49]

And yet Donnelly would agree to run for political office again, and as a Democrat, no less. The opportunity to defeat one of the younger brothers of Elihu Washburne, the man he had called out in his infamous congressional feud, proved too enticing to resist. This time Democrats asked Donnelly to run on their ticket to prevent the Republican William D. Washburn, a favorite son of the lumber, railroad, and milling industries, from winning the House seat in the Third District. Though both the Democratic Party and the Greenback Party rallied behind Donnelly as their collective choice, the campaign struck many as counterintuitive from the start. In accepting the Democratic nomination, Donnelly went on record as saying he was not a Democrat but would gladly fight for select Democratic causes with which he agreed, such as the eight-hour workday and the regulation of child labor. Recognizing that only someone with Donnelly's name recognition could hope to defeat a powerful member of the Washburn clan, Minnesota Democrats accepted his terms, and yet the relationship of convenience was doomed to fail from the start.

Donnelly—who perceived in his opponent the twin scourges of corporate monopoly and corruption—campaigned vigorously, benefiting from the endorsement of Harlan Hall, founder and publisher of the *St. Paul Daily Globe*. A dedicated Democrat, Hall found himself in unfamiliar territory endorsing a perennial party-switching ex-Republican. Still, he put everything he had behind the candidate he endorsed, sending a canvasser with Donnelly everywhere he went on the campaign trail. The combination of the charismatic Donnelly on the stump and the *Globe* coming in the mail proved a formidable one, as Hall's subscriptions in rural counties soon rivaled that of other daily newspapers.[50]

Donnelly and Hall's all-out effort nearly put Donnelly, the unlikely Democrat, over the top, as ultimately he managed to reduce a sizable Republican majority in the district by two-thirds while losing by a narrow margin of three thousand votes in an election marred by alleged fraud on the Republican side.[51] The cost of waging the hard-fought battle had been steep, however, and Donnelly was compelled to sell his beloved newspaper and personal mouthpiece, the *Anti-monopolist*, to repay his debts and to help his backers mount a legal challenge. A congressional investigation of alleged bribery on behalf of his Republican opponent dragged on for weeks, and though it found ample evidence of irregularities, it refused to overturn the official election results. The losing fight left Donnelly more indebted than ever, and it emboldened partisan Democrats in the Third District, for whom the loss was proof that nominating a perennial party switcher on their ticket had proved to be a serious error.

The loss of the contested election of 1878 against the brother of his longest-standing political enemy marked a low ebb for Donnelly, who blamed fate and damned circumstance for an "unconscionable run of miserable fortune."[52] His hopes rebounded, however, when friends and allies, convinced of evidence showing bribery, fraud, and illegal voting, compelled him to file a contested election suit. But Donnelly's case could not be heard in Congress until January 1879, and though on hearing the testimony, the House Committee on Elections voted to remove Washburn from his seat based on evidence of voting improprieties, a second, seemingly larger controversy arising from Donnelly's election fraud suit prevented the whole-House vote needed for Washburn's expulsion. When the spin-off controversy, dubbed the Springer Affair after an anonymous bribe letter to House Committee on Elections chair William Springer, persisted into the late spring of 1880, Donnelly lost all hope of occupying the Third District House seat that would have been opened for him upon a full House vote for Washburn's removal. As he saw it, Washington politicians had chosen expediency over ethics and political skullduggery over common sense. Once again, it seemed, fate had conspired to return him to the lonely spot in the library of his home in Nininger City, where he traded political imbroglio for a retreat to his long-neglected studies in archaeology and ancient civilizations.

By 1881, Donnelly's once thriving Nininger City had become something of a ghost town. Touring the village on assignment for the *St. Paul Sunday Globe*, the unidentified reporter described the place as "decayed" and "not quite so remarkable in its desolation" except for one pleasant surprise: Donnelly's stately home. Invited in, the roving correspondent described a feeling of "spaciousness" and "hospitality," a feeling punctuated by the fine company of its owners. Donnelly, the reporter observed, was "the very incarnation of the bountiful host," with a "mental range . . . embracing wit, anecdote, personal experiences, and political reminiscences." Above all, the reporter insisted, a visitor leaves with an "unalterable conviction of [Donnelly's] goodness and his kindness of heart. The more you see of him the more steadfast is your belief in the fatalistic motto '*che sara, sara*'—what will be, will be." Was the great Donnelly a has-been, a washed-up politician stuck in the crumbling village he had helped found, or simply a strange genius who had beaten his retreat from the madding crowds? And what sort of man, the reporter wondered, would leave lucrative work as a youthful Philadelphia attorney for a life lived on the Minnesota frontier, at the center of a paper town whose best days lay decades in the past? On these existential questions, in particular, the reporter reflected at considerable length:

> So in this hamlet with its dismantled warehouse, and blighted enterprise legible in its very air lives, and studies, and dreams, one who threw away pecuniary success in early life . . . to wage war with

stout heart, and vigorous brain, with the forces banded to cheat, and annihilate him if possible.

And then wasn't it worthwhile to have left Philadelphia if only to have made that anti-Washburne speech never-to-be-forgotten while any of the name survives to suggest the Donnelly brand.

And finally, if pecuniary success had tempted him to stay in Philadelphia, Mrs. Donnelly's glorious contralto would have been lost to the State, and what a privation it would be.

Minnesota was best for Ignatius Donnelly after all.[53]

And maybe it was. In the early winter of 1881, a newly inspired Donnelly began making notes for his first serious work of book-length nonfiction, traveling to bookstores in nearby St. Paul to read scientific journals and books on subjects ranging from mythology and literature to anthropology and historical geography.[54] Drawing on lessons learned on the lecture circuit, he attempted to synthesize information gleaned from science, literature, folklore, religion, and mythology into a persuasive package digestible for lay audiences. As a writer he would also go his own way, eschewing conventional interpretations of existing scholarship for bolder, more idiosyncratic takes. He believed that the truth could be arrived at via a unique combination of creativity, intellectual curiosity, and what one Donnelly biographer called "tenacious conviction."[55] Energized by what he found in his research, he wrote feverishly, completing his manuscript in months rather than years. By late winter he traveled to New York with a complete draft of *Atlantis* in hand, hoping against hope that publishers would find his daring treatment of the world's most famous lost civilization as compelling as he did.

In late March of 1881, neither the Sage of Nininger nor his chosen New York publisher, Harper & Brothers, knew that the book he dropped off that spring day would soon become an international sensation.

CHAPTER 2

Atlantis: The Antediluvian World

Ignatius Donnelly read the glowing review of his new nonfiction book, *Atlantis: The Antediluvian World,* in the usually hostile pages of the *St. Paul Pioneer Press* with what was surely shocked disbelief. "Plausible, perspicuous, buttressed by many curious and recondite facts," the review declared, "an instance of what marvelous force may be imparted to any theory by the simple application of intellectual power."[1] In the past, the publication had maligned the former lieutenant governor and congressman at every possible turn, casting him as a tempestuous political threat. And yet even it could not deny the importance of the work on which he had ceaselessly toiled since a series of bruising election defeats sent him back to his study. "It is my eldest child," Donnelly wrote in his diary of the manuscript that had been waiting in press for nearly a year. "It may grow up to be an imbecile but the fibers of my heart will cling to it."[2] Working mostly in the isolation of Nininger City, he could do little more than speculate about how his brainchild would be received in the wider world. The fatalist in him feared the worst.

Donnelly sampled early reviews of *Atlantis* on trips into nearby Hastings, Minnesota, where he picked up the regional newspapers that served as his intellectual lifeline during hard winters spent in the small hamlet he had helped found along the Mississippi River. The book he worried might ruin what was left of his political brand was being received with unexpected enthusiasm. In nearby St. Paul, the *Daily Globe* led its review with that it considered a novel headline: "Ignatius Donnelly as an Author."[3] The notion of the former lieutenant governor and congressman as a popular scribe would, it seemed, take some getting used to, especially in an upper Midwest where Donnelly's name was synonymous with podium-thumping politics.

And yet even the legions of detractors couldn't deny the power of the politician turned public intellectual. The *Daily Globe*'s teaser of a subheading avowed that the Sage of Nininger's debut work of nonfiction was a "curiously interesting, entertaining, and valuable work." It was, the newspaper claimed, a sensation, and one still more exceptional because it had been written by a frontier Minnesotan rather than a New York intellectual. Any work written by Donnelly would, the editors insisted, command the interest of the curious public he had passionately served. In its glowing assessment, the newspaper seemed eager to ease its readers into Donnelly's earth-shaking, even heretical thesis: Atlantis was real, not fable; the Biblical flood referenced in Genesis was the very same that had inundated the Atlantean world, submerging the island kingdom and bringing its reign of cultural dominance to an abrupt end. "The fact that the story of Atlantis was for thousands of years regarded as a fable proves nothing," the *Daily Globe* reminded its readers, quoting Donnelly's own language exactly: "There is an unbelief which grows out of arrogance, as well as skepticism which is born of intelligence. The people nearest to the past are not always those best informed concerning the past."[4] Across the Mississippi River in Wisconsin, the *Janesville Daily Gazette* agreed, vowing that Donnelly's ingenious book had made the paper's editors believers. As Donnelly moves seamlessly from "one distinct and novel proposition to another," they said, readers begin to believe, in spite of themselves, that there "actually did exist such a piece of terra firma as Atlantis."[5]

Donnelly made no attempt to blunt the drama inherent in his thesis. Lawyer-like, he led with thirteen bold propositions of whose ultimate truth he hoped to convince his jury:

1. That there once existed in the Atlantic Ocean, opposite the mouth of the Mediterranean Sea, a large island, which was the remnant of an Atlantic continent, and known to the ancient world as Atlantis.

2. That the description of this island given by Plato is not, as has been long supposed, fable, but veritable history.
3. That Atlantis was the region where man first rose from a state of barbarism to civilization.
4. That it became, in the course of ages, a populous and mighty nation, from whose overflowings the shores of the Gulf of Mexico, the Mississippi River, the Amazon, the Pacific coast of South America, the Mediterranean, the west coast of Europe and Africa, the Baltic, the Black Sea, and the Caspian were populated by civilized nations.
5. That it was the true Antediluvian world; the Garden of Eden; the Gardens of the Hesperides; the Elysian Fields; the Gardens of Alcinous; the Mesomphalos; the Olympos; the Asgard of the traditions of the ancient nations; representing a universal memory of a great land, where early mankind dwelt for ages in peace and happiness.
6. That the gods and goddesses of the ancient Greeks, the Phoenicians, the Hindus, and the Scandinavians were simply the kings, queens, and heroes of Atlantis; and the acts attributed to them in mythology are a confused recollection of real historical events.
7. That the mythology of Egypt and Peru represented the original religion of Atlantis, which was sun-worship.
8. That the oldest colony formed by the Atlanteans was probably in Egypt, whose civilization was a reproduction of that of the Atlantic island.
9. That the implements of the Bronze Age of Europe were derived from Atlantis. The Atlanteans were also the first manufacturers of iron.
10. That the Phoenician alphabet, parent of all the European alphabets, was derived from an Atlantis alphabet, which was also conveyed from Atlantis to the Mayas of Central America.
11. That Atlantis was the original seat of the Aryan or Indo-European family of nations, as well as of the Semitic peoples, and possibly also of the Turanian races.
12. That Atlantis perished in a terrible convulsion of nature, in which the whole island sunk into the ocean, with nearly all its inhabitants.

13. That a few persons escaped in ships and on rafts, and, carried to the nations east and west the tidings of the appalling catastrophe, which has survived to our own time in the Flood and Deluge legends of the different nations of the old and new worlds.[6]

A veteran of the lecture circuit, Donnelly anticipated the sensation these opening statements would cause, and he took pains to remind skeptics that legends of buried cities like Pompeii had been considered mere myths until the mid-1700s. Herculaneum, another lost city excavated in the early eighteenth century, had also been considered pure invention by many. If these cities could be real, he reasoned, why not Atlantis?

A decade before Donnelly published his account of the antediluvian world, Jules Verne reintroduced Atlantis to the popular imagination with the first English translation of *Twenty Thousand Leagues under the Sea*. In the novel, Nemo, captain of the submarine *Nautilus*, explores the mysteries of the deep accompanied by Professor Pierre Aronnax, a French marine biologist and the story's narrator. *Twenty Thousand Leagues* had been a sensation in France, where it was first published in serial form in the children's magazine *Le magasin d'éducation et de recreation* in the spring of 1870. The popularity of the tale among readers of *Le magasin* had prompted the editor Pierre-Jules Hetzel to publish the book in a stand-alone French edition later that same year, thought it would have to wait until 1872 for its first printing in English.

Pigeonholed as children's literature by most US newspapers and literary reviews, the book's popularity spread slowly in the United States, with *Twenty Thousand Leagues* waiting two full years after its first translation into English for a dedicated review in the *New York Times* alongside Verne's subsequent novels *A Journey to the North Pole* and *The Field of Ice*. The *Times* review cast the Frenchman as "an author widely celebrated among children and young folks generally," and an "immense sensation in the juvenile world."[7] It noted the exceptional verisimilitude of tales so lifelike that their author could "scarcely be accused of exaggeration." In Verne's breathtaking fictional account, Captain Nemo and Professor Aronnax witness the wonders of Antarctica, the South Pole, and the great Kelp Forest, but their most memorable exploration is of a seemingly endless field of ruins at the bottom of the Atlantic. A man of science, Aronnax marvels at the sight of submerged Tuscan temples, crumbling aqueducts, and broad deserted streets. Declaring the ruined civilization sprawled out before him "a perfect Pompeii escaped beneath the waters," the professor wonders aloud, "Where was I? I must know at any cost." Noting Aronnax's confusion and wonder, Captain Nemo picks up a piece of chalkstone to inscribe his one-word answer—*Atlantis*—on a black-rock outcropping.[8]

Verne's fictional depiction closely parallels Plato's description of the island in *Critias*, a dialogue devoted almost entirely to what the philosopher believed to be a historical account of the lost island civilization. Like Professor Aronnax, Plato describes an acropolis and a marvelously engineered city located on a plain divided by aqueducts and surrounded by verdant mountains. In Verne's novel, the erudite Aronnax serves as a fictional proxy for Plato's historical authority, as he appears to confirm the existence of the legendary civilization, effectively debunking scholars who dismissed it as legend. Aronnax becomes a believer, exclaiming, "What a light shot through my mind! Atlantis! the Atlantis of Plato, that continent denied by Origen and Humbolt, who placed its disappearance amongst the legendary tales. I had it there now before my eyes, bearing upon it the unexceptionable testimony of its catastrophe." Led by what he calls "the strangest destiny," Aronnax and Nemo touch the "ruins a thousand generations old and contemporary with the geological epochs."[9]

One month after the first English translation of *Twenty Thousand Leagues* appeared in Britain, Verne's speculative fiction mingled unexpectedly with newspaper headlines, as the HMS *Challenger* expedition left Portsmouth, England, on December 21 for what would become a sixty-eight-thousand-nautical-mile scientific journey to plumb the secrets of the world's oceans. Though the *Challenger* had originally been built as a Royal Navy ship, most of the vessel's guns had been removed to make room for the dredging, sounding, and sampling equipment needed for an ambitious scientific expedition. Aboard were the prominent naturalists Charles Wyville Thomson, Henry Nottidge Moseley, and Rudolf von Willemoes-Suhm, along with the oceanographers John Young Buchanan and John Murray.

The results produced over a three-year journey that astounded credentialed scientists and the general public alike, and included the cataloging of over four thousand previously unknown species.[10] Via a combination of deep-sea soundings, bottom dredges, and open water trawls, the crew planned to study the chemical structure of the ocean floor, the physical and chemical composition of deep-sea deposits, and the distribution of organic life at varying depths. But privately the hopes for exploration were even more ambitious and competitive. While the

Challenger sailed south toward Portugal in early January, in the Caribbean, naturalist Louis Agassiz declared that representatives of "earlier geological periods" might well be found in the world's deepest waters.[11] The great naturalist had just returned from the island of Barbados, where, he wrote a colleague, in just four dredging hauls at between 75 and 125 fathoms he had collected specimens sufficient "to occupy half a dozen competent zoologists for one year."[12] The English biologist and anthropologist Thomas Henry Huxley further excited expectations in an article written for *Popular Science Monthly*, hinting at "zoological novelties; or, better still, zoological antiquities" intact in the ocean depths, including those that would represent the "predominant population of a past age."[13] The *Challenger* was then traveling into the region most likely to house the zoological antiquities to which Huxley referred, as it steamed from Portugal to Gibraltar to Madeira and the Canary Islands. Each of these volcanic peaks had long been considered possible candidates for, or geological analogs of, the lost continent. While the expedition would not attempt to confirm or deny a scientific basis for what it referred to as Plato's myth, it nevertheless felt compelled to acknowledge that the very idea of the sunken island continent had "not been without influence on studies intimately connected to oceanography."[14]

An avid reader of popular science periodicals, Donnelly seized on the scientific evidence turned up by the *Challenger* expedition. As a frontispiece to his book, he included a sounding illustration, "The Profile of Atlantis," subtitling it "deep-sea soundings of H.M. *Challenger* and U.S. Ship *Dolphin*."[15] Resembling a seismograph, the chart showed a broad peak projecting from the ocean floor—1,000 nautical miles wide and approximately 2,500 fathoms (15,000 feet) deep—with two distinct spikes emerging above the ocean's surface. The easternmost peak represented the Portuguese islands of Madeira, followed by several more spikes several hundred nautical miles away, representing the archipelago of the Azores. Undergirding these islands, the chart suggested, was an underwater volcanic mountain sufficiently wide to have hosted Plato's lost civilization. Donnelly drew additional support for his theory of an antediluvian world from the chief scientist aboard the *Challenger*, Sir Charles Wyville Thomson, who reported that the burnt-looking mountains of the Azores were in fact composed of lumps of porous black lava that, as the zoologist put it, "must have been ejected as volcanic bombs in a glorious display of fireworks at some period beyond the records of . . . history."[16] Writing for the *Westminster Review*, the Scottish historian William Henry Oliphant Smeaton agreed with Huxley and Donnelly, asserting that confirmation of the story Plato told in *Timaeus* could be seen in the Azores, where geological evidence pointed to an ancient volcanic explosion of a "gigantic scale" sufficient to have sunk an island empire.[17]

Titling his chapter on the oceanographic evidence "The Testimony of the Sea," Donnelly assigned the appellation "Dolphin's Ridge" to the widest portion of the undersea mountain he felt certain was the rock on which Atlantis stood.[18] The name paid tribute to the USS *Dolphin* under the direction of the American oceanographer Matthew Fontaine Murray, whose soundings of the Atlantic revealed what would later come to be known as the Mid-Atlantic Ridge running from northeast of Greenland all the way to the South Atlantic. From the sounding data obtained from the *Dolphin* expedition, Murray hypothesized the existence of what amounted to the world's longest mountain chain—with its highest peaks emerging as rugged islands like Iceland and the Azores. Donnelly's original map of the Mid-Atlantic Ridge delineated what he called a three-pronged form of a giant undersea range, with one prong pointing toward Ireland, another connecting with the northeast coast of South America, and a third near or on the west coast of Africa. The broadest portion of Dolphin's Ridge ran through the Azores archipelago, and here, he claimed, perhaps two thousand feet below the sea, lay the submerged Atlantis. The motion of the ocean currents, in Donnelly's view, further corroborated the existence of a Mid-Atlantic Ridge. The Gulf Stream's abrupt turn to the northwest as it approached Dolphin's Ridge from the southwest, he conjectured, must be a response to the Atlantean land mass buried in the middle of the sea, impeding its path.[19]

Donnelly's Dolphin's Ridge hypothesis reflected an original, inferential read of the literature, connecting the dots between archaeological, anthropological, zoological, and geological data. As the so-called Sage of Nininger, he was free to write and research as his conscience dictated, taking his conjectures well past the point where timid scholars turned away for fear of impropriety or public condemnation. The Dolphin's Ridge theory offered a case in point. While most scholars considered the alleged discovery of a lost civilization sufficiently sensational, Donnelly followed the evidence he had synthesized to two still more startling conclusions: first, that ancient people had traveled the ridges between continents, accounting for otherwise inexplicable cultural similarities in cultures half a world away; and second, that the Garden of Eden, whose location had never been firmly fixed by the Bible, was in fact a cultural memory of the near-perfect civilization cultivated for a time by the Atlanteans.

Concerning the first hypothesis, Donnelly hastened to add that the three-pronged connecting ridge lay almost completely submerged in the time of Atlantis, and therefore it would be incorrect to assume that movements to and from the island were easy or frequent. Instead, over time, seafaring peoples from Europe, North America, and Africa, including the Egyptians, Greeks, and Phoenicians, would have visited the kingdom only to return to the mainland with stories of its marvels. Donnelly worried that the second of these two conjectures, which made Atlantis synonymous with Eden, would sound heretical to Christian readers, and yet he persisted. While he arrived at this startling claim by a preponderance of the anthropological, theological, archaeological, and zoological evidence available to him, the basis of his conclusion rested on similarities between Genesis and Plato's narrative of the rise and fall of Atlantis. "The Bible agrees with Plato in the statement that these Antediluvians had reached great populousness and wickedness," Donnelly wrote, adding that it was on account of their wickedness that God resolved to destroy them.[20] In both cases the inhabitants of the doomed land were destroyed in a great flood. Likewise, the Bible claimed that in an earlier age, before its destruction, humankind had lived in a peaceful, sinless condition in a Garden of Eden; Plato, Donnelly pointed out, claimed the same of the Atlanteans. Even the description from Genesis of a river departing from Eden, from whence it divided and became four tributaries, closely aligned with Platonic descriptions of Atlantis. The Four Rivers of Paradise that marked the biblical location of Eden corresponded with the great irrigation ditch that encircled Atlantis, into which streams flowed down from the mountains. Its shape—three tributaries encircled by a fourth river—could be seen in the emblem of the cross surrounded by a circle, which, Donnelly argued, had been accepted as the symbol of the Garden of Eden since pre-Christian times.[21]

Donnelly braced himself for widespread public condemnation but found praise instead. The *New York Times* lauded his new release in a two-paragraph item. "There has always been a singular fascination about the Greek philosopher's story of the great island continent that once existed in the Atlantic Ocean," the review began, adding, "It has remained for Mr. Ignatius Donnelly to . . . bring it up again for serious consideration."[22] While noting the author's reliance on deep-sea soundings from the *Challenger* mission, the review praised Minnesota's onetime congressman for his ingenuity and talent for inductive reasoning, cautioning that the tome was far from idle reading. "Mr. Donnelly's collation of exact knowledge and the results of ethnological research is excellent," the newspaper conceded, "and few who take up his volume will dispute his right to his theory." One week later, on February 25, the *Cincinnati Commercial* summarized for its readers the bold claims made by "the versatile Mr. Donnelly." The book, it noted, was a "singularly interesting one" presented with "much ingenuity and painstaking care."[23] As if in an afterthought, the review closed, "And it is also very well written." The *Boston Post* brought the title's first two weeks on the market to a satisfactory conclusion with yet another favorable assessment. Like the *Times* and the *Commercial*, the *Post* seemed almost taken aback not just by the sheer originality of the analysis but also by the author's tone, which seemed at times to be so self-assured as to be beyond "the limit of mere speculative thought."[24] For these early reviewers Donnelly sounded more like a sage than a scholar.

And yet for all the work's bravado, the confidence that distinguished it did not translate to the personal life of the author. Scarcely more than six weeks before its publication, Donnelly dared to dream in the pages of his diary that *Atlantis* would bring him success, honor, and relief from the debts he had incurred pursuing legal remedies for his contested election suit. At the same time, the fatalist in him feared that his literary achievement would be lost on the wider world, because, as he put it, "I am a provincial in location and a nobody in the scientific world; for mankind always looks to Jerusalem, and think it impossible that any good thing can come out of Nazareth."[25] Now, three months removed from that dark night of the soul, he reflected in hindsight, "I feared my baby stillborn; that my golden egg was addled; that the cloud of adverse fate would never lift."[26]

But it did lift. Based in part on the strength of earlier reviews, Harper & Brothers asked Donnelly to begin making corrections for a second edition. Early sales in England suggested transatlantic appeal. On March 26, Donnelly received a letter postmarked London that helped reassure him of the lasting contribution *Atlantis* would make. The four-page missive from British prime minister William Ewart Gladstone nearly caused him to issue a "war hoop of exultation."[27] Gladstone's personal note felt like redemption, as it reaffirmed the David-beats-Goliath theme on which Donnelly built both his personality and his political career. In his journal he savored the irony of it all: "I looked down at myself, and could not but smile at the appearance of the man who, in this little, snow-bound hamlet, was corresponding with the man whose word was fate anywhere in the British Empire. . .. The leg of my pants was torn; my coat was nearly buttonless . . . and I was trimming the kerosene lamps."[28] The author was surely prone to exaggeration, but it was true that political life had not been as remunerative for him as it had for many of his less scrupulous colleagues. Instead of growing richer in Washington, DC, he had seen his financial fortunes rapidly decline since the Panic of 1857 had reduced the boom town of Nininger City to a hard-pressed agrarian outpost clinging to existence. At twenty-six, flush with cash from successful real estate ventures in Nininger and elsewhere, Donnelly had been a millionaire,[29] but now it was all he could do to keep the home fires burning.

Harper & Brothers marketed *Atlantis* energetically, sensing the reading public's appetite for texts on history, literature, and classical studies. Among the titles in its catalog of new books and editions for the winter of 1882 were books on English, French, and American history, alongside edited editions of Herodotus, *Hamlet*, and *Measure for Measure*.[30] Readers in the United States and Great Britain were in a mood to trace cultural origins, to expand their minds, and to reacquaint themselves with the classics of antiquity. Sandwiched between *The Making of England*, by John Richard Green, and *Old Greek Education*, by John Mahaffy, in Harper & Brothers' list, *Atlantis: The Antediluvian World* matched the zeitgeist perfectly.

In Minneapolis–St. Paul as well as in nearby Hastings, an enthusiastic homegrown readership boosted sales. In a column called "City Globules," the *St. Paul Daily Globe* noted that demand for Donnelly's book had been so great that one local bookseller had already ordered five hundred copies of the second edition.[31] In the author's childhood hometown of Philadelphia, demand for the book at the iconic Lippincott & Co. continued swiftly on the heels of a review that called the author's hypothesis "unquestionably ingenious." *Atlantis*, it vowed, was sufficiently compelling that it could singlehandedly stimulate popular interest in historic and prehistoric research.[32] In St. Albans, Vermont, the *Daily Messenger*, avowing that a perfect synergy had been found between author and subject matter, remarked on the fruitful concordance between the "strange" Ignatius Donnelly and the "strangely interesting" volume *Atlantis*.[33]

And yet even the formidable combination of Donnelly's ambition and Harper & Brothers' publicity machine could not insulate the iconoclastic *Atlantis* from its fair share of mixed and negative reviews. Quoting the *New York Commercial*, the *Warrenton Gazette* in North Carolina pointed out Donnelly's tendency to "take for granted what he should have proved," especially in his earnestness to clinch an argument. "If in every instance he does not succeed in convincing his reader, he at least interests and amuses him," the reviewer opined, while conceding that, in the main, the writer wove facts together with "great ingenuity" while building his case with "ability and industry."[34] Across the country in Salt Lake City, the conservative *Deseret News* struck a similar chord, saying that while it could neither confirm nor deny the book's marvelous theories, it was nevertheless well worth reading. Apart from the controversial theory the volume extolled, it was a literary work "worthy of great commendation."[35]

Predictably, the strongest pushback came from newspapers in the Bible Belt. The *Central Presbyterian* in Richmond, Virginia, chastised the *Chicago Interior* for a fawning review of the new book, writing, "We are a little amused that so learned a journal as the Chicago *Interior* should be half carried away with the fanciful book of Mr. Ignatius Donnelly on 'The Lost Atlantis.'"[36] The *St. Louis Post Dispatch*, quoting the *Cincinnati Enquirer*, registered similar amusement at the book's claims, pointing to the author's infamous dustup with the politically powerful Washburn family as proof of his penchant for dramatic overstatement. "The audacity with which this book is cut out is truly worthy of Donnelly," noted the especially cynical reviewer, who added that the author-politician's current theology reflected the loss of faith "a good Catholic will come to after he has been some years in Congress." Titling his review "Another Crank," the critic maintained that in his gift for selling dubious dogma, Donnelly was akin to Brigham Young, intending no compliment in the comparison.[37] The *Chicago Daily Tribune* picked up the theme, closing its review by reminding readers that the author of *Atlantis* had previously represented Minnesota in Congress for several years. "This," the wags at the *Tribune* noted, "accounts for two things: his fondness for subjects of very remote origin" and his "occasional misapprehension of fiction for fact."[38]

The successful launch of the title in the spring of 1882 commenced a significant period of reevaluation and recalibration in Donnelly's life. With *Atlantis* generating additional income and acclaim, he began to reconsider his postcongressional identity as a farmer-landowner, and much of the impetus for this reassessment came from his wife. Kate Donnelly saw the publication of *Atlantis* not only as an opportunity to pay back farming debts but also as a chance to convince her husband to abandon the yeoman's life in favor of the more urbane, intellectual pursuits she considered his true strength. The Donnellys had moved to the Minnesota frontier from the East, and neither they nor their children were natural farmers. "When I think of farming—I get almost sick," Kate wrote in early May. "Think how hard they work—and they invariably come out in debt—& then comes borrowing next—& then misery—life is scarcely worth having."[39] While Donnelly kept the cropland he predicted would prove indispensable in a future wheat boom, he partially acquiesced to his wife's request, selling fifteen city lots and additional farming ground further afield in Stevens County, Minnesota.[40]

In the six months following the publication of *Atlantis*, the author's bleak fortunes had turned. In November he had lamented his circumstance in far-flung Nininger, admitting to his diary that he "grieved sometimes over the hard fate that chains me and mine . . . to this lonely spot." Even so, he promised, he would try to make the best of it, and count his blessings. "And yet, it squeezes one's heart," he added, "to see the years slip away, while he does nothing—is nothing."[41] Now, with his first book selling well in its fourth month on the market, he had repaid many of his most pressing debts and won back the public esteem he feared he had lost completely. But he had not yet heard en masse from the constituency whose support he now sought. The scientific and academic community known for its rigorous appraisal had yet to weigh in on *Atlantis*.

By late summer of 1882, the popular appeal of *Atlantis: The Antediluvian World* caused the American Association for the Advancement of Science to offer Donnelly membership in its elite ranks, despite growing discontent with the upstart book among credentialed scientists. Charles Darwin had received a gift copy of the book from the AAAS and reportedly read it with skepticism.[42]

While Donnelly made little to no mention in his diary of particular articles that inspired *Atlantis*, a review of the newspapers and periodicals that discussed the lost island from 1877 to 1881 suggests a likely paper trail. In July 1877, an article entitled "Glimpses of Atlantis" ran in a supplement to *Scientific American*. Published without a byline and intended to translate emerging science relevant to Atlantis to the broader reading public, the article was reprinted in dozens of newspapers across the United States, including several in the Midwest. "The lines of scientific thinking were converging," the author of "Glimpses" summarized, in support of "the truth of the ancient story, long considered mythical, in regard to the geologically recent occurrence of that remarkable catastrophe." The article advanced its core argument in plain language: namely, that archaeo-geology had demonstrated that "the memory of man runs back vastly farther than history has been willing to admit, so that there remains no inherent improbability in the [Atlantis] story the Egyptian priests told Solon." To further substantiate its conclusions, it recited findings from the sounding expeditions undertaken by the *Dolphin* and the *Challenger*, which had overturned conventional wisdom that the bottom of the Atlantic was shaped like a regular trough or basin rather than a series of dramatic canyons. In fact, the shape of the Atlantic floor was closer to a double trough, soundings revealed, with two deep depressions separated by a mountainous ridge running north to south. On the western side of that ridge—the North American side—lay a series of hills and valleys of the sort that could have been created only if those features had once been on dry land. The popular article anticipated Donnelly's argument, using many of the same terms, before concluding that "here, unquestionably we have the backbone of the ancient Atlantic continent." It went on to claim that the final disappearance of the ridge that marked Atlantis's highest elevations had occurred relatively recently, corroborating theories of a Europe-to-America land bridge put forward by the Austrian botanist Franz Unger and, to a lesser extent, by the naturalist Asa Gray's research into the European origins of the California sequoias.[43]

Recent discoveries from archeologists and ethnographers working in Mexico and Central America, such as Charles Étienne Brasseur de Bourbourg, had suggested that Central American narratives of a great country to the east that disappeared beneath the sea were relatively widespread among Mesoamerican peoples. It was Brasseur de Bourbourg who first pointed out that the words *Atlas* and *Atlantic* lacked clear precedents in the Old World, though the *Atl* prefix was a part of the Nahuatl language in Mexico and Central America. Given the concurrence of historical testimony from both sides of the Atlantic—from ancient Egypt and Greece on one side and the Maya on the other—concerning the existence of an island kingdom, the *Scientific American* concluded, "We are not aware of any geological reason for doubting the possibility of the lingering of Atlantis as an archipelago down to post-tertiary times, and its final submergence with the period man appeared."[44] Such speculations were reinforced by Brasseur de Bourboug's references to Plato's descriptions of the culture of Atlantis, which he believed was carried on by the Maya after catastrophe struck the island. In his book *Quatre lettres sur le Mexique*, Brasseur de

Bourbourg drew extensive parallels between Mayan and Egyptian pantheons and cosmologies, implying that they had a common source on the lost continent of Atlantis.[45]

In October 1879, the aspiring archaeologist Edward Herbert Thompson synthesized the work of Brasseur de Bourbourg and others in his article "Atlantis Not a Myth." Published in *Popular Science*, Thompson's article made the most accessible, engaging argument yet for the existence of the antediluvian kingdom. Written while Thompson was still in his twenties, the piece bristled with youthful confidence and testified to a mind, and an era, hungry for new discovery. Condemning the "spirit of bigotry" that had caused prior scientists to scorn the likes of Galileo, Thompson insisted that a spirit of open-mindedness was sweeping the scientific world, one that "tells men to look upon a new idea or theory, even if it does run outside of the accustomed rut, with a reasoning if not favorable eye." He predicted that an Edison-like figure would soon emerge with an intellect sufficient to "bring together the faint voice of the prehistoric past and the bright, clear voice of the present." Such a genius would find among the Mayan artifacts an American Rosetta Stone that would reveal the complete chain of human history—a chain that ran through Atlantis.[46]

Thompson's article added little to the scientific argument for the ancient continent, but it summarized the case for it more succinctly, and more imaginatively, than any that had come before it. The author conjectured so convincingly that his speculations sounded like facts to many lay readers. He wrote of an ancient peninsula extending from Mexico and Central America to modern-day Madeira and the Azores. This peninsula was fair and fertile and inhabited by a people well versed in the arts of war and civilization, and whose domain stretched well into Europe and Asia. Then, Thompson claimed, "the whole fair land was engulfed by the sea, in a mighty convulsion of nature." Plutarch, Solon, Herodotus, and other ancient writers spoke of the island as a known fact, Thompson pointed out, adding that Seneca's writing in *Medea* also suggested a belief in the submerged kingdom. Plato, he insisted, was well known as the most cautious of ancient philosophers, a fact that made his detailed account of Atlantis all the more compelling. Thompson quoted Plato's claim that the greatest deed of Athens was its military defeat of an army that "came across the Atlantic seas, and insolently invaded Europe and Asia." The army from the West hailed from an island that was larger than Asia and Libya combined, and from it one could pass easily to the other islands, and from these to the continent beyond. The continent beyond, Thompson surmised, was the Americas, where Mayan culture flourished as the westernmost outpost of an Atlantean empire.[47]

The enthusiastic reaction to Thompson's bombshell article in *Popular Science* likely boosted Donnelly's confidence that a book-length treatment of the subject would capture the public imagination. In fact, Thompson's article moved Stephen Salisbury III, the chief benefactor of the American Antiquarian Society and a fellow Mayanist, to support Thompson's nascent career in archaeology and, ultimately, to secure the younger man a post as an American consul in the Yucatan. Still, by the early 1880s, Donnelly's national platform and name recognition far exceeded Thompson's renown. A generation older, Donnelly had the time, the library, and the intellect to forward the case for Atlantis to a national and international audience.

For all their popular appeal and intrigue, however, the views of Brasseur de Bourbourg, Thompson, Salisbury, and other so-called Mayanists were far from mainstream in the scientific community. And as Donnelly's *Atlantis* achieved wider readership, established scientists agitated to counter its claims. Darwin's alleged lukewarm reaction to Donnelly's treatise echoed that of many of the ethnologists and naturalists who read the book in the six months after its publication. Some periodicals, hoping to capitalize on the book's popularity by challenging it, summoned experts in an attempt to expose the Sage of Nininger as a pseudoscientist. In Brooklyn, the *Daily Eagle* commissioned the New York Supreme Court justice and ethnologist Daniel M. Tredwell to bring Donnelly down from his pedestal. Tredwell filled three tabloid columns in a spirited attempt to discredit Donnelly's theories and, by extension, Plato's. Calling Plato's secondhand account of the Edenic island a "foolish" and "fragmentary story," Tredwell agreed with Donnelly on one important point: determining the origins of Grecian, Phoenician, and Egyptian civilization was one of "the most perplexing ethnological problems ever presented to human understanding."[48] His observation explained the strength of feeling on both sides of the debate: if Plato's narrative could be corroborated and Donnelly's theories proven, the history of Western civilization would have to be rewritten.

Tredwell's claim of a fiction at the heart of the Platonic narrative was conventional. Lacking the evidence to confirm or deny its substance, ethnologists questioned instead the provenance of the story, which had come to Plato via the priests of Sais, in Egypt, who in turn shared it with the Greek traveler Solon. From there, Tredwell points out, it was passed down from Critias to Socrates, Timeas, Hermocrates, and Plato, losing accuracy in each recounting. The story suffered from Greek "interpolation," Tredwell insisted, and it had been further misinterpreted in Donnelly's accounting.[49]

Tredwell's attempt at debunking was systematic and methodological. First he disagreed with Donnelly's idea that the Greeks, Phoenicians, and Romans had, in effect, been civilized by the Atlanteans to their west; on the contrary, imports in the region at that time had largely come from the East. Language and myth, he maintained, moved in a similar east-to-west direction. Atlas, the alleged patron and ruler of Atlantis, was very likely a Greek adaptation of characters found in the Vedic hymns of India. Even *Atl*—the root of *Atlantis* and *Atlas*—was etymologically alien to the Greek tongue, and to European languages more generally. Once the root of the word itself had been pinpointed, Tredwell claimed in his philological analysis, the real location of Atlantis, if such a place existed, could be geo-located. The watery kingdom, he argued, was more likely to be found in the volcanic islands of the Pacific Ocean between Easter Island and the Marianas, which were also located above a deep-ocean trench.[50]

As comprehensive as Donnelly's research had been, he lacked the field-specific knowledge brought to bear by scholars conducting original research in the discipline. Among the top periodicals reviewing *Atlantis* that late spring and summer, *Harper's Monthly* staked out a middle ground halfway between Donnelly worship and Donnelly condemnation, writing, "If occasionally we are staggered by the insufficiency of the premises and proofs on which some of his cherished conclusions are based, and are amused at the facility and extravagance of some of his deductions, his reasoning is ingenious." Donnelly's gift, the periodical suggested, lay in his ability to interpret complex scientific and historical scholarship for a broader public, resulting in a work that was "entirely free from the technical shibboleths which render scientific works sealed books to average readers." The author, the review granted, was so "full of his subject" that only an "abnormally dull and unsympathetic reader" would not catch the contagion of his enthusiasm."[51]

Though *Harper's* conceded Donnelly's charisma, its review echoed the familiar criticism that the author had inadequately traced the lineage of his theories to predecessors who had made similar points decades if not centuries earlier. For example, in his book *Lettres sur L'Atlantide de Platon et sur l'ancienne histoire de l'Asie* (Letters on the Atlantis of Plato and on the ancient history of Asia), the French astronomer Jean Sylvain Bailly had defended the truth of Plato's accounting in *Timaeus* and *Critias*. Addressed to his fellow French philosopher Voltaire, an Atlantis skeptic, the first of Bailly's letters established a Donnelly-like premise: just because we do not have direct scientific proof of a phenomenon does not mean that phenomenon cannot exist. As Bailly put it: "Doubt is always permitted in science; it is the touchstone of the truth. However, doubt must have boundaries; all truths cannot be demonstrated like mathematical truths."[52]

A skilled astronomer credited with helping calculate the orbit for Halley's comet, Bailly drew eclectically on science, classical mythology, linguistics, and Orientalism to make his case, arguing that the Brahmans who had shaped Indian civilization were more likely Sanskrit-speaking Atlanteans. Like Donnelly, Bailly noted the similarities in the Atlantis theogony, as reported by Diodorus of Sicily, to that of the Egyptians, the Phoenicians, and the Greeks. He deduced that each of these countries had been "civilized" by a sophisticated society capable of spreading its belief systems and cultural influence. This island's imperial reign had lasted until the eruption that Plato references in *Timaeus* caused its destruction.[53]

Bailly was a polymath, capable of reading and synthesizing complex research in multiple disciplines. And like Donnelly he was also a successful politician, elected first as the president of the French National Assembly and later as mayor of Paris in the days immediately following the storming of the Bastille. Unlike Donnelly, however, Bailly believed Atlantis was centered in the far North, closer to the Arctic, either in Spitsbergen or in Greenland. He claimed its people moved south toward the Mediterranean as the Earth cooled, spreading their culture as they migrated.

In *Lettres*, Bailly prods the eighty-five-year-old Voltaire with the idea that, as he puts it, "It is difficult to find interest in people we did not know."[54] Because Voltaire had read the Eastern philosophers and developed an admiration for Vedic wisdoms, it was understood that he would have difficulty properly valuing Atlantis: "You must feel some aversion in casting them [Vedic philosophers] off for those teachers lost in the night of antiquity," Bailly observes, "forgotten by the ingratitude of men, and whose names and memory have almost been erased by time. One creates a society, and chooses friends by reading history."[55] In so many words, Bailly implies that Voltaire has chosen the wrong historical friends and, moreover, that the wisdoms of Sanskrit, spoken and written from roughly 900 BCE to 1500 BCE, must have come from somewhere else, and that somewhere else could not have been from a relatively youthful culture like Greece. Using archaeo-astronomy, Bailly estimates the apogee of Atlantean culture at around 3900 BCE. Then, working backward, he computes the following peak dates for other ancient civilizations:

Egyptians, 3000
Chaldeans, 2473
Phrygians, 2700
Persians, 3209
Indians, 3000
Chinese, 2952
Scythes, 2924[56]

Bailly arrives at his approximate dates by examining ancient texts of recorded celestial events, enacting the name for the field he helped pioneer: archaeo-astronomy. Egypt's date is calculated according to the periodic cycles of the heliacal rising of the star Sirius (Sothis), which corresponded with the flooding of the Nile. Dates for Persia are computed using ancient manuscripts that reference the four stars indicated by the cardinal points: the Eye of Taurus and the Heart of Scorpio related to the two equinoxes, while the Eye of Leo and the southern Fish corresponded to the two solstices. Bailly arrives at his date for Chinese civilization using astronomical accounts of the first emperor of China, though he cautions that his time frames represent the date of a renaissance, or flowering of astronomical culture, not a beginning or founding date. Like Plato, he dates the founding of Atlantis to around 9000 BCE and its development of an advanced economy and culture to approximately 6000 BCE. The reason that the Egyptians, the Chaldeans or the Persians, the Indians, the Chinese, and the Scythians or the Tartars all experienced a cultural renaissance at around 3000 BCE could be explained by early visits to them by a people who had since mostly disappeared from the face of the earth: the astronomy-gifted Atlanteans. Sanskrit, Bailly claims, offers a linguistic artifact testifying to the passage to India of an ancient maritime people located in the northern Atlantic. While some of Bailly's notions struck contemporaries and colleagues as far-fetched, his notion of a language, and therefore culture, dispersing from west of India—for example, from areas around the Caspian Sea—and flowing to the East had gained wider acceptance by the time Donnelly published *Atlantis*.

While Bailly may have been Donnelly's most direct eighteenth-century predecessor in terms of style, tone, and claim, the archaeologist and photographer Augustus Le Plongeon arguably influenced *Atlantis* more than any other Donnelly contemporary. Le Plongeon was a fascinating, mercurial, and controversial figure himself. He had been conducting fieldwork in the Yucatan for nearly a decade by the time *Atlantis* was published, and though Donnelly cites him by name only once in nearly five hundred pages, the arguments of the two men closely resemble one another. Donnelly quotes Le Plongeon's controversial claim that one-third of the Mayan tongue was "pure Greek."[57] A dedicated Mayanist like Thompson and Brasseur de Bourborg before him, Le Plongeon believed that the Mesoamericans, not the Indians of the Far East, were the chief diffusers of language, religion, and culture. And, like Donnelly, he believed that the ancient civilizations had been cultured from west to east. Le Plongeon, however, believed that the Mayans predated the Atlanteans and used Atlantis as a literal and cultural bridge to reach the Egyptians, the Phoenicians, and the Greeks.

Le Plongeon's interest in Atlantis was, in fact, secondary to his interest in the Maya, but in order for his theory of Mayan interchange with Egypt and India to hold water, it needed an ancient intermediary in the mid-Atlantic capable of explaining the cultural progression from west to east and, at the same time, convincing those skeptical of the Mayans' abilities as sailors that as a people they could simply have island-hopped from Atlantis and other islands on their way to Africa and beyond. To justify his theory, Le Plongeon traces the lineage of scholars and philosophers who had written about the island kingdom, beginning with Plutarch's *Life of Solon* and *De facie in orbe lunae*.[58] Diodorus Siculus, he maintains, attributed the discovery of the island continent to the Phoenicians, describing the land as mountainous while at the same time warm and temperate. The Byzantine historian Procopius alludes to Atlantis as an enormous island several thousand stadia, or about 350 miles, from Ogygia, an island mentioned in Homer's *Odyssey*. Theopompus and Cicero reference its immense size, while Aristotle refers to a decree made by the city of Carthage in 509 BCE, limiting the outmigration of Romans to the "Western Lands" presumed to be Atlantis. The belief in the former existence of extensive lands in the middle of the Atlantic, Le Plongeon points out, was acknowledged by scientists well into the fifth century CE, the general understanding being that the archipelago had been submerged as a result of cataclysmic seismic activity. He quotes Proclus in his commentary on *Timaeus* as saying, "The famous Atlantis exists no longer, but we can hardly doubt that it did once, for Marcellus, who wrote of Ethiopian Affairs, says that such and so great an island once existed, and that it is evidenced by those who composed histories relative to the external sea."[59] Le Plongeon blames catastrophic events like the fall of Carthage and, later, the burning of the Library of Alexandria, Egypt, for the loss of a more robust paper trial.[60] The closing of the academies at Athens and the schools of Alexandria and the burning of additional libraries at Serapeum had further abetted the West's cultural amnesia.

Donnelly largely refrained from Le Plongeon's potentially anti-Christian rhetoric, focusing not on the cultural whitewashing of Atlantis from the collective memory by missionaries, but instead on the scientific and cultural evidence for the island's existence. Perhaps wishing to distance himself from the kind of fanciful mythologizing Le Plongeon and his wife, Alice, proffered in their interpretation of Mayan theology, he preferred to think of his argument for Atlantis as a legal briefing or an appeal to a jury, organizing his initial chapters as thematic "testimonies."

While Donnelly was seldom embraced by the credentialed scientists whose esteem he sought, the popular appeal of Atlantis stirred the general public, placing him at the center of a cultlike obsession with the submerged civilization that continued long after his book's publication.[61] No doubt inspired by Donnelly's bestseller, New Orleans planned its Mardi Gras parade around the theme, dedicating twenty floats to illustrate the "fabled splendors of the lost continent."[62] In Baltimore the annual Oriole Pageant reprised the Edenic kingdom not just in a parade but at a grand ball held at the Academy of Music, wherein a tableau had been created to represent this mid-ocean "terrestrial paradise." Hundreds of thousands turned out to see the Atlantean-themed pageant billed as a "spectacle of Oriental Splendor and magnificence."[63]

The inherent appeal of Donnelly's argument translated into remarkable book sales abroad, both in England, where the prime minister's endorsement had spurred demand, and elsewhere in Europe. Harper & Brothers issued seven editions of the book in 1882 alone while approving multiple foreign-language editions.[64] Indeed, by the winter of 1883, Donnelly had simultaneously managed both to resurrect the story of Atlantis and to renovate his own personal reputation. The Sage of Nininger, observers claimed, had become one of the most talked-about figures outside the professional and intellectual circles expected to debate the existence of ancient civilizations.[65] The genius of *Atlantis* lay not so much in original research as in its outreach to tens of thousands of readers who were typically excluded from matters of scientific conjecture. Readers eagerly posted letters of appreciation to Donnelly, with some enclosing evidence of attempts to solve the mystery of the ancient civilization for themselves.[66]

Donnelly had fired the public's imagination, and the public responded by filling the nation's newspapers and magazines with news, reviews, and verse inspired by the fabled island. In the heart of the Great Plains, the *Weekly Kansas Chief* celebrated the cultural craze by featuring a poem about Atlantis on its front page. Penned by the New York novelist and poet John Townsend (J. T.) Trowbridge, the verse lines celebrated the romantic allure of the submerged isle, describing "a realm of rivers, vales, and valiant men: / Be it a myth or well-preserved tradition, / Today in fancy we may build again / That early vision."[67] In Milwaukee, the *Weekly Wisconsin* followed suit, running its own anonymous ode to the Edenic island atop page 2: "Beautiful aisle of the ancient sea / Long lost Atlantis come up to me!"[68] In Iowa, the *Fairfield Tribune* decorated its pages with a remarkable one hundred verse lines penned by the writer-historian A. R. Fulton from Des Moines. With a clear nod to Donnelly, Fulton concluded, "All this was far in the past, but still / A mystery doth haunt us; / For neither books nor wisest sages tell / Where sleeps the lost Atlantis!"[69]

Inspired by Donnelly's findings, poetic odes to the fantastical undersea realm ran in newspapers as far away as Troy, Kansas, where the outspoken editor Solomon Miller found a kindred spirit in Donnelly's iconoclastic notions. Like the onetime congressman from Minnesota, Miller had been a politician, serving terms in both the Kansas House and Senate. And like Donnelly he was an acknowledged master of the homespun political put-down, leveling his opponents with epithets such as "dirty dog," "skunk," and "hare-brained jackass."[70] *Atlantis* captured Miller's fancy, as it did many midwestern editors eager for a native son to tackle the suffocating sanctimoniousness they perceived among intellectuals on the Eastern Seaboard. Like many Middle American readers, Miller was especially intrigued by Donnelly's claim that the mound-building Native Americans of the southern and midwestern United States were, like the Mayans, descendants of the Atlanteans. Miller mentioned Donnelly's illustrations of anthropomorphic representations of the mound-building indigenous peoples of the Midwest who raised earthen mounds to represent animals, like the elephant, not known to exist in the New World. Ancient Mexican and Central American drawings also consistently depicted elephants, suggesting contact between the ancient civilizations of the East and West. Miller went so far as to declare "highly probable" Donnelly's notion that Native Americans had been refugees from the great cataclysm that had inundated that island kingdom, and he vowed to reserve space in future editions of his newspaper for ongoing updates on the all-consuming Atlantis question.[71]

Spurred on by the impressive sales for *Atlantis* and the freethinking spirit of the times, Donnelly began working on a follow-up volume in May 1882. Like its predecessor, this new work of nonfiction would grow from interdisciplinary research in fields ranging from geology to ethnology to history and theology, and like its predecessor, it would be written quickly in dedicated sessions in Nininger City, with occasional trips to favorite bookstores in St. Paul to retrieve necessary texts. "It grew within me from small beginnings like an inspiration," Donnelly noted in his journal, with a flush of excitement similar to that which he had experienced in drafting *Atlantis*.[72] His new brainchild soon attracted the attention of the *St. Paul Globe*, which reported that Donnelly would leave for New York City in early July to "arrange with Harper Brothers for the publication of another book" that would "outrank Atlantis" in the interest it would kindle in literary circles.[73] Donnelly left for New York just two months after beginning to draft his latest manuscript, hopeful that Harper & Brothers would buy his new effort on sight. As he had with *Atlantis*, he dropped the manuscript off for consideration before returning to his hotel, hopeful he would have a contract in hand by the time he left the city. Instead, he returned to the Harper offices to find that they had refused to publish his new work on the grounds that it would be condemned by the scientific community and rejected by the general public, which would find its thesis too radical.[74]

Scribner's rejected the manuscript next, sending Donnelly into a familiar tailspin of self-doubt.[75] He had made the trip to New York flush with excitement for his sequel to *Atlantis*, but now the bustle of the city he had looked forward to visiting served only to deepen his depression. On the train back to his childhood hometown of Philadelphia, the specter of Ignatius Donnelly as defeated politician and American crank reared itself once more, conjuring the old demons that fueled his often fatalistic thinking. Viewed through a haze of disappointment and depression, New York was little more than a cauldron of writhing humanity he was all too glad to leave.

Still, for all his gloom, Donnelly understood that he had found a second calling that would allow him a midlife reprieve from the capriciousness of public service. He noted in his journal, "One thing is certain: —my books have lifted me out of the dirty cesspool of politics, nasty enough at all times, but absolutely foul to the man who doesn't win."[76] While its sequel had yet to find a publisher, there was little doubt that *Atlantis* had been a winner.

CHAPTER 3

Ragnarok: The Age of Fire and Gravel

Back in his natal hometown, Donnelly arranged an interview with a newspaper friendly to his cause, the *Philadelphia Press*, making no public mention of his new manuscript's recent rejections. Pennsylvania's native son had traveled east for the purpose of delivering his latest effort, the *Press* reported, which was true enough.

In Philadelphia, Donnelly jumped at the chance to make his pitch in the pages of a major metropolitan daily. In its July 25 edition, the *St. Paul Globe* reprinted the lengthy interview he had given to the *Philadelphia Press* about his new work. The *Press* had done him a publicity favor, it seemed, trumpeting in big bold type that the Sage of Nininger's forthcoming nonfiction book would attempt to prove that the "legends of olden time"—floods, fire and brimstone, and the fall of man—were literally true. The newspaper explained to its readers the special significance of Donnelly's unusual title, *Ragnarok*: in Old Norse, it meant a "darkness of the gods" or "twilight of the gods" that precipitated the destruction of the world. The book contained another, bigger bombshell, one that Donnelly had waited well into his interview to reveal: namely, that the "drift" layers of rock, dust, and gravel assumed by geologists to be "diluvium" soils deposited by flood, glacier, or ice sheet had instead been caused by a catastrophic impact from a comet.[1]

"I feel that any statement of the purpose of my book before its publication would scarcely do it justice," Donnelly cautioned his interviewer. "It is an argument which attacks many preconceived opinions." On first blush, he conceded, the public might well dismiss the theories animating his latest manuscript as "impossible, if not absurd," but, as with *Atlantis*, he hoped they would give the copious evidence he had curated a fair hearing. "I hope that those who read the book will lay it down with the feeling that if I have not proven my case, I have at least made a plausible argument," he told the *Press*.[2]

Donnelly made his comments with the stinging rejection from Scribner's still fresh. The publisher had taken the unusual step of sending a manuscript intended for a general readership to a scientist whose report on the book, once delivered, had made the press think better of extending a contract. While the reviewer admitted that the book was "well written," it was, he added, "scientifically ridiculous—worthy of Jules Verne."[3] Humbled perhaps by the review's caustic tone, Donnelly assumed a less bombastic demeanor in the Philadelphia interview, though privately he continued to insist that if his theories weren't exactly right, they were at least plausible. The near-constant dismissal of his notions as pseudoscience by credentialed experts rankled him, causing him to arrive at the cynical conclusion that a hidebound scientist-reviewer would take offense "at the idea of an extra-terrestrial origin of anything found on earth from the soul of man to a paving stone."[4]

While he hoped to remain coy about the exact hypotheses his manuscript would advance, Donnelly's gift of gab got the better of him. By the close of his interview with the *Press*, he had revealed his argument in considerable detail. To make his case, he would need to establish the fact that comets weren't made up only of gases, as many supposed, but of what he termed "ponderable material," such as rock and clay dust. It was this dusty, rocky "gravel," he claimed, that had been ejected across most of the Western Hemisphere after the comet's devastating impact, settling on the earth from above like a heavy snowfall, rather than being slowly deposited by moving glaciers or ice sheets. Comets weren't as rare as the general public assumed, he insisted, but were instead as common as fish in the sea. Even a single impact from a comet would gravely injure life on earth, and with some comet tails as lengthy as the distance between the earth and the sun, even a fragment from a portion of one, if ripped free or sheared off by the sun's gravitational forces, could cause a horrific strike.[5]

Second, in order to ensure a fair hearing of his theories, he would have to put on public trial the flawed theories of what Donnelly called the glacialists. These proponents of the ice-sheet theory failed to adequately explain how the ice and snow of the continental sheets had come to be created in the first place, or how the drift-soil layer documented all across the Western Hemisphere could have occurred along the equator if the soils of the equatorial regions were locked away beneath an impenetrable layer of ice. Or this quandary: how could temperature-sensitive tropical plants such as the banana have survived an alleged equatorial ice age and a mass extinction if mild frost is known to kill them?

In this, his first metropolitan press interview dedicated to his new project, to sell his book's more novel notions, Donnelly relied mostly on the scientific knowledge he had assembled in his research. But the material that most excited him he mentioned only at the conclusion of the interview: the nearly two hundred pages he had filled with ancient legends from across the world that gave credence to a comet impact. Great floods, early humans sheltering in caves to avoid destruction, evaporation of prodigious amounts of seawater into clouds that covered and chilled the globe—all had been depicted in the artifacts and legends of earlier civilizations. The Norse legend of Ragnarok was "a correct, literal, historical account" of these geological and climatological phenomena, he maintained. The fall of man, the expulsion from paradise, the darkness that "rests on the face of the deep," the destruction of Sodom and Gomorrah, and other events relayed in the Bible also aligned with the theory. Though his merger of geology and astronomy with myth, folklore, and theology was unorthodox, it stood to prove Donnelly's potentially heretical notion that "science and religion are, in some respects, not as far apart as has been supposed."[6]

The interview wrapped with a note from the *Press* that readers might expect to see *Ragnarok* in a month or two, though, truth be known, Donnelly had yet to secure a contract for its publication. Fortunately, his efforts bore fruit shortly thereafter, when O. B. Bunce at D. Appleton & Company in New York City offered to publish the work. The author would have to make some unusual concessions to get the book into print, however. He agreed to forego royalties altogether on the first one thousand books sold, while conceding to just 10 percent commission on the second thousand—the same rate offered him by Harper & Brothers for all sales on *Atlantis*.[7] After two thousand copies, the royalty would increase to 15 percent, reaching a maximum of 20 percent after the first four thousand units sold. The author framed his willingness to sign such a contract as proof of his absolute confidence in the title's salability, though the financial rewards it offered him were shockingly modest for the scribe behind the best-selling *Atlantis*, which had already entered a fifth US edition.

Though publication took closer to four months than the two Donnelly had predicted, *Ragnarok* appeared to considerable fanfare in time for the 1882 holiday shopping season. In early December, Donnelly's allies at the *St. Paul Daily Globe* announced its publication, letting the public know that the volume could be had for two dollars at the St, Paul Book and Stationery Store. While the *Globe* promised to withhold judgment on the literary merit of the book "pending a perusal and review of the work," the news item was clearly crafted to boost holiday sales. Preempting skepticism from those who might wonder why Harper & Brothers hadn't published the sequel to *Atlantis* as expected, the *Globe* made a special point of referring to Donnelly's third-choice publisher as the "well-known [publishing] house of D. Appleton, New York." Beyond that, it could only advise its readers that the illustrations and typography of this latest effort made it a "gem," and its "novel theories" and the "well-known ability of the author" would, the newspaper predicted, make it a success.[8]

Donnelly would have to wait for the *Chicago Daily Tribune* review on December 3 for a more expansive evaluation of his *Atlantis* spin-off. To the author's surprise and the publisher's delight, the *Daily Tribune* devoted a full broadsheet to a work it considered truly remarkable. Run under the headline "*Ragnarok*: A Book That Is Certain to Attract the Attention of Scientists," the subheadings that followed, ranging from "The Earth alleged to have been in collision with a comet" to "Some hard knocks dealt to long accepted scientific theories," hinted that the Sage of Nininger had succeeded in lodging yet another novel thesis. The assessment opened with a reminder to midwestern readers that the author of *Ragnarok* was the very same as the one behind the phenomenal *Atlantis*, which it called "a semi-scientific argument" built as much on a literary method as on a scientific one. Although few scientists had come forward to endorse the findings revealed in *Atlantis* during its first nine months on the market, the book, with its accessible style and admirable audience awareness, had stimulated serious discussion. The newspaper predicted that *Ragnarok* would be a "tour de force of a similar sort."[9]

In sum, the evaluation was a positive one, the reviewer concluding that comet impacts had indeed previously devastated the earth and that they would doubtless do so again. The *Tribune* was particularly impressed with the author's ability to locate support for his theories in myth, legend, and sacred texts, lauding his talent for marshaling disparate disciplines in defense of his comet-impact thesis. The titular Ragnarok received particular attention as a kernel of the larger human story: the death of the gods in heaven, resulting in a reign of fire, wind, and storm so fierce that relatively few could survive it. While the reviewer conceded that they could not hope to shed proper light on the book's many paradoxes or necessarily vouch for the accuracy of its scientific evidence, they stood in sheer admiration of the expansive intellect that had fashioned it. "However we may discredit the author's conclusions, it is impossible to withhold respect for the ingenious logic and industrious scholarship which mark its pages," the review concluded.[10]

The *Tribune*'s lengthy appraisal drew immediate reactions from readers, including a letter to the editor from a Chicago resident identified only by his initials, H. G. B., urging readers to give Donnelly's work careful consideration. H. G. B.'s story was a personal one. As a boy he had grown up in rural western Ohio, where rocks known locally as "hardheads" were strewn throughout the fields and forests. "Even the most ignorant and unlearned in geology of the inhabitants agreed that these rocks could not have 'grown' where they were found," the letter writer noted. As he grew up and became conversant in glacier literature, he realized that neither the glacier theory nor the continental ice sheet theory could account for the size, smoothness, and breakage patterns in rocks that were twice as heavy and dense as any other kind of rock in that part of the country. After reading *Ragnarok*, the letter writer had become convinced that "even to an amateur geologist, the presence of these 'hardheads' can be far more plausibly accounted by comet contact than by glacial and drift periods." While H. G. B.'s story lent anecdotal support to Donnelly's theories, it was his conclusion that resonated most with *Tribune* readers tempted to dismiss the comet-impact theory out of hand. Because the human mind was wired to cling to established theories before embracing new ones, the correspondent pointed out, Donnelly's work might not receive the serious attention it warranted from credentialed geologists and scientists. But even these hardheaded scholars, he predicted, could not long ignore the "germs of mature study, shrewd and far-seeing deductions" and "evidence of the closest observations of the results of cause and effect" inherent in Donnelly's theories, which in due time would "attract the attention they deserve from the best of our learned men."[11]

From Nebraska, E. F. Test wrote to say that he had been reading *Ragnarok*, finding it "hair-raising in places" and altogether "ingenious," especially in its reinterpretation of Genesis in light of the comet-impact theory. But Test said that Donnelly missed the mark when it came to the creation of heaven and earth. The Bible's account of a six-day creation, beginning in darkness and followed by light, should be regarded as literally true, he argued, whether the result of a comet impact or not. Test asserted that Donnelly's account of a cataclysm was in keeping with the Bible, but the author had been wrong to classify Genesis as a "legend," as it appeared to the letter writer to be a "statement of literal truth endorsed by the almighty on Mount Sinai." In other words, Test implied, Donnelly's comet-induced cataclysm and the Old Testament could both be true. The comet had perhaps created the darkness, fire, flood, and chaos, and from this darkness God had "merely fitted up this earth, having a previous existence of ages, for the habitation of mankind, in the six days recorded by the Bible."[12]

Two days before Christmas, the *Quad City Times* in Davenport, Iowa, gifted *Ragnarok* with its most glittering review yet, saying of the new work, "It is not an exaggeration to say that *Ragnarok* is one of the most striking productions of the times." No mere summary would do the work justice, the editors noted—readers would have to read it for themselves. But there was little doubt that the book would meet with the "hostility of those who have devoted their life to proving that all the gigantic phenomena of the Drift were due to the action of ice."[13] If Donnelly's comet-impact hypothesis proved correct, it stood to put the conventional ice-sheet theory, and the scientists who had vouched for it, on the hot seat.

Born of feverish, around-the-clock research and writing, *Ragnarok* explodes existing conventions of scientific communication. In lieu of treating readers as an abstract entity or expedient authorial invention, Donnelly treats them like the flesh-and-blood folk who attended his popular lectures at fairs, folk gatherings, and chautauquas. "Reader, let us reason together," he opens, before launching into a series of questions he feels confident his readers will be sufficiently intelligent to entertain.[14] Liberally using interrogatives and imperatives, Donnelly engages with his audience directly, as he might with a jury, writing, "So far as possible, [as I shall in all cases speak by the voices of others]

I shall summon my witnesses that you may cross-examine them. I shall try, to the best of my ability, to buttress every opinion with adequate proofs. If I do not convince, I hope at least to interest you." Referring to readers using the familiar second-person appellation "you," Donnelly uses bulleted lists of evidence, annotated illustrations, and clearly signposted quotes from other authorities and scholars to invite the lay reader into complex scientific questions. "Let us go a step further," he exhorts, invoking the hortative *let* coupled with the second-person plural *us* to signify that the scientific inquiry ahead will be a collaborative undertaking: "Let us try to conceive the effects of the fall of the material of the comet upon the earth." Donnelly asks his readers to picture the most severe storms they have endured in their lifetimes, and then to magnify them a thousandfold in order to approximate the abject fear that early humans would have felt as fragments of a ruined comet rained from the sky.[15]

The writing is at once dramatic and apocalyptic, joining the charisma of a preacher with the intellectual energy of a gifted public scholar. The author urges his reader:

> Fancy a storm of stones and gravel and clay-dust!—not a mere shower either, but falling in black masses, darkening the heavens, vast enough to cover the world in many places hundreds of feet in thickness; leveling valleys, tearing away and grinding down hills, changing the whole aspect of the habitable globe. Without and above it roars the earthquaking voice of the terrible explosions; through the drifts of debris glimpses are caught of the glaring and burning monster; while through all and over all is an unearthly heat, under which rivers, ponds, lakes, springs, disappear as if by magic. . . .
>
> Look out at the scene around you. Here are trees fifty feet high. Imagine an instantaneous descent of granite-sand and gravel sufficient to smash and crush these trees to the ground, to bury their trunks, and to cover the earth one hundred to five hundred feet higher than the elevation to which their tops now reach! And this not alone here in your garden, or over your farm, or over your township, or over your county, or over your State; but over the whole continent in which you dwell—in short, over the greater part of the habitable world![16]

Elsewhere, and in the most colorful terms, he reminds his readers of the sheer scale of comets that had passed overhead during their lifetimes, including the comet of 1811, which, at its widest, tallied nearly 14 million miles, with a length estimated at 116 million miles. Calling the comet a "monster," he invites readers of *Ragnarok* to "imagine such a creature . . . with a head *fifty times as large as the moon*, and a tail one hundred and sixteen million miles long, rushing past this poor little earth of ours." At approximately 7,925 miles wide, the earth would "simply make a bullet-hole through that tail, fourteen million miles broad, where it passed through it!—a mere eyelet-hole—a pin-hole," and yet in that fleeting moment of contact, the side of the earth facing the comet might be covered with hundreds of feet of debris.[17]

Donnelly's exuberance, and his willingness to translate the abstractions of numbers and theories into concrete language the lay reader could understand, troubled the sort of scientists who relayed their results primarily to academic colleagues in what they hoped would be an unemotional, impartial tone. While the style and substance of *Ragnarok* made a lasting impression on *Daily Tribune* readers, for example, others in Chicago were not so convinced. The editors at the *Inter Ocean* were in no mood for more of the former congressman's far-fetched apocalyptic theories. What was the connection, a cynical *Inter Ocean* reviewer mused, between the month of December and the publication of books seeking to undermine established truths? Did the cold somehow stimulate the part of the brain devoted to conspiracy theory? Tongue firmly in cheek, the reviewer reasoned that such a mind of winter must persuade "intellectual amateurs" to "assail the solid masonry of popular opinion with all the assurance of a battering ram."[18]

The lengthy, unsigned assessment that ran in the newspaper's Saturday edition established a playbook that future anti-Donnelly reviewers would return to again and again, representing the midwestern sage as little more than a quack whose strange genius could be responded to only with humor, if it was responded to at all. Previously, venom directed at Donnelly had focused on his lack of formal training in the sciences and his flair for literary style, but increasingly it carried an urban bias against the author's provincial home in Minnesota, characterizing the place as the sort of far-flung God-forsaken hinterland that could only breed an American crank. Calling Donnelly the "son of blizzards" and the "Oedipus of Minnesota," the *Inter Ocean* wondered how the former lieutenant governor of Minnesota could make such short work of problems that had vexed the likes of the naturalist Louis Agassiz. Reciting a purposely reductive reading of Donnelly's theories, the reviewer concluded by needling Donnelly once more, in parting, for his northern home: "Such, in brief, is the reconciliation of science, tradition, and sacred history, as effected by what might be called the blizzard theory." The Sage of Nininger, the piece concluded, had proven himself so adept at "solving the insolvable" that he should now turn his attention to the "unguessed riddle of all philosophy—the cause of the cause of the thing caused."[19]

Two weeks later, the *New York Times* echoed the *Inter Ocean*, expressing skepticism about Donnelly's take on the science while nevertheless acknowledging his growing influence as an explicator of scientific phenomena to a wider public. While the *Times* had been mostly sympathetic to *Atlantis* in a review published some nine months earlier, it had since grown circumspect in its regard for the upstart Minnesotan's trademark iconoclasm. Publishing its review of *Ragnarok* as New Yorkers scurried about the metropolis buying last-minute holiday gifts, the publication served notice of its sentiments with unusually damning language, observing, "The arguments he [Donnelly] advances are drawn from every possible source and are decidedly crude." *Times* readers were advised that the author had stated the existence of natural phenomena that had no known basis in fact. The newspaper accused the author of imagining many of his "wild," discredited, or altogether outdated theories, which he then "lugged in and presented" in a "filamentous condition." It singled out Donnelly's reference to research showing the remains of organic matter in some meteors fallen to earth; for Donnelly the evidence suggested that comets contained the detritus of exploded planets that had once contained life, though the *Times* insisted that still more recent scholarship had debunked the existence of life in meteorites.[20] While subsequent science would prove Donnelly's theory nearer to the truth, the authority carried by the *Times* name was sufficient to confirm many readers' suspicions that the excitable Donnelly had not quite done all his homework.

While the *Times* review didn't explicitly name Donnelly's provincial location as a factor in research it alleged to be inadequate or inaccurate, a geographic critique could easily be read between the lines. In truth, Donnelly's home in remote Nininger City did in some respects disadvantage his research relative to his more metropolitan peers. Simply retrieving the day's newspapers required a three-and-a-half-mile journey into nearby Hastings. A trip to the nearest bookstore of note—Merrill's on East Third Street in St. Paul—entailed a crossing of the Mississippi River and nearly twenty-five miles of difficult travel. And unlike most of his fellow intellectuals, Donnelly preferred to conduct his literature review in the more populist surroundings of a shop selling books to the general public, rather than cloister himself away in archives. Even on occasional trips home to Philadelphia, he preferred to work among the people at the public library.[21]

While he could buy most of the scientific and literary periodicals he needed at Merrill's, academic journals proved more difficult to acquire, and his exchange of views with professional scholars in the fields relevant to his research was practically nonexistent. And because Donnelly relied primarily on previously published research that would be accessible to him in Twin Cities bookshops, his conclusions could not take into consideration soon-to-be-published research of the sort traded between scholars rubbing shoulders. On the opposite side of the ledger, however, he was exceptionally well versed in the content of the nation's newspapers, and his familiarity with current events and political happenings far eclipsed that of many ivory tower intellectuals. Then, too, the relative isolation of Nininger boosted his reputation as sage or soothsayer—the sort of oracle for whom distance from teeming cities enabled prophetic vision. While it questioned the currency of his science, the *Times* review conceded that Donnelly was at his best, and most prescient, when reciting the oral traditions that substantiated his comet-impact theory.[22]

In Part III of *Ragnarok*, entitled "Legends," Donnelly opens by briefly arguing his premise: namely, that "construction of the intellectual nature varies no more, from age to age, than the form of the body or the color of the skin; the generations feel the same emotions, and think the same thoughts, and use the same expressions." This continuity should be expected, the author argues, if the psyche is as inheritable as, say, the color of the eyes. Expressing the esprit de corps of mythologists and folklorists, he writes, "If a tale is told at a million hearth-fires, the probabilities are small, indeed, that any innovation at one hearth-fire, however ingenious, will work its way into and modify the narration at all the rest."[23] Early humans could be counted on to repeat, rather than materially alter, the stories that had been handed down to them. And when stories, folktales, and legends overlapped and intersected, a careful reader-listener could hear in the similarities a shared "heritage of humanity."[24] At root the shared legends prove "the absolute fidelity of the memory" of all who had come before. Thoughtful readers who invest in the essential truth of these overlapping folktales and legends will discern a common cultural narrative across religions and belief systems, in which man, after dwelling on a benign and temperate earth for thousands of years, would witness an "appalling and sudden calamity."[25] Indeed, Donnelly spends the entirety of Part III quoting cataclysmic fall-of-man narratives in texts ranging from the Norse *Ragnarok* to the Bible.

While the United States' newspaper of record praised Donnelly's command of the world's mythological and folkloric traditions, even this—the strongest testimony in the book—was hampered by what the *Times* called the "mental dyspepsia from having swallowed much more than [Donnelly] can digest." To further make the point, the review inventoried the book's eclectic subjects, which, listed together, might strike readers as, at best, tangentially related to one another: "comets, drifts, conflagrations, ages of darkness, Chicago Fires, moraines, stratifications, Neanderthal skulls, primeval storms (with a harrowing illustration), stone images from Ohio, copper coins (engraved with an acid and passed through a milling machine, found in Illinois 114 feet under the ground)." The author, perhaps fearing that his theories would not be believed, had overstuffed his chapters with digressive or distracting phenomena that risked overwhelming even the most patient of readers. The *Times* concluded its evaluation on a high-handed if not patronizing note, admitting that despite *Ragnarok*'s shortcomings, no possible harm could come from reading it. "It is undoubtedly our author's privilege to speculate to his heart's desire," it conceded, while adding, "but to take this book au serieux is the only mistake." Scientific men would find Donnelly impertinent, but "those who like to dream about what might have been the past life of this world" might indeed find *Ragnarok* to be a pleasurable read.[26]

Where, exactly, had Donnelly misunderstood the science? Scientists themselves were mostly silent on the specifics of any alleged errors, preferring instead to dismiss his treatise in its entirety or to question the author's credentials to speculate on such weighty scientific questions. Certainly, the flaws in Donnelly's method of argumentation were apparent to many: he tended to overgeneralize, to conflate cause and effect, and to cite scholars outside the mainstream whose assessments agreed with his own. The dates he conjectured for cataclysmic events were sometimes inaccurate; for example, in linking the extinction of Neanderthals to a comet impact approximately thirty thousand years in the past, he most likely missed the mark by at least five thousand years. In speculating that a comet impact roughly thirty thousand years ago knocked the earth further off its axis, he badly underestimated the number of years scientists would later posit.

Donnelly's eager mind tended to make connections, ipso facto, between events that may have been coincidental. For example, if a cruder Neanderthal skull and a finer Engis skull were found relatively near one another hundreds of feet underground in the drift layer, it did not necessarily follow that the two men preexisted the cataclysm or even that the bones of the animals around them that would soon go extinct could be used to date either the death of the two men or the impact of the alleged doomsday comet. Donnelly often failed to see the possibility of covariables in natural phenomena, succumbing to black-and-white mutual exclusivity. A case in point is his complete dismissal of the ice-sheet theory on the grounds that ice sheets could not possibly have enveloped the entire earth because, if they had, they would have extinguished nearly all plant life; such logic, while sound, neglected the fact that ice sheets advanced and retreated over time. While earth's most severe ice ages may not have completely frozen the tropics, they may have made it colder and significantly more muddy.

Scientists scoffed at many of Donnelly's conclusions, dismissing some of his more dramatic theories as radical while treating the ideas they could not discount as self-evident or jejune. In the East, criticism of *Ragnarok* tended to carry with it an urban bias that implied that only a provincial mind could come up with such nonsense. The editor of the *Evening Journal* in New Jersey treated the midwesterner's findings as naive if not juvenile, writing, "Mr. Ignatius Donnelly, the author of *Atlantis*, holds that the ponderable material in the tail of a comet is probably stones and clay dust, of which the drift is composed. Mr. Donnelly now lives in Minnesota. He had better move a little further west. Everybody east of Minnesota knows that the South African diamond field came from the swab of a comet's tail."[27] In the eyes of critics in the scientific community, *Ragnarok* and its ilk amounted to so much bunkum or humbuggery, pseudoscience fed to a public hungry for conspiracy theory and helpless before the illusionary or inconclusive claims of cranks. Amounting to a kind of scientific show business practiced for profit, sensationalist treatments like Donnelly's, critics argued, consisted of what one scholar later described as a "quintessentially antebellum American mixture" made up of "pseudo-science" and "entertainment."[28]

Despite the scientific dismissal, the book-buying public voted with its dollars for the Sage of Nininger's visionary ideas, causing the author, by his own admission, to begin "strutting like a turkey cock" as 1882 gave way to 1883. Sales continued apace in December and well into January, during which time the book sold some 3,500 copies—an amount that easily exceeded the sales record for *Atlantis* during its first weeks on the market. Four months later in April, Appleton would sell out of the entire first edition of 5,000 copies, though the publisher reported that the rate of the sales had slowed significantly.[29]

In response to the spring sales decline, Donnelly suggested that Appleton's O. B. Bunce arrange for a review of the book in *Popular Science*, which operated as a sort of subsidiary of the D. Appleton Company. When the editor of the magazine, E. L. Youmans, refused Bunce's request, Donnelly pressed the issue until Appleton shared with him the contents of a letter Youmans had written in protest, the most damning excerpt of which read, "There has not been any extended attempt to refute the position of the author of *Ragnarok*; nor is it probable that there will be, because the minds that are taken with that work are in a very unpromising condition to reason with. The book being absurd. . . . What would you think of a man who would gravely reply to . . . the romancer Jules Verne."[30] Donnelly's "dubious science" and "attempted profundity," as one Donnelly biographer later put it,[31] made him a convenient straw man to the sort of scientist who hoped to limit the field to credentialed practitioners.

Donnelly understood that Youmans had an axe to grind. First, Youmans was a fierce defendant of the independence of scientists, and he had made it clear that Bunce had overstepped his bounds in requesting a favorable review in a periodical purportedly dedicated to scientific impartiality. Second, Youmans had been a very public proponent of evolutionary theory, and Donnelly's attempt to reconcile science with religion struck him as dangerously antiscientific. In a letter written to Bunce, the author defended his work against the charges Youmans had leveled at it, clarifying, "Now I do not say that my theory is absolutely true beyond question. That can be safely asserted of few things in this world. But what I do claim is that it is not 'absurd and ridiculous' in itself & that it is entitled to fair consideration in the hands of thoughtful men."[32] Bunce replied diplomatically but forcefully, reminding the author that D. Appleton did not consider his work science per se and would not market it as such.[33]

Though sales of *Ragnarok* had peaked by the summer of 1883, Appleton kept the book in print, reissuing it in multiple editions. While Donnelly could take solace in the work's longevity, the repudiation of his ideas in scientific circles had convinced him that science itself was a flawed system that boiled down to "congeries of schoolmasters repeating what someone else has told them."[34] His developing disdain for elite scientists and other so-called experts aligned him with the growing number of midwestern regionalists who had come to decry the intellectual dominance of the East, where, they believed, intellectual culture was dangerously derivative of that in England and Europe. If an American thinker dared to suggest a novel scientific notion, Donnelly concluded, it would be rejected as pseudoscience until such time as it had been endorsed and sanctioned by educated elites abroad. An American genius would necessarily be more plainspoken, practical, and populist than the likes of Darwin or Spencer or Agassiz, he maintained, and to expect otherwise would be akin to asking a zebra to change its stripes.

While the publication of *Ragnarok* had helped solidify Donnelly's reputation as a sort of strange genius sequestered in a distant American hinterland, it had come at a cost. The mostly private life he had made for himself after retreating from national politics had become public again, and the Donnelly name had now become synonymous with pseudoscience and conspiracy theory. Political enemies who feared the growing political platform his publishing success might provide used his unorthodox theories as a punchline. In poking fun at what it considered his pedantry, the *St. Paul Pioneer Press* offered a blueprint for how Donnelly's newfound literary fame might be used against him: "Donnelly is still seeking his lost Atlantis, which sunk beneath the waves in the tempest of clouds and fire in 1868. . .. For he is own Ragnarok too—or would be if his dream could come true. There is a pleasant suggestion of allegory in the part he assigns to comets in the phenomena of physical disturbance. For that is the part he always assigned himself in the phenomena of political disturbance."[35] The criticism sounded cruel, and yet it introduced an intriguing premise: that a Donnelly free from political allegiances was as dangerous as a speeding meteor pointed toward political earth, demanding to be reckoned with or else. The dramatic rise and fall of his political fortunes seemed almost cosmic in magnitude, like the revolutions of a rogue planet wobbling dangerously in its orbit.

The bestselling author of *Atlantis* and *Ragnarok* appeared to understand the metaphor implicitly. The diary entries Donnelly made for his fifty-second birthday manifest the allegory the *Pioneer Press* had inscribed, and yet with far more vulnerability than the newspaper might have imagined. He confessed to his journal, "It hurts one to think of how little space he occupies in the universe; how for a few short years he has a chance at sunshine and the air & then is not." If dust could not perish, he observed, and if matter was indeed indestructible, then how could life ever be truly extinguished? Donnelly's habit of writing extraordinarily lengthy, deeply introspective journal entries on or near his birthday perennially produced his most poetic thoughts on mortality and personal legacy. And this birthday entry proved no exception: "And so our hurt vanity finds compensation in the hope that though we may be whisked away from the sunshine here we may reappear elsewhere, under a brighter sun and in a fairer world."[36]

Chapter 4

The Shakespearean Cipher

By the election season of 1882, Ignatius Donnelly had become a literary meteor. Though his conclusions in *Atlantis* and *Ragnarok* had been dismissed by many experts as so much sophistry and pseudoscience, they had been embraced by readers with hearts open to the uncanny and minds inclined to alternative truths. He had begun acting the part of the reclusive genius, bunkering down in his library at Nininger City, determined to witness political squabbles at safe remove. "Ignatius Donnelly has done one wise thing," the *Sterling Bulletin* noted, reprinting an apt commentary from the *Kansas City Journal*. "He has kept out of politics long enough to write an interesting book."[1] He followed through on his pledge to stay out of politics that autumn, with the exception of a paid stint as a deliverer of stump speeches in favor of A. A. Ames, Minneapolis mayor and current Democratic candidate for Congress in Minnesota's Fourth Congressional District, and against his old nemesis, William Washburn.

On November 4, he took the stage in St. Paul's Market Hall to blast the crookedness of the Washburn family in a speech transcribed by stenographic report for the *St. Paul Daily Globe*, which subsequently published the address in its Monday edition. In a lecture punctuated by laughter, Donnelly dazzled as author-politician-humorist, cracking self-effacing jokes as easily as he invoked fiery political invective.

Assuring the crowd that he had sincerely intended to permanently retire from public life, he continued:

> I did not suppose you would hear my musical voice again. [Laughter] I made up my mind to devote myself to literature. I wanted to study back to some period of the earth's history anterior to the time when the Washburn family began to run for office; [Laughter] and the result was, my friends, I wrote a book that dated back before the deluge. [Laughter] Well, I have written another book . . . the object of which is to demonstrate that long ages ago this earth of ours was struck by a comet's tail [Laughter] and I would say to you, confidentially my friends, that on Tuesday next Bill Washburn will conclude that the comet has come back again and hit the world another whack.

Turning serious, he insisted that humanity could be divided into two classes, "those who eat and those who are eaten"—into "the wolves and the sheep." While he conceded that the Republican Party had begun with a noble impulse, it had since degenerated, he said, into a "party of rascality and . . . a party of robbery." Exhorted by the crowd to keep his marathon speech going, the author-statesman promised to speak until he dropped, so long as some kind spectator would bury him in St. Paul.[2]

The indefatigable Sage of Nininger was still standing on November 7, when he appeared at a packed Turner Hall in an event billed as the last grand rally of the season, held on the "eve of the battle." A receptive Minneapolis crowd, reported the *Globe*, soaked in his sophistry, "anxious to listen to the exposure of W. D. Washburn's rascality." As the night's featured speaker, he took the stage "in his happiest vein," eager for a final takedown of enemies deserving divine retribution, and fully capable, as always, of winning the sympathies of the crowd "as if by magic." The *Globe* duly reported that the bestselling author's speech "sparkled with wit and humor" balanced by "sophistry and argument." As he had two nights earlier, Donnelly accused Washburn of buying votes and selling away the people's public land to barons and ringleaders given sweetheart deals for pennies on the dollar.[3]

Despite a week's worth of Donnelly's charismatic public addresses, Ames lost the election in Minnesota's GOP-leaning Fourth District by nearly double digits. Except for that seven-day period of last-ditch stump speeches made on his friend's behalf, Donnelly had managed to stay out of politics in the autumn of 1882, insisting to all who asked him to enter the fray that he was focusing his energies on writing and superintending his wheat crop. Buoyed by his identity as a popular, if controversial, author and gentleman farmer, Donnelly began a new writing project by which he hoped to delve further into a lifelong passion: Shakespeare. As in *Atlantis* and *Ragnarok*, he would be seeking to substantiate a dramatic hunch harbored for many years: in this case, that the poorly educated "William Shakesper" of Stratford could not be the same as the erudite William Shakespeare whose name appeared on the world-famous plays and sonnets. As early as 1878, Donnelly had recorded in his diary his intention to reread the Shakespeare plays with the goal of locating a cipher hidden within them that would reveal their true authorship.

The obstacles were time—of which, in the midst of a frenetic wheat harvest, Donnelly had precious little—and the difficulty of accessing a facsimile of the 1623 Shakespeare First Folio in rural Minnesota. When finally he did receive a copy, he took it with him to Stevens County for the harvest, resolved to pore over its contents at night. Not long after, he noted in his diary that he had been working diligently at what he thought might well be a "great discovery revealing a cipher in the plays pointing to Francis Bacon as their real author."[4] Finding the mathematical key needed to unlock the cipher, he confided to his diary, was "hideously complicated and perplexing," occupying his waking thoughts and infusing his dreams and nightmares.[5] Already, his counting system had turned up key words such as "Bacon," "Francis," "William," "Shake," and "Speare" hidden in the text. He was "certain there was a cypher," and that it "cannot be by accident."[6]

With marketing and publicity for *Ragnarok* still occupying much of his time, Donnelly would need to scrutinize every word of the nine hundred-page First Folio, containing thirty-six plays, as well as manage his agricultural enterprise. Despite the obstacles, he pressed on, believing that he was drawing ever nearer to the key that would break the code, despite difficulties in consistently finding sequences that would reveal Bacon's authorship. The intricacies of the message Bacon was attempting to transmit became the latest in a series of obsessions. "I think about it all day & dream about it all night," Donnelly remarked in his diary.[7] Had he heeded them, his diary entries that December of 1883 might have served to warn that the cipher he believed to be buried within the Folio was beyond his ability to decode, in terms of both the time he could afford to devote to the problem and the mathematical acumen required to execute the decipherment. Still, he stewed in the conundrum he had identified, resolved to reach out to others who shared his doubts about Shakespeare's authorship.

Atop the list of would-be supporters was Appleton Morgan, a New York copyright attorney and author of a book published in 1881 entitled *The Shakespearean Myth*. Already, Morgan noted, Shakespeareans had begun to reconsider their overly rigid "cast-iron theory" that "every page, line, and word of the Shakespearean drama was written by William Shakespeare demi-god, and by none others." In exhibiting even the slightest bit of openness, he wrote, they had "perhaps even opened a path through which the unbelievers may become, in due time, orthodox."[8] A natural iconoclast and an indefatigable investigator, Morgan shared a spirit with Donnelly, one that delighted in challenging age-old assumptions. Children studying geography in Norway had lately been taught as fact the existence of a whirlpool off the coast that drowned ships; American and European children had been encouraged to think of William Tell as a flesh-and-blood man rather than a folkloric figure. If such "facts" as these could later be exposed as legends, it was equally possible that Shakespeare's authorship had been a myth perpetuated by ignorant schoolteachers and hidebound historians.

Donnelly's letter to Appleton, in which he claimed that he could prove that Bacon was the author of the plays, soon prompted an in-person meeting between the two men. The *Minneapolis Daily Tribune* broke the story under the headline "Donnelly's Shakespeare." The big bold type in the article's summary headline promised drama, mentioning "secret keys," "ciphers," and "alleged proof" to be offered by Minnesota's homegrown sage in a forthcoming book. Bylined "Editor, Tribune," the front-page article intimated that a momentous development had occurred in the Twin Cities: "A discovery has been made in this State which is certain to produce a worldwide sensation. The Hon. Ignatius Donnelly of Hastings, Minnesota, author of *Atlantis* and *Ragnarok*, found . . . in the writings of Francis Bacon, a description, twice repeated, of a cipher whereby one writing could be enfolded and hidden in another 'omnia per omnia.'"[9]

Bacon had foreshadowed the cipher method in his 1623 work *De Augmentis Scientiarum*, wherein he writes of "secrets of knowledge" revealed in "obscurity of delivery" decodable only by "wits of such sharpness as can pierce the veil." Donnelly, the *Daily Tribune* claimed, had pierced the veil. Morgan likewise offered a qualified endorsement on his visit to Minnesota, saying that if what Donnelly had found was not a cipher, it was at the very least "a most marvelous sequence of identical coincidences, and one forbidden by any known or conjectured law of chances." Donnelly had thus far refused to provide the details of his alleged key, except to say that he had honed in on *Henry IV* and *The Merry Wives of Windsor* as texts in which the words "Bacon" and "William" were repeated a conspicuous number of times. Beginning with these textual clues, the *Daily Tribune* stated, he had "discovered the rule and . . . enough of the cipher story to show that the plays contain a narrative of Bacon's own life, and secret history of the reign of Elizabeth."[10]

Donnelly had not intended to reveal the existence of the cipher until it had been more thoroughly worked out, but now, with the reason for Morgan's visit to Minnesota made public, he had little choice but to beg for more time to divine the hidden message. Making the time crunch worse, George Gillitt, the editor of the *New Era* in nearby Hastings, Minnesota, had begun a movement to draft Donnelly to run against the Republican Horace Straight in the Third Congressional District. Once publicized, Gillitt's vision quickly caught on among a coalition of supporters from the Farmers' Alliance and the Democrats, who nominated Donnelly to run against Straight—an invitation he reluctantly accepted. Since the campaign would distract him from his literary investigations, and since his book would not be ready for at least another year, he had come forward on the advice of friends to claim his discovery and to ask for more time to complete the "slow and tedious" job of counting every word in the First Folio. A single mathematical error, the *Tribune* cautioned, "would throw out the work of whole pages."[11]

In August, Donnelly had narrowly won the Democratic nomination, despite the protestations of the party faithful aghast at the idea that someone so recently a Republican could swap his party affiliation with the ease of a man taking off a dirty shirt. While prominent nominators publicly dissented, he delivered an address meant to mollify them, thanking convention attendees for the "magnanimity and generosity" shown in selecting as their nominee a former Republican who had "dealt [them] many blows in hard-fought campaigns." Sounding a distinctly populist, almost nonpartisan note, the party's new nominee characterized his prior affiliation as dutiful allegiance to a group that had lost sight of its duty to the people and that now amounted to a "sinking ship" that, in his loyalty to the republic, he had been reluctant to abandon. He assured concerned Democrats that his appeal would cross party lines, attracting disaffected Republicans and avowed antimonopolists to the Democratic Party. "Why should traditional prejudices keep us apart?" he asked, closing a conciliatory acceptance speech with the sincere hope that voters could rise "to a higher level" by "forgetting party prejudices."[12]

In this, his latest comeback, Donnelly would once again be juggling the twin callings of politics and literature. In September, when word of his cipher first broke, he had been something of a long-shot candidate with only a glimmer of hope of winning the solidly Republican district. But his ability as a charismatic speaker on the stump offered voters a bright contrast with the stoical Straight. The voters of the Third District appreciated the underdog, and the huge crowds Donnelly drew as he canvassed the southern half of the state suggested they embraced the idea of the writer-politician's upset win. On October 6, Donnelly took his upstart campaign to Shakopee, Minnesota, where Straight had served as a three-term mayor prior to his election to Congress. Expecting trouble, the *St. Paul Globe* dispatched a special correspondent to cover the event, and the reporter came away genuinely moved by what he called the "singular spectacle" of "one man, all alone, fighting money, power, patronage." The atmosphere promised unrest if not all-out anarchy. Law enforcement was quickly called in to restore order and remove a particularly noxious heckler, only to have Donnelly demand that his tormentors be allowed to stay so that he might attempt to win them over.[13]

In Shakopee, Donnelly announced his intention to take the moral high ground by refusing to attack Straight in his hometown. From the rostrum he declared, "I have not in this canvass uttered one unkind word against Major Straight personally. I have simply discussed his congressional record. On the other hand Major Straight has a horde of speakers at my heels who are attacking my private character and striving to cover me with mud and filth." Claiming that his opponent's negative campaigning would backfire to the tune of hundreds of lost votes, he delivered what the *Globe* characterized as a "magical" speech that eventually silenced into thoughtfulness even those Straight supporters who had come to drive him from the stage. As the *Globe* saw it, the Sage of Nininger posed a unique dilemma for the political opposition resolved to defeat him. If the Straight campaign attempted to dismiss him as a "low-down demagogue and blackguard, full of base instinct and habits," impartial voters would naturally ask themselves whether "these charges be true of a man who has written two of the most scholarly and thoughtful books of his age, that are read with delight in both the old and new world." Donnelly lacked an entourage to answer criticism on his behalf, the newspaper readily conceded, and yet his philosophical books had "lifted him above the reach of . . . malice."[14]

Despite his opponent's gang of hecklers and unruly "whippersnappers" doggedly appearing at each of his appearances,[15] Donnelly kept a breakneck schedule. During the day he traveled; at night he spoke to large crowds in places like Beaver Falls, Granite Falls, and Richland, where supporters packed meeting halls to see the famed author-politician. At many stops he was left to fend off men the Straight campaign had planted in the crowd to derail him. "To follow a man, night after night, simply to lie about him behind his back disgusts all men who love fair play," newspapers quoted Donnelly as saying. In tiny Manannah, Minnesota, 120 miles northwest of Nininger City, fervent supporters filled the rural schoolhouse to hear him speak for an incredible two and a half hours to a standing-room-only house and several threshing crews. The sight of Donnelly, an ex-Republican now running as a Democrat, surrounded by diehard Republican farmers willing to switch parties to support him, spoke volumes not only about the candidate's personal appeal but about a changing political landscape wherein old party ties were weakening. "There is a general breaking up of old party lines," the *Globe* observed, "and if the Republicans think that Minnesota is to continue among the undisputed Republican states they will find themselves mistaken."[16] To Donnelly's benefit, Scandinavian farmers and laborers were "breaking loose in all directions" and had soured on Strait's and the *St. Paul Pioneer Press*'s negative campaign tactics.

Donnelly struggled not to take the vicious political attacks personally. Feeling his good name tarnished or defamed, he would often answer his critics directly in letters printed in newspapers across the state. In October he responded to a man who wondered whether Straight's accusation that Donnelly had sold out to the railroad interests could possibly be true, since Donnelly had a reputation as one of the nation's fiercest opponents of railroad monopolies. In a lengthy reply, Donnelly claimed that Straight's nonsensical accusations "only show[ed] what a contemptible thing political bigotry is." Later in the same letter of self-defense, he observed, "The lies that are circulated against me in this contest are so multitudinous and possess such infinite variety, that I feel like exclaiming, with the worthy German, the first time he saw a monkey, 'Mine Gott, vot vill der Frenchman make next!' "[17]

With the dark horse Donnelly gaining on Straight late into October, several of the major Minneapolis–St. Paul newspapers refused to allow the party-switching candidate to project himself as above the fray. The *St. Paul Pioneer Press* worked to curb his momentum by casting him as a has-been who would do better by the people of Minnesota by sticking to his bookish pursuits. If the independent-minded Donnelly tried to convince the Republican farmers downstate to cross party lines and vote the Democratic ticket, they warned, he would be sent rudely back to Nininger City, to the "cool shades of literary seclusion which he had been enjoying for some years with great advantage to himself and to the public at large."[18] Little more than a month after breaking the news of the cipher, the *Minneapolis Tribune* followed up with an article suggesting that Minnesota's homegrown sage had merely fallen in line with the long history of "cranks" who had questioned Shakespeare's existence. "Mr. Ignatius Donnelly," the *Tribune* observed, "whose active interest in Democratic politics has led him to the development of ingenious antiquarian theories, has now hit on one that is as absurd as it is ingenious."[19] The implication was clear: Donnelly's second life as a man of letters did not qualify him for Congress any more than this political life had credentialed him to be a scientist-author. Meanwhile the *Pioneer Press* doubled down on its earlier attacks equating Donnelly the resurgent political candidate with Donnelly the writer of unfounded theories, waiting till the eve of the election to publish unsubstantiated claims that Donnelly had plagiarized much of *Atlantis*.[20]

When that charge failed to lodge, the newspaper accused him of writing a letter in 1880 that allegedly offered a $5,000 bribe to elect his political nemesis William D. Washburn. Without evidence, the *Pioneer Press* alleged that the congressional committee charged with reviewing the disputed Donnelly-Washburn election had found Donnelly complicit, when in fact he had been exonerated in the so-called Springer Affair.[21] In reply Donnelly announced his intention to file a libel suit against the editor of the *Pioneer Press*, with the *St. Paul Globe* taking his side in characterizing the pending lawsuit as a "libel suit against a liar." The repetition of such misleading public accusations against the Sage of Nininger would, the *Globe* said, only stamp the offending editor "with the brand of willful, deliberate, and malicious liar" who would "now have an opportunity to be legally recorded the scoundrel which he is."[22] Newspapers as far away as New York covered Donnelly's threatened lawsuit, describing the former congressman with a long list of titles ranging from Democratic politician to "statesman, historian, archaeologist, etc.," while labeling a "delusion" Donnelly's claims of $20,000 in damages to his personal reputation.[23]

With ad hominem attacks against him reaching a fevered pitch, Donnelly lost yet another heartbreakingly close race, one in which he exceeded nearly all expectations, losing by less than one thousand votes, or about 3 percent of the total cast. Donnelly, who had dared to hope that the political winds had blown back in his favor, took the loss hard, and doubly so when he was refused a position of political patronage in the newly elected Grover Cleveland administration. He had hoped for a lifetime judgeship, an ambassadorship overseas, or a position in the Department of the Interior, such as surveyor general of Minnesota.[24] Indeed, he traveled to Washington, DC, multiple times after the election to call personally on allies he hoped would help secure him a position.

When all desirable appointments were refused him, he cried foul, alleging a series of conflicts of interest and quid pro quos from top to bottom in the Minnesota political establishment, including wealthy railroad icon and *Pioneer Press* part owner James J. Hill, St. Paul merchant and Democratic Party leader Patrick Kelly, and Democratic Central Committee chair and St. Paul banker Michael Doran. In making his allegations public, Donnelly opted for a scorched-earth policy that alienated him both from the Democrats Kelly and Doran controlled and from the Republicans from whose ranks he had defected more than a decade earlier. In his diary he bemoaned his damned political fates, noting that he was now as completely ostracized under Democratic rule as he had been for nearly two decades under a Republican regime.[25] His election-season letters to President-Elect Cleveland had not helped his cause much either. Adopting a moralizing tone, the communiques encouraged Cleveland to fight against the advent of political bosses in the Midwest and urged him to make good on his promise to fight corruption. "You should not give a few men, base, greedy grasping men power to enrich themselves at the expense of the people & the cost of the party's future," he warned.[26]

Donnelly's popularity with the people of his adopted home state correlated almost inversely with his electoral fortunes. "It shows how popular you are with the people," Kate Donnelly wrote in a letter of consolation to her husband, adding that the close results proved that he was "not a dead man" given how much money it had taken to defeat him.[27] Kate lobbied her husband to pursue a federal appointment even if it meant pulling his punches against Doran and Kelly; politics, she reminded him, lacked decency.[28] Donnelly was inclined to agree with her, while reassuring himself that he could live without office and hold his head high, that even the wealth and power of Hill, Kelly, and Doran could not destroy his reputation with the people. In letters to friends and supporters, he claimed to feel that he had, paradoxically, more influence than ever before on the fate of his home region, an influence he attributed to his populist fight against the robber barons and ringleaders he had battled at his own expense and to his political detriment.

And the defeat in the election of 1884 carried with it another silver lining too, as Donnelly the politician could now yield to Donnelly the author, allowing him to return to the cipher whose inner workings he had had to put on hold for the sake of the campaign. While he had fought hard to regain a seat in Congress, the nation had continued to wait for the code break he had promised. In Tucson, Arizona, the editor at the *Sunshine and Silver* reported that Donnelly had been working on his monumental decipherment for four years and would soon release it to the world; so great was his confidence in the sage that he worried in advance how he might feel when Shakespeare was dethroned. "It affords no pleasure to have a myth dispelled," the editor observed in a piece reprinted in St. Paul by the *Daily Globe*, reflecting the sentiments of many who were less than eager to grapple with the prospect of a fraudulent Shakespeare. "For one who has stood by Shakespeare's grave . . . under the shade of the noble oaks of England, and listened to the murmuring Avon, it will be no joy to learn that Shakespeare's plays were written by Lord Bacon."[29]

By the late winter of 1885, Donnelly had returned to his ciphering with renewed urgency, both because he hungered for the popular esteem such a historic achievement would elicit and because he badly needed the money a successful book would bring. His losing campaign, coupled with multiple trips he had made to Washington, DC, to plead his case for a patronage appointment after his bitter electoral defeat, had badly depleted his funds, making it necessary for him to have his book royalties paid directly to his sons to avoid pending liens.

In March 1885, a reporter at the *Washington Republican* found Donnelly hard at work at a DC-area library, with the 1623 First Folio opened to *Henry IV*. Its pages were covered, top to bottom, the newspaper reported, in marginal notes. Eager for any attention paid to his cause, Donnelly pointed out that Shakespeare did not publish a single play in his own name during his lifetime and made no claims of authorship. "I have long been convinced, from the voluminous evidence on the subject, that Bacon wrote these plays," Donnelly told the *Republican*, adding that Bacon, a chancellor of England, had become during his lifetime highly proficient at writing messages in codes in order to safely convey government secrets. "In studying the subject merely with historical evidence," he said, "it occurred to me that possibly Bacon had made some reference to his authorship in a cipher woven in the text of the plays. . .. I began re-reading them and found that they were from beginning to end one marvelous mosaic work of internal narrative arranged by a system as accurate, unvarying, and precise as a sum in arithmetic."[30]

By autumn, Donnelly's quest for the cipher had, for some, begun to take on the quality of a lost cause. Still angered by the libel suit he had threatened, the *Pioneer Press* in St. Paul publicly taunted him to make good on his promise to produce a worked-out cipher. Newspapers around the country jumped on the bandwagon, making sport of the unfulfilled pledge. Several made quips at Donnelly's expense when a man named William Shakespeare was appointed postmaster of a small Michigan town, prompting the *St. Paul Daily Globe* to quote this glib dig from the *Pittsburgh Dispatch*: "He is prepared by cipher, as well as in other devious occult ways, that Bacon is entitled all favors given to Shakespeare."[31] In a lengthy write-up, *The Sun* in New York City claimed that Donnelly had leveled "the most audacious claim of literary discovery ever put forward by any human being." The editors wondered at the strange calculus, declaring, "Either he has determined to throw away for the sake of short-lived notoriety a well-earned reputation, and to make himself for all time a ridiculous and despised figure in literary history or he has in fact hit upon proof that Bacon was the real Shakespeare." The peril of Donnelly's premature public pronouncement that he had found the cipher was that it left no middle ground. Unlike claims made by previous Shakespeare skeptics, his methods did not rely on circumstantial evidence or any other "cloudy scheme or forced construction." Given the "astounding claim advanced by a gentleman of established literary reputation and unquestioned personal character," *The Sun* stated, the newspaper would, like the rest of the world, "await with great interest the fulfillment of Mr. Ignatius Donnelly's extraordinary promise to demonstrate to a mathematical certainty the Baconian authorship of Shakespeare's plays."[32]

To many observers it appeared that Donnelly was either stalling for time to find, ex post facto, the embedded secret narrative he had promised, or leveraging the long delay to stir up interest in his forthcoming work. Several of his personal letters on the subject found their way into the popular press in the spring of 1886, including a letter sent to an unidentified British correspondent, in which he enthused that Bacon's code-within-the-plays was a "most marvelous work" and was "no less impressive than the plays themselves." In his view Bacon appeared to have written both the plays and the code, "reckless of the trouble it would give him to work the words into the plays," from which Donnelly had deduced that "the plays were bent and twisted to conform to the Cipher, not the Cipher to the plays." To readers who disbelieved the notion that the world's greatest body of drama could be written as a vehicle for a hidden narrative, he hastened to point out that the Elizabethan era had been a time of intense suppression that necessitated unprecedented levels of secrecy. As he dug deeper into the code, he claimed to have found not just a simple statement of Bacon's clandestine authorship but a complete hidden history of Elizabethan intrigue and skullduggery, a record of the latter part of Queen Elizabeth's reign "with all its plots and conspiracies and their effects on great historical events." The plays were Bacon's appeal to posterity and a kind of intellectual revenge for the persecution and suppression he had faced—the "gall and bitterness of a tortured life embalmed in poetry and the merriment of comedies."[33] Bacon's supreme ability to leave intricate clues to his existence behind in the text, Donnelly believed, rendered him godlike.

In his letters to a British colleague, Donnelly acknowledged the astounding nature of the intellectual test he believed Bacon had set, noting, "As I work the marvel grows upon me, how any human brain could be ingenious enough to construct such a wonderful mosaic work." He expressed confidence that the "publication of the cipher and my work will place Bacon upon an irreproachable height in human estimation."[34] In the meantime he labeled as absurd concerns expressed by others that he was attempting to foist an untruth on unsuspecting readers, a topic to which he dedicated a lengthy paragraph, beginning with a prescient rhetorical question: "Why should I assert that I have found such a cipher—not a hop-skip-and-jump Cipher but a mathematically accurate rule—if I have not? I ask no money from anyone. If I published a book that was a fraud or a delusion, the few copies which might be sold before the truth was discovered would surely not compensate me for the everlasting shame and ridicule which would fall upon me." The missives he dispatched overseas revealed the immense pressure under which he had placed himself and suggested the intensity of the public's scrutiny of his claims: "Can anyone believe that I would concoct a deliberate lie, which only a few months would explode? And for what? Not for notoriety; I have enough of that already. Is it to be believed that

I would imperil whatever little honor I may have gained by my exceptionally successful books *Atlantis* and *Ragnarok* by a pretended claim to a great discovery?"[35]

As Donnelly deliberated over the supposed cipher in the plays, he perpetuated a vicious cycle: the press printed leaked letters in which he had promised great discoveries to eager correspondents, and the publication of these letters, in turn, intensified the growing demand that he produce the promised key. And the tension inherent in the race to produce definitive results proved palpable in many of the nation's periodicals. "The man who proves beyond the possibility of a doubt either that the Shakespeare plays were written by William Shakespeare or that Francis Bacon was their true author will be the benefactor of the human race and a foremost figure for all time in literary history," *The Sun* surmised, adding, "Mr. Ignatius Donnelly promises to settle the controversy in a few weeks in favor of Bacon."[36]

Exasperated by the public's incredulity, overwhelmed by the mathematical difficulties of the cipher, and anxious to secure an advance publishing deal that would make his labors remunerative, Donnelly found himself stuck in what seemed a never-ending loop. In early March 1886, the *St. Paul Daily Globe* reprinted a letter—written months prior—from Donnelly to Morgan, who now served as the president of the New York Shakespeare Society. Morgan, whose earlier visit to Minnesota had helped whet the public's appetite for an imminent decipherment, agreed with Donnelly that Shakespeare had not authored the plays but favored the idea that Shakespeare had been just one of many collaborators. In the leaked letter, Donnelly attempted to lift any lingering doubt as to Bacon's hand: "I say to you, my friends, dismiss all theorizing. Francis Bacon was the real Shakespeare. The Mecca of the world is St. Albans, not Stratford. This will be made as plain in a few months as that two and two make four." There was, he declared, "no getting away from the arithmetic." In his letter he rejected Morgan's notion that the most famous plays in Western literature could have been written by committee. Morgan's theory, he argued, implied the "contemporaneous existence of a half dozen Shakespeares," whereas five thousand years of history had produced only one such man. To suggest a cadre of some five or six would be to suggest that phenomenally gifted scribes were as "thick as blackberries," and that those blackberries, by some miracle, had all ripened in London at the same time.[37]

Morgan was pleased to have an influential ally in his argument against Shakespearean orthodoxy, and while the two men differed as to the true hand behind the work, they at least commiserated on the difficulty of the task before them. "I don't mind the flings of the daily press," Donnelly reassured him, adding, "The witlings must have their quips." What he most objected to wasn't the occasional provocation or lighthearted joke but the lack of a fair hearing given him by publications presenting themselves as fair and unbiased. He recounted one instance in which an eastern newspaper had sent a correspondent all the way to Minnesota to interview him, and, in a moment of candor, the journalist admitted that he had been sent with instructions to make light of Donnelly and to debunk his findings. Ultimately, that same reporter had come away so thoroughly convinced of Donnelly's hypothesis that he refused his editor's request, siding with the Sage of Nininger instead. The sheer scope of the media bias sent Donnelly searching for a historical analogy: "Fancy a Spanish journal, if one such had existed, refusing to notice Columbus's return from the new world unless he paid advertising rates for the same!" In his view a discovery like his, which would reveal "all the hidden marvels of the sixteenth and seventeenth century, and the wonderful secret of the greatest mind that ever lived," was "little less extraordinary" than Columbus's discovery of the New World.[38]

While several of his letters in defense of his cipher were shared with the press without his knowledge, Donnelly penned others directly to writers and editors he felt lacked the intellectual capacity to understand the breadth of his project. Half amused and half incredulous, he responded to the *Daily Globe* article entitled "Donnelly's Delusion" in a letter calling Shakespeare's contemporaries to the stand for a mock trial in which their claims of authorship were all summarily rejected, including Milton, who, Donnelly pointed out, was eight years old when Shakespeare died. He closed his rebuttal, "He laughs best who laughs last."[39] All humor aside, every sling and arrow Donnelly felt obligated to rebut or redress caused him to fall further behind on the necessary work of applying the cipher, and with election season in the offing, demands on his time would only increase in the coming autumn.

In early July, Donnelly's disgruntlement with the Democrat Party establishment in the Twin Cities found an outlet in an "anti-boss" conference organized to send a message to Democratic Party operatives, and the monopolies that bought their loyalties, that corporate cronyism must stop. The *Daily Globe* described the antimonopoly gathering of 133 attendees in big bold type as "Donnelly's Day" and declared, "Wherever the Sage of Nininger Led the Convention Followed." Donnelly sparked the meeting's first fireworks by proposing a resolution that called out the offending railroads by name while declaring the antimonopolists "in cordial and earnest sympathy with the farmers" of Minnesota. Judge Eugene St. Julien Cox objected both to formally naming the railroads as public enemies and to Donnelly, of whom he warned his colleagues, "He could disorganize the Democratic party. As a disorganizer he is a great success." To widespread merriment in the auditorium, Donnelly retorted, "I never disorganized myself," in response to which Cox promptly quipped, "You disorganized Shakespeare."[40]

Donnelly had had his day in July, and by September a nascent populist group called the Minnesota Farmers' Alliance appeared viable as a third party. Donnelly saw a coalition of farmers and laborers as the best way to end the iron grip on the Minnesota political machine enforced by Twin Cities Democratic operatives like Kelly and Doran. In an attempt to defuse growing tensions between liberal Democrats and Donnelly, state Democratic platform committee chair Judge Lars M. Rand offered Donnelly a chance to undertake a literary challenge of a different sort: authoring the state Democratic platform. If Donnelly, the wordsmith, composed the platform anonymously as a kind of ghostwriter, Minnesota's liberal Democrats would be more likely to accept it. Donnelly refused to take the bait, however, casting his lot with a third party in replying, "I will not be used as an instrument to transfer the people to the power of Jim Hill." He added, "I have nothing in the world but my voice and my influence and I am resolved to use both for the benefit of my fellow men not their injury."[41]

In September, following through on his pledge to represent the working men and women of Minnesota, he played a leading role in a joint convention that brought together delegates of the Knights of Labor, the Farmers' Alliance, the Patrons of Husbandry (Grangers), and the Trades and Labor Assembly. The gathering of so many diverse reform groups lacking formal political-party status was unprecedented in state history, and it seemed fitting that the fiercely independent, protean Donnelly would serve as the chief author of the forward-thinking platform that emerged from the joint convention, one that championed such progressive causes as the prohibition of child labor in mines and factories and the incorporation of trade unions.[42]

Donnelly had cast his lot with the working men and women of Minnesota and against the monopolists, and the state Farmers' Alliance rewarded his loyalties by nominating him as its candidate for the Minnesota House of Representatives. Donnelly claimed not to know about the nomination before it was made, but he ultimately agreed to run in deference to the request. Remarkably, he had been nominated as a no party/independent candidate on the basis of support from a fragile coalition of the farmers of the Farmers' Alliance joined together with the Democratic-leaning Knights of Labor. The coalition Donnelly put together displeased dogmatic leaders on both sides, but discontent was especially keen among the leadership of the Knights of Labor, who waited until Donnelly walked across the stage at the convention to disavow his representation of their organization. Whether the ploy was pure political theater or sincere disdain for the party-crossing politician, even the Donnelly-hating *St. Paul Pioneer Press* noted the audacious move made by the leaders of the Knights of Labor, remarking, "Such a humiliation has never before been witnessed in any public place" in the Midwest.[43] Once Donnelly had been removed from the hall, however, the conventioneers accepted the very Alliance-Knights shared platform he had been instrumental in crafting, though Donnelly could take little solace. When the Knights of Labor subsequently voted to endorse the mainstream Democratic candidate for governor, A. A. Ames, he believed the labor union had, in effect, endorsed the forces of bossism, corruption, and monopoly. "The saloon element & railroads are triumphant," he noted in his diary, adding, "and my star sets behind a huge black cloud."[44] He understood that while his personal popularity might win him a seat in the statehouse, the Democrats' fear of bucking Doran, Kelly, and Hill would limit his ability to build a cross-party coalition by and for the people.

To the surprise of many who had long ago declared him dead as a politician, Donnelly won his November 1886 race for the Minnesota House, noting with satisfaction in his diary that he had earned approximately 85 percent of the vote in Nininger City and more than 66 percent in nearby Hastings—a testament to the strength of support he received from those he counted as neighbors.[45] With Donnelly headed back to the statehouse in St. Paul, Twin Cities newspapers feared a cult of personality would once again form around the charismatic former lieutenant governor, who had demonstrated a mercurial—some said dangerous—willingness to support whatever party best represented the interests of the people at any given time. The *Pioneer Press* suggested that he would merely use his seat in Minnesota's lower house as a means to construct his own personal political party, and from there earn election as Speaker of the House.[46] Meanwhile, the *Globe* conjectured that he would use his win in a mostly Republican district as a springboard for a future campaign for US senator.[47] Both newspapers implied that the Minnesota House of Representatives would risk becoming the House of Donnelly, though a closely divided election and renewed partisanship convinced more sanguine observers that any cult of personality would be kept in check.

Duly elected to the Minnesota legislature, and with railroad monopolists like James J. Hill firmly in his crosshairs, the protean Donnelly shifted his identity once more to match the populist spirit of the times. The *Globe* reported that he had been solicited for a short biography as a newly elected public official. Initially Donnelly had listed his occupation as "Farming and Literature," only to think better of it, crossing out the words "and Literature" to leave simply "Farming."[48] For the moment, the shoe seemed to fit. While he continued to solve the Shakespearean cipher at home in Nininger City, Donnelly turned his attention to an equally vexing political riddle: how to curb the growing monopoly power of the railroads. The antirailroad bill he crafted was to be his signature legislation, and in various iterations it called for everything from an amendment to the Minnesota Constitution relegating railroad transport within the state's borders, to paid state inspectors posted at each major railroad stop to guard against price gouging at the public's expense, to guaranteed special shipping rates for the state's food producers, from whom the railroad companies excessively profited. His antirailroad legislation drew comment from newspapers throughout the upper Midwest and Great Plains, as editors and readers across the region hardened their views into pro-Donnelly or anti-Donnelly positions.

In the winter of 1887, the *Globe* reprinted reactions from around the Midwest in a full-page feature it called "Voice of the People." The broadsheet might as well have been called "the Donnelly Vent," as nearly three-quarters of its contents were devoted to readers' feelings about the controversial lawmaker. The *Herald* in St. Peter, Minnesota, declared him a "giant among small men" in the legislature, to such an extent that in the future, when old legislative records were exhumed, "some stranger will wonder whether or not he was the only member of the House of [18]87." The *Republic* in Jackson, Minnesota, lauded Donnelly's newfound discipline, asserting that he had learned to "bridle his tongue." The *Advance* in Clearwater, Minnesota, split the difference, arguing that he would have been one of the era's great politicians if only he had not talked so much. Conceding that he was the "directing power" of the Minnesota Statehouse, the *Advance* nevertheless complained that who "Donnelly cannot convince he laughs down. . . . Pity there is so little stability to the man!" The *Republican* in Hudson, New York, wholeheartedly concurred, criticizing him for his "political gymnastics" while adding, "It would take more than a Bacon-Shakespeare cipher to trace out the history of Donnelly's political career." Meanwhile, the *Herald* in Anoka, Minnesota, warned the "eloquent" and "brilliant" sage that his continued abuse of the press would lead to his ruin. The *New Richmond North Star* in Wisconsin countered that he was a "leading light," maintaining that the legislation he sponsored was unfailingly "characteristic of his wisdom and . . . better judgement." He was, they cheered, the "nemesis of the monopolists and the railroads." The *News-Ledger* in Litchfield, Minnesota, acknowledged that on top of his ceaseless work on the cipher, Donnelly was "straining every nerve . . . to make himself recognized as the people's champion" and had been "astonishingly successful."[49]

Donnelly's persistent desire to enact the will of the people drew him inexorably into yet another public controversy in which he was determined to side with the populists. This one involved the heated debate over the possible pardon of the infamous Younger brothers—Cole, Bob, and Jim—for their role in the attempted robbery of the Northfield, Minnesota, bank alongside Frank and Jesse James in 1876. In July 1886, former Minnesota governor William R. Marshall had published a three-thousand-word letter in the *Pioneer Press* in favor of pardoning the Youngers, in which he argued that the brothers were "not as black as much falsehood, much prejudice, and the dime biographers have painted them."[50] Marshall, a Civil War veteran himself, believed that Cole Younger's record of meritorious service in the Confederate army, coupled with his exemplary behavior during the prior decade of incarceration, should merit his early release. Donnelly joined Marshall in the campaign for clemency for the brothers, a move that created a contentious interstate dispute between Minnesota, which had successfully tried and convicted the Youngers for a crime committed on its soil, and the border state of Missouri to the south, where the James and Younger brothers were regarded by many as native sons and folk heroes. Many members of the Missouri legislature, and dozens of prominent public officials throughout the Midwest and Great Plains, petitioned for the release of the Youngers. In Minnesota, Donnelly and Marshall were among the few prominent public figures to support the call for clemency. Despite the opposition from politicians in his home state, Donnelly, according to the Missouri journalist Robertus Love, "fought for the Youngers with a zeal as fiery as that evinced in his contention for the Baconian cryptogram theory."[51]

To counter his growing populist mandate, opponents in the legislature tried every possible means of thwarting Donnelly's favored causes, opposing his support for pardoning the Youngers and sending his railroad bill back to committee while Donnelly was away from the legislative chambers.[52] One especially determined House member was alleged to have offered $250 to his colleagues if they would vote against the railroad regulation measure. Despite dogged resistance from his colleagues, however, Donnelly ultimately prevailed in his efforts to implement labor- and farmer-friendly legislation, passing eighteen of the laws he spearheaded in original or amended form, against some fifty-seven bills he had introduced, for a success rate of more than 30 percent.[53] In praising his remarkably productive term in the House, the *Globe* lamented that the "legislature wasted a whole session in attempting to bury one man. . . . There is well-settled popular conviction that on the issues over which the legislature quarreled Mr. Donnelly was nearer right than the legislature."[54]

But even Donnelly's efforts to pass common-sense populist reforms had met with consistent headwinds, causing some to believe that his personal and political power had begun to wane. The St. Paul newspaper that covered him most closely cautioned those prepared to celebrate his political demise. The man had an elastic nature, it reminded readers, one that readily changed shape only to bounce back: "It is not an uncommon thing for Donnelly to be turned down, but he is not a man to be kept under. . . . That he is erratic and lacks ballast is admitted by his best friends. That he often permits his impulses to run away with his judgment has had too frequent demonstration to be doubted. And that he too frequently assumes dictatorial bearing where more modest pretentions would suit the occasion better is lamentably true. Yet notwithstanding all these defects, the man who questions Mr. Donnelly's preeminent abilities writes himself down a fool." The Sage of Nininger, claimed the *Globe*'s editor, was widely understood by the people of Minnesota as "the brainiest man in the state," and the people invariably affirmed his "intellectual worth." Donnelly enjoyed more widespread public support than ever, the newspaper pointed out, as he increasingly sided with the people.[55]

By the late spring of 1887, constant needling from skeptics on the literary front moved Donnelly to submit two articles to the *North American*

Review in an attempt to make good on his earlier promises. In the second essay, he revealed the most concrete information yet concerning the cipher on which he had been ceaselessly toiling, illustrating his claims with facsimiles of two hand-annotated pages from the first part of *Henry IV*. In the margins of the reproductions, readers of the *North American Review* could now see for themselves Donnelly's marginal notes and dizzying mathematical computations of the number of hyphens and brackets on each of the analyzed pages of the First Folio. But in sum, the two *Review* articles revealed little of the new information for which bibliophiles had been clamoring, and Donnelly took care to preempt an application of his cipher beyond the first and second parts of *Henry IV* by saying that if he continued to publish his research in article form, it would soon constitute the promised book itself. Instead he concluded with yet another request for more time, conceding that four years after word of his cipher had been leaked to the press, he had only begun to unravel the hidden narrative in the first and second parts of *Henry IV*—one play out of thirty-six. Further progress, he explained, had been delayed by "the very immensity of the story." A full report would take him yet another year, though he would, he promised, publish a small part of the story that very year and "satisfy the incredulous of the truth of the discovery."[56]

He closed by remarking on the fierce resistance his ideas had encountered in the United Kingdom. Since his research proposed only to "take the mantle of immortality from the shoulders of one Englishman and place it on the shoulders of another Englishman," he could not see what place "national feeling" should have in resolving such a scholarly question. He ended his piece on a particularly high-handed note, declaring, "The world can afford to wait until the evidence is in, before it passes final judgement on the grandest and most gifted of all the sons of men." Donnelly could promise only that he intended to have his book in the hands of a printer by later that fall, at which time he hoped to "satisfy fully the expectations of the world."[57]

CHAPTER 5

The Great Cryptogram

The headlines of the Sunday, August 28, 1887, edition of the *Minneapolis Star Tribune* broke the news: the strange genius from Nininger had once again succeeded in shocking the world. "Ignatius Donnelly's Forthcoming Work Heard From via New York," the newspaper trumpeted, adding, "New and Startling Theories Announced by the Sage of Nininger." Skeptics worldwide, the article blustered, had been "well-nigh converted."[1]

By the time the second of his two articles ran in the *North American Review* in July 1887, Donnelly had secured a subscription publisher for the book-length work with which he had long teased the world's literati. Grandly titled *The Great Cryptogram*, the book would be printed by R. S. Peale of R. S. Peale & Company of Chicago, who bought into Donnelly's wishful estimate that the volume would sell an estimated one hundred thousand copies.[2] At a royalty rate of approximately $1.00 per volume sold, Donnelly stood to earn as much as $10,000 for publishing his iconoclastic theories. An "edition de luxe" would be made available for as much as $25.00, while a more affordable version would cost something closer to $4.50.[3] In either case, the book would be prohibitively expensive for all but the most dedicated Donnelly fans and devotees of literature, though Peale hoped such readers might justify the price of the tome as an investment. Beautifully typeset with engraved titles, copious illustrations, and a lovely frontispiece, *The Great Cryptogram* would be produced as a kind of keepsake that bibliophiles at home and abroad might savor.

Donnelly's "new and startling theories" were, in fact, not entirely new. In January 1856, Delia Bacon published her essay "William Shakespeare and His Plays: An Inquiry concerning Them" in *Putnam's Monthly Magazine*, dismissing the Bard of Avon as a "stupid, ignorant, illiterate, third-rate play-actor" wholly incapable of generating the greatest body of work in Western literature.[4] Rather than hang the mantle of greatness on a single unlearned and rude performer, she advocated a collective authorship theory, maintaining that "Shakespeare" was in fact authorship by committee under the directorship of Lord Bacon. The alleged goal of the Francis Bacon–led group of subversive Elizabethan writers and thinkers was to weaken the hold of the monarchy by embedding, as allegory, prescriptions for populist political reform deep inside the plays.[5] As evidence of the Shakespeare disconnect, Delia Bacon pointed to the anonymous plays produced in London across a period of many years that only later bore Shakespeare's name, explaining that several of the dramas central to the Bard's canon had been staged years before they came to be associated with the Stratford actor. "Such a nucleus of the Shakespeare drama there was already," she reminded her reader, "when the name which this actor bore, with such orthographical variations as the purpose required, began to be assumed as the name and device."[6] Like many Shakespearean skeptics, she paid dearly for what critics considered her insolence. In his book *The Shakespearean Myth*, her fellow Shakespeare skeptic Appleton Morgan described how Delia Bacon was "pelted with a storm of abuse, derision, and merciless malice, until in poverty, sickness, and distress . . . she passed out of sight forever."[7]

Inspired by Delia Bacon, Judge Nathaniel Thomas published *The Authorship of Shakespeare* in 1866. Thomas's book, more than Bacon's article, offered the most obvious precedent to *The Great Cryptogram*, as Thomas specifically pointed to a single author, Francis Bacon, as the creator of the plays. Early in his seven-hundred-page opus, Thomas disagreed with Delia Bacon's multiple-author theory, stating that his purpose was "to show that the whole genuine canon of Shakespeare was written by this one and the same author."[8] That one author, of course, was Francis Bacon, who the author maintained possessed the erudition and poetic sensibility sufficient to author the plays, unlike Shakespeare, whose formal education had apparently ended at the free grammar school of Stratford-upon-Avon. Moreover, Thomas points out, no original manuscript of any play, poem, or letter, or other prose composition in the handwriting of William Shakespeare, had ever been discovered.[9] By the six-hundredth page of his book, the judge expressed his certainty in the most unequivocal terms, writing, "'Our Shakespeare' was no other than Francis Bacon himself; and William Shakespeare ceases to be that 'unparalleled mortal' he has been taken for, that title being justly transferred to the man to whom it more properly pertains."[10] Wisdom, vigor, imagination, knowledge, perceptivity, genius, wit, brevity—all the ringing virtues conveyed in the plays could be traced back to Lord Bacon.

While Donnelly agreed with Thomas's single-author theory, the "startling" new discovery he had made was not merely linguistic or lexical but arithmetical. While his predecessors could be dismissed by some as idle literary speculators, Donnelly hoped to be classed as what the critic Susanna Ashton later called a "prominent cryptographer" if his method yielded results.[11] A cipher hidden in the plays—logically derived and unerringly divined—would constitute the closest thing possible to a final mathematical proof.

Recognizing the book's blockbuster potential, R. S. Peale's company sought to stoke advance publicity for its release, arranging for the *New York World* to tease the forthcoming title in its Sunday edition. To maintain some semblance of journalistic integrity, the *World* commissioned the mathematics professor Thomas Davidson to interview Donnelly and to evaluate the cipher's logic and legitimacy. Davidson visited Nininger in the late summer of 1887 and came away impressed with the author's method, writing to Donnelly shortly thereafter, "I am very impressed with your work and have almost become a Baconian without the cipher!"[12] Davidson's lengthy review in the *World* was laudatory, though the professor mostly focused on the accuracy of Donnelly's counting method and the consistency with which he had applied the rule or key he had devised to decode Bacon's alleged secret message. Davidson had been given access to the proofs of the forthcoming book and had found them convincing on balance. But the number of caveats his review offered made his endorsement sound cautious. He confessed that he had not been able to "test the cipher" and that the "actual workings of the cipher" had not been explained to him. By way of disclaimer, he wrote, "I am not in a position to satisfy entirely the public curiosity with regard to this matter." The commissioned expert acknowledged that while the Sage of Nininger had explained the nature and method of the cipher to him, "he still left, and that intentionally, one point dark." What that one crucial point was, Davidson did not say. "Certainly," he acknowledged, "I do not know the ultimate law of the cipher. Indeed, Mr. Donnelly is not sure the same cipher runs through all the plays." Ultimately, Davidson concluded that he was not in a position to determine the reality of the cipher, though it was "difficult to doubt it."[13]

In Chicago, Joseph Medill, owner and managing editor of the *Daily Tribune*, responded cautiously to Peale's requests for press coverage of the new release, commissioning an expert of his own to independently appraise the soundness of Donnelly's argument and evidence. Medill employed the services of the astronomer-writer Professor Elias Colbert of the University of Chicago to read the book, interview Donnelly, and return a report. To Medill's surprise, Colbert concurred with the iconoclastic author that there was indeed a cipher running through the plays. "I am obliged to indorse the claim made by Mr. Donnelly that he has found a cipher in some of the plays. . .. I do not say, nor does he claim, that he has discovered the complete cipher, and I think it is quite probable that some of the readings he gives will bear modification in light of subsequent knowledge," Colbert wrote. Despite these shortcomings, he concluded, "But the cipher is there, as claimed, and he has done enough to prove its existence to my satisfaction."[14] Neither Colbert nor Davidson could successfully reproduce Donnelly's results—in part because Donnelly refused to share the complete key with them. But to the extent that both men accepted his premise, their independent evaluations, coupled with the author's persistent claims, successfully challenged what Ashton terms "Stratfordian complacency."[15]

While Medill refused to endorse *The Great Cryptogram* in his newspaper even after receiving the positive assessment, Peale and Donnelly regarded Davidson's and Colbert's expert reports as ringing endorsements. Davidson's evaluation, in particular, had produced sufficiently complimentary language that it could be mined for promotional quotes and laudatory blurbs. *The Sun* in New York City, however, was less impressed, bemoaning that the *World* had sent an expert all the way to Minnesota to return with "nothing very lively." It claimed that Donnelly had "purposefully refrained from disclosing any facts which would enable anybody to test the genuineness of the cipher" and complained that Davidson's review had done little to advance public knowledge of the Sage of Nininger's much ballyhooed theory. Those who were waiting on a concrete cipher to either "demolish it as a humbug or establish it as a fact, the most marvelous in the history of literature," had learned little from Davidson's visit. *The Sun* suggested that readers would be wise to lower their expectations, reasoning that if Donnelly had made great progress on his calculations, a visit from a commissioned expert would have brought new information to light; because it had not, it only stood to reason that "those who buy and read Mr. Donnelly's book will find themselves, when they get to the finish, in the same state of unsatisfied curiosity and mystification." The newspaper saw two likely options: that Donnelly had not succeeded in further decoding the Baconian text-within-the-text, or that he was withholding information for a possible sequel; after all, it conceded, the author was "a most interesting man."[16] Perhaps this was a case of the wise man playing the fool.

Donnelly dealt with the pre-press publicity given *The Great Cryptogram* cautiously and with an eye toward thwarting the potential theft of his intellectual property. To guard against prepublication leaks, typesetters, editors, and publishers involved in the project would be kept in the dark as to the exact workings of the cipher for as long as possible, typesetting and editing discrete portions of the manuscript without ever having the text before them in its entirety.[17] These safeguards meant that Peale himself remained ignorant of many key aspects of the manuscript, including the fact that Donnelly had deciphered only 1,700 words—not 17,000—of the secret story of Elizabethan intrigue Bacon was said to have enfolded within the plays. Even as Peale set sail for London to arrange for a foreign edition, he remained clueless as to the cipher rule, finding Donnelly unwilling to provide the sort of supporting material the publisher could readily understand. When Peale arrived in the United Kingdom, he found the British press dubious, and sometimes openly hostile, at the prospect of reporting on such a seemingly heretical work. The editor of the *London Daily Telegraph* declared that Donnelly "might as well expect the English people to give up their belief in the Constitution as their belief in Shakespeare."[18]

As he had during the writing of *Atlantis* and *Ragnarok*, Donnelly suffered grave eleventh-hour doubts about the reception his work would receive. He acknowledged to his diary that a financial failure for the book could prove devastating for his family, especially since he had already received an advance against royalties to pay down his debts. The unrelenting Minnesota winters made the task of finishing his final chapters feel like a prison sentence: "All is white and desolate, no one comes to see me from weeks end to weeks end; I work from 10 o'clock in the morning until 11 at night, with a few minutes intermission for meals & one hour's lonely walk." Authorship, so often glamorized by the public, was, under the circumstances, "not a delightful occupation." Donnelly bemoaned the fact that he was "chained to the stake" and could not "fly," and he looked forward to a time when he would "rejoice when the great task is finished, no matter how the book turns out."[19]

And turn out the book did. Beautifully typeset and richly illustrated, the final version totaled nearly one thousand closely argued and detailed pages. The volume's subtitle boldly asserted its claim—"Francis Bacon's Cipher in the So-Called Shakespeare Plays"—and its frontispiece illustration, a painting of the lordly Bacon in place of the Bard, made the argument implicit: Shakespeare would be supplanted. In the epigraph to *The Great Cryptogram*, Donnelly deployed lines from *Henry IV* coyly selected to reinforce his daring thesis:

> And now I will unclasp a secret book
> And to your quick-conceding discontent
> I'll read you matter deep and dangerous
> As full of peril and adventurous spirit
> As to o'er walk a current loud
> On the unsteadfast footing of a spear.

The tone of the frontmatter is vintage Donnelly, combining grandiosity and audacity with a palpable sense of vulnerability, fallibility, and even fatalism. On one hand he announces his intention to "do justice to the memory of Francis Bacon," declaring it a "noble privilege" to lift the "burden of injustice from the shoulders of long-suffering merit." He will, he says, battle "against the great high walls of public prejudice" that had elevated Shakespeare beyond the status he deserved. The cipher would turn out to be the long missing key that, once turned, will "unlock a vast history, nearly as great in bulk as the Plays themselves." The hidden narrative, the author promises, will tell a "mighty story of one of the greatest and most momentous eras in human history," duly described by Bacon, whom Donnelly calls "the most gifted human being that ever dwelt upon the earth."[20]

Elsewhere in the book, however, the discoverer of the great cipher presents himself as self-effacing and apologetic. As early as the first page, the author of *Atlantis* and *Ragnarok* begs his readers' indulgence for what he describes as "the shortcomings of the work." He confesses that he has penned his opus "in the midst of many distractions and interruptions" and that the manuscript lacks "the perfection which ampler leisure might possibly have given it."[21] What those exact distractions and interruptions were, Donnelly declines to say, but it's clear from context that financial worries, farm superintending, political wrangling, and familial duty combined to delay the long-promised revelations.

In book 1, part 1, unambiguously titled "William Shakespeare Did Not Write the Plays," he unfolds the checkered biography of the Bard, highlighting the many inconsistences between the man and his work, ranging from the preponderance of French- and Italian-sourced language in the oeuvre of a man universally acknowledged to have a poor reading knowledge of both, to the inclusion of complex legal language by a playwright said to know precious little about the law. Donnelly alleges that Shakespeare was the first in his family to be able to read and write, and asserts that he grew up in a bookless house within a "bookless neighborhood." It would be, he writes, a "gross improbability" for a young man raised in such conditions to become the greatest writer of his or any era, and it would be a true miracle if "out of this vulgar, dirty, illiterate family came the greatest genius, the profoundest thinker, the broadest scholar that has adorned the annals of the human race." It was theoretically possible, Donnelly concedes, but any thinking person would readily admit that it was "scarcely probable."[22]

The first seventy-five pages of *The Great Cryptogram* trace the scant, ignominious facts of Shakespeare's life through to an unremarkable and undignified end that finds the legendary writer leaving behind "not a single tradition or memorial that points to learning, culture, refinement, generosity, elevation of soul, or love of humanity." Donnelly closes with a quote in which Ralph Waldo Emerson laments of Shakespeare, "I cannot marry the facts to his verse."[23] Shakespeare was most certainly not a lawyer, but Francis Bacon was, the author points out, arguing that the court scene from *The Merchant of Venice*, among many others, is "so saturated with the law the writer must have been in daily practice of the law, and in hourly converse with men of the same profession." [24] Put simply, only Bacon had the sort of political, ideological, and intellectual chops to write the plays. Bacon's extant essays and letters, Donnelly maintains, prove that he possessed the poetic skill and sensibility to have carried off the task, but his position as an aristocrat and courtier of Queen Elizabeth would have prohibited him from publicly participating in a craft—playwriting—considered beneath his station.[25]

Donnelly devotes the first half of *The Great Cryptogram* to a circumstantial case for Bacon's authorship, painstakingly quoting the work of other scholars and commentators who believe Shakespeare's authorship to be a myth. Book 2, titled "The Demonstration," contains the alleged proofs. It begins with the author's anecdotal recollection of his original epiphany concerning the existence of a cipher within the plays. He recalls how, years earlier, he encountered a chapter on ciphers in one of his young son's books, a chapter that cited Bacon as having devised the "most famous and complex cipher" ever written. The volume went on to explain the ingenious method behind Bacon's code, which functioned by substitution, such that, for example, *aaaaa* stood for the letter *A*, *aaaab* stood for *B*, *aaaba* stood for *C*, and so on through the alphabet. Using such substitutions it was possible to encode a shorter, secret message within a much longer block of text. Bacon's cipher was significantly more complex—such that the authors of the cryptography chapter estimated that one in a thousand had any hope of discerning it, let alone translating its carefully embedded syntax word for word.[26]

Donnelly recalls for his readers that Bacon had once traveled to France to write a book, *De Augmentis Scientiarum*, in which the great politician-naturalist-bibliophile made his case for having one's own private alphabet. Such a private alphabet, or "word cipher," could be useful for avoiding persecution and suspicion. "Let a man have two alphabets," Bacon wrote in *De Augmentis*, "one of true letters, the other of non-significants; and let him unfold in them two letters at once, one carrying the secret, the other such a letter as the writer would have been more likely to send, and yet without anything dangerous." Any hostile agent who discovered the missives would be able to make sense of only the "exterior letter" and, finding it to be probable, would "not suspect anything of another letter within."[27] Bacon further insisted that the ultimate effectiveness of the cipher required artfulness and intelligence on the part of both the encoder and the decoder if both parties were to preserve the "secret of princes."[28] By skillful presentation, the encoder and the decoder could present the exterior epistle as meaningless or pedestrian while sharing between themselves and other sympathetic parties an intimate secret.

For most of his adult life, Bacon had served as a decipherer of such messages from European courts, putting the "secrets of princes" into practice. Throughout, he espoused a belief in what he called the "enigmatical method" of the ancients, the intention of which was to signal a secret meaning to those souls thoughtful enough to have "received the interpretation of the enigma through teachers" or those of the requisite wit and discernment to "pierce the veil" for themselves.[29] In Bacon's

Elizabethan era, near-constant political foment, royal intrigue, and incessant power struggles made cipher writing common practice among the young statesmen of London, in an environment in which writing *omnia per omnia*—translated as "signifying anything with anything"—proved both fashionable and practical.

To further corroborate the circumstantial evidence for a great cryptogram embedded in the body of work falsely attributed to Shakespeare, Donnelly points to a particular passage in Bacon's will, which had been altered at the eleventh hour to read, "I leave my memory to the next ages and foreign nations, and to my own countrymen after some time be passed."[30] The last phrase, "after some time be passed," appeared to suggest Bacon's foreknowledge of delayed gratification, in a manner consistent with an author or playwright who expected his popularity to grow with some dramatic posthumous revelation. Donnelly's supposition that Bacon had enfolded a secret message within his will was heightened by a later change in the passage to read, "For my name and memory I leave it to men's charitable speeches, and to foreign nations, and to the next ages."[31] Donnelly suspected that the "after some time be passed" in the original had struck Bacon as too obvious a nod toward his secret authorship of the plays. After Bacon's very public fall from grace later in his career, a deathbed admission of secret authorship would only have furthered the public distrust that had been growing since Bacon's unpaid debts and alleged bribes had become public knowledge. The internal narrative Donnelly felt certain Bacon had hidden in the plays functioned as an exposé of the clandestine court skullduggery that, if decoded in Bacon's lifetime by his many enemies, would surely have brought "serious penalties to his kinsfolk, his family, his very body in the grave." Bacon's master plan for posterity could be seen as perfectly intelligible, Donnelly believed, and he summarized it thusly: "When his corpse was dust, his blood extinct, or diluted to nothingness in the course of generations; then, when all vanities of rank and state and profession and family were obliterated; when his memory and name were as a sublimated spirit," only posthumously, after some time had passed, would he, through the cipher narrative, restore his proud legacy.[32]

Donnelly next provides his readers with a summary of the logic underlying his decipherment. He posits that if Bacon had wished to convey his authorship of the plays, one would expect to find words such as "Francis," "Bacon," "Shake," "Speare," "Shakes," and "peer" used within the dialogue. Adhering closely to this hypothesis, he focuses on occurrences of the word "Bacon" and "William" in *The Merry Wives of Windsor* deployed in instances that feel otherwise contrived or tangential.[33] Most conspicuous in the author's mind is the complete absence of the word "William" from older pre-1623 versions of *Merry Wives*, suggesting that the name had been added at a later date despite its seeming irrelevance to the plot of the play. To substantiate his claims, he quotes the experts Richard Grant and Thomas Middleton, who likewise note the superfluous scene introducing "William" in the 1623 First Folio that had "nothing whatever to do with the plot." In act 4, scene 1—in a portion entirely missing from earlier versions—the word "William" is used eleven times, and the word "hog" and "bacon" are used several more, inclusive of the expression "hang hog," a term widely associated with a quip made in a court proceeding presided over by Nicholas Bacon, Francis's father. In the scene immediately following, Donnelly finds the words "Shakes" and "peere," used in ways altogether different from those used in earlier versions of the play, suggesting edits had been made, post facto, for the purpose of embedding the cipher in the Folio. Donnelly wants his readers to pay close attention to "the extraordinary way in which the typeset words are bracketed and hyphenated" within belatedly introduced portions,[34] since he has come to believe that brackets and hyphenations are instrumental to the key, that, when turned, unlocks the secrets carefully hidden in the text. Recited all together as a litany of evidence, repetitions of "Francis" (inclusive of variants such as "Francisco" and "Frank") and "William Shakespeare" (inclusive of "shake, "shakes," "speare," and "peere") amount, in Donnelly's eyes, to "so many fingers extended pointing the attention of the sleepy-eyed world" to something beneath the surface—"exclamation points that Bacon believed would, sooner or later, fall under the attention of some reader of the plays."[35]

The key appeared to lay in the eccentric if not erratic pagination and printing of the First Folio, published well after Shakespeare's death. Donnelly undertakes an extensive explication of the importance of this posthumous edition, with a panoramic view of what he considers the most revealing aspects of its broader historical context: By 1623, Shakespeare had been dead seven years, Queen Elizabeth had passed and James was now king, and the plays had not been staged by a major playhouse in at least a dozen years. Meanwhile, Bacon had concluded his tenure in the highest station in Britain, Lord High Chancellor, two years earlier in 1621. Concerned as never before with the preservation of his legacy, Bacon filled his personal correspondence with references to creating "banks or mounts of perpetuity, which will not break," to recreational writing beyond his well-known essays, and to an author's natural desire to seek publication of such recreational writing before his death. Lord Bacon sent his closest friend abroad, Sir Tobie Matthew, "a great and noble token" of his work, only to have Matthew respond enigmatically, "The most prodigious wit that I ever knew, of my nation and of this side of the sea, is of your lordship's name, though he be known by another." Donnelly suggests that the great and noble token sent to Matthew was, in fact, a copy of the Folio of 1623, printed by Bacon's allies according to his specifications, with its inaccurate page numbers, brackets, and hyphenations constituting the key to the cipher buried inside.[36]

For Donnelly, the inexplicably egregious errors riddling the First Folio could suggest only an ulterior motive. For example, had the laws of continuous pagination been obeyed, *Henry V* should have begun on page 103, but instead it began on page 69; similarly, *Troilus and Cressida* should have begun on page 234; instead it commenced on page 79, followed by 80, with the remainder of the pages of the script left mysteriously unnumbered.[37] Given the historical evidence that the printers cared enough about accuracy that they stopped the print run on several occasions to make corrections, and given that the printers' signatures indicated many eleventh-hour insertions, including the insertion of four additional pages in *Henry IV*, it strikes Donnelly that such inconsistencies were "made to order."[38] He asserts that the errors intentionally inserted into the manuscript by the printers operationalized the cipher key.

Redoubling his efforts in light of this discovery, Donnelly revisits the most prominent use of the word "Bacon" on page 53 of Shakespeare's historical plays. Counting downward from the top of the column on that page, and counting only the spoken words that precede the word "Bacon," makes "Bacon" the 371st word in the column. He next divides the number 371 by the number of the page, 53, to yield 7—a mathematical anomaly with a 1-in-938 chance of occurring.[39] He conducts the same test on page 67, where he had earlier found printed the words "S. Albones" (a corruption of the name of Bacon's hometown, St. Albans) in act 4, scene 2, as the 402nd words on the page. Applying the same mathematical operation (402 divided by the number of the page in the Folio, 67) yields a quotient of 6—the exact number of italicized words in the column containing the words "S. Albones." In each of these two cases, and in several more delineated by the author, a single change in hyphenation or italics would render the supposed cipher code invalid. Donnelly's analysis of the six total columns extant on pages 53 and 54 yields a tantalizing first line of a cipher: "Francis Bacon Nicholas Bacon's Son." Nicholas Bacon, Francis's father, was a member of the British Parliament later named Lord Keeper of the Great Seal by Queen Elizabeth.

Once commenced, Donnelly's combing of the text for cipher clues yields an abundance of telling anomalies, including nearly a thousand bracketed words in *1 Henry IV* and *2 Henry IV* and well over three hundred hyphenated words across the same two plays. Donnelly deems the use of abbreviations such as *K.* for "King" and *Ch.* for "Chief" to have been alterations made in accordance with the cipher pattern, which required a certain number of words per column to preserve the all-important arithmetic.[40] Other smaller clues reveal themselves in comparisons made between earlier published versions of the plays, the Quartos, and the definitive Folio edition of 1623. For example, the *b* in "bacon" had been lowercased in the play's earlier publication, but the same word was printed with a capital *B* in the Folio, for no apparent reason other than to signal the identity of the play's true author.[41] The very fact that fully half of the plays collected in the Folio were new to that volume confirms for Donnelly that Bacon had been waiting for both Shakespeare and Queen Elizabeth to pass before publishing his cipher versions, further suggesting that the great statesman believed any immediate danger in his identification as the playwright had expired by 1623.[42]

"Francis Bacon Nicholas Bacon's Son" is just the beginning, however, of the secret story the Sage of Nininger susses out in the so-called work of Shakespeare. The next steps are far more uncertain, leaving the decipherer to lament, "A more brain-racking problem was never submitted to the intellect of man."[43] It is one thing to follow a mathematical rule involving five words repeated across as many columns, but it is a far more sophisticated arithmetical challenge to decode cipher words sufficient to tell a complete story running across the entire breadth of the plays. Here Donnelly pauses to explain, by analogy, the thorny enormity of the task before him: "It was as if one had taken me into a vast forest, and told me that, on certain leaves of certain trees was written a clew [*sic*] to know the . . . trees on which the words were to be found. If I had climbed into and searched the branches of those trees, and collected with infinite care, the words upon them, I was still at my wits' end. How was I to arrange them?"[44] Elsewhere, he resorts to metaphor not just to describe the magnitude of the task but to explain to readers why he has not yet worked out the entire hidden story. He explains, "I have been tempted to go on and on, working out the marvelous tale; and I have heaps of fragments which I have not now time to put into shape for publication. I have been like Aladdin in the garden; I turn from one jewel-laden tree to the other, scarce knowing which to plunder, while my publishers are calling down to the mouth of the cave for me to hurry up."[45]

Donnelly declares that the decoders of the famous Rosetta Stone had a simpler task, though he claims to have found the answer to the inner workings of the cipher machinery in five root numbers—505, 506, 513, 516, and 523—that he insists unlock the cipher story in *1* and *2 Henry IV*. But he is purposely coy as to how he arrives at those root numbers, saying only that they are the product of "multiplying certain figures in the first column on page 74, by certain other figures."[46] He withholds the exact explanation, intending that in the future, when time allowed, he would apply his rule to both the first and second parts of *Henry IV*.

In the meantime, he pauses in his nearly one-thousand-page opus to brood over the unhappy prospect of other scholars and code breakers applying his mathematical rule before he would have a chance to publish a more complete deciphering. This would be a great indignity, for he could not copyright his method, and were it to be pirated, he would have worked for years for the benefit of others with no recompense, a theft of intellectual property that, he said, could best be understood by analogy: if the inventor of the telephone or the telegraph could protect profits made from these new and novel uses of electricity, then certainly similar protections should be extended to "the one who by years of diligent labor has lighted a new light in literature and opened a new gate in history."[47]

In any case, Donnelly maintains, no reasonable man would object to his withholding from the public his hard-won key, though he intimates that the cipher he has discovered is purely arithmetical and precisely regular. He arrived at his formula by breaking each Folio column into subdivisions—for example, those natural breaks created by exits and entrances of characters, at the ends of scenes, and at the ends of columns. Counts would then proceed from the first word of each of these many subdivisions, excluding stage directions—not just by counting down from the first word of each subdivision but by counting up from the last word. Hyphenated words could count as either one word or two words, according to "the requirements of the cipher rule."[48] Different pages would have different numbers of subdivisions. For example, the two columns on page 73 each contained three subdivisions.

To decode exact words in the cipher story, Donnelly makes approximately twelve calculations for each page. For example, on page 73—constituting the last page of *1 Henry IV* in the First Folio—the cipher necessitates the following calculations:

words in the first subdivision of text
words in the second subdivision of text
word in the third subdivision
words in the column
words from the last word (and including the last word) of the first subdivision to the end of the column
words from the last word of the first subdivision (and including the last word) to the end of the second subdivision
words from the first word of the second subdivision (and including the first word) to the end of the column
words from the first word of the second subdivision (and including the first word) to the end of the second subdivision
words from the top of the column to the end of the second subdivision
words from the top of the column to the beginning of the third subdivision
words from the beginning of the third subdivision to the end of the column
words from the beginning of the third subdivision, potentially plus or minus any hyphenated words.[49]

The flow of the cipher across the pages of the Folio requires Donnelly to derive what he calls "multiplier numbers." These multipliers could be ascertained by counting the number of bracketed words, the number of hyphenated words, the number of bracketed words plus any hyphenated words also included in brackets, and the total number of bracketed or hyphenated words. To show his math, he directs his publisher to include an illustration showing some seventeen pages of the Folio, including the margins wherein he has made his counts.[50]

Disappointed readers inferred from this limited sample that Donnelly had deciphered Bacon's clandestine cipher story only in portions of two of Shakespeare's historical plays, meaning that the larger secret narrative said to span the entire oeuvre would remain, for now, untold.

But the cipher story derived from just two of the histories proves sufficiently sensational. Donnelly maintains that it speaks to the controversy created by the performance of the play *Richard II* and reveals an attempt by Queen Elizabeth to learn the real identity of the playwright she strongly suspected was not William Shakespeare. The cipher story intimates that Elizabeth believed the play was treasonous because it intended to incite the kind of civil unrest that would lead to her being deposed from the throne. It describes how she sent royal officials to arrest Shakespeare and torture him into a confession of being the pen behind *Richard II*, and of Shakespeare needing to flee Britain for the Continent to escape persecution. The cipher story goes into further detail about Shakespeare's youth and old age; his syphilitic condition; his marriage to Anne Hathaway; his alleged beating and imprisonment; and the claims made by the 1st Earl of Salisbury, Robert Cecil—Bacon's cousin—that Shakespeare is not the author of the plays.

All these Donnelly dutifully reveals in successive chapters, in each instance showing the mathematical calculations used to derive certain cipher words and syntax, including the pages and columns on which the cipher words could be found. Whole, grammatical sentences emerge in his decipherment, though some allowance must be made for homonyms, puns, and figures of speech Bacon allegedly used to hint at the characters involved in the drama without naming them directly. For example, in the portion of the hidden cipher story wherein Robert Cecil—Queen Elizabeth's spymaster in charge of security of the state—alleges that Shakespeare did not author the plays, Donnelly's cipher translation reads, "Seas ill says that More low or Shak' st-spur never writ a word of them." In the fashion of allusions in the Elizabethan era, homonyms were used to conjure important persons without naming names; hence Donnelly concludes that "Seas ill" is a homonym for "Cecil," "More low" for Marlowe, and "Shak' st-spur" for "Shakespeare." He derives this particular "chapter" in the hidden story from words used on just three pages—74, 75, and 76—of *2 Henry IV* and asks skeptical readers whether there could be four columns on three consecutive pages anywhere in the world where six such significant words could be discovered. And in the unlikely event there were six such words on three consecutive pages, could they be located not just by the same root number but by the same modification of the same root number—in this case, the root number 516? "If you can indeed do this in a text where no cipher has been placed," Donnelly quips, "then the age of miracle is not yet past."[51]

By page 844 of *The Great Cryptogram*, Donnelly—presumably fearing that he has not yet convinced dubious critics—blames his publisher for the fact that he has applied his cipher rule only to *1* and *2 Henry IV*. He begins chapter 19 with the curiously intimate admission, "My publishers write me that the book now contains 900 pages, and that the *edition de luxe* 'looks like a Chicago directory!' "[52] Donnelly's curious aside inscribes a kind of vicious circle. The more he feared that his cipher would be rejected by scholars and critics, the more words he wrote in an attempt to convince them; the more words he wrote, the more uncertain his publisher became about the profitability and reliability of the book; the more concerned the publisher became about the value of the book in the eyes of the reader, the more inclined Donnelly was to argue for the greater length and complexity offered by additional sections, tables, illustrations, and arithmetical proofs. In chapter 29 he musters a curious combination of laments, excuses, and certainties, avowing to his reader, "I regret to leave the story of Shakspere [*sic*] unfinished."[53] As partial consolation, and perhaps to tease an eventual sequel, he delivers enticing fragments of the remaining cipher stories buried in the plays—sentences here and there that he has worked out as evidence of the shocking revelations a further deciphering of the internal story would beget—for example, an alleged suicide attempt by Bacon and an attempted robbery by a youthful Shakespeare forced to flee Stratford for London.[54]

Because Donnelly was a politician accustomed to delivering for his constituents, the unfinished nature of the cipher troubled his conscience. He admits as much in the penultimate chapter of book 2, in which he references, with all due circumspection, the more audacious claims he made in the original prospectus of the book. He had not, for example, solved the cipher of Bacon's attempted suicide, nor had he worked out the complete internal story of Bacon's clandestine contact with Shakespeare in Stratford, via Bacon's personal assistant and quasi literary executor, Henry Percy. While Donnelly had set out to elevate Bacon belatedly to the status of greatest Western writer of all time, Bacon instead emerges as an almost pathetic figure. By book's end, he seemed to some readers, as one Donnelly biographer puts it, like a pitiable "prisoner in the dock, defended by an able attorney unafraid of excesses."[55] The attorney in the analogy was, of course, Donnelly.

Since the publisher had sold *The Great Cryptogram* via advance subscription, Donnelly worried that any significant departure from the original proposal might cause readers to demand their money back.

Indeed, the depth of the author's self-consciousness explains an entire chapter inserted at the end of book 2, included under the title "A Word Personal." Donnelly notes the irony: "I began this book with an apology; I end it with another." Thereafter he acknowledges that the book in its final form had been compiled with "the utmost haste and under many adverse circumstances." He describes his misfortune in having announced in 1884 that he had found a cipher in the plays. Sufficiently startling, the claim was not easily forgotten by readers and critics, who began demanding that he come forward with his proofs, and when he did, insisted on branding him a lunatic. Goaded by the naysayers, Donnelly confesses that he had been too quick to seek publication of a work meant to satisfy their doubts. The strain of keeping his commitment to his publisher, while also campaigning and serving in elected office, he says, thwarted the more thorough investigation he desired. In many other ways, however, he insists that he has overdelivered: instead of the promised seven hundred pages, he has given readers nearly one thousand, including a large chunk of the cipher story describing Shakespeare's marriage and the character of his wife, Anne Hathaway.[56]

While he may have failed by his own exceedingly high standards, Donnelly's core conviction—that a cipher existed within the plays—won numerous converts. And with his own mea culpa placed so near the end of a thousand-page tome, where many readers would never find it, the book generated intense public interest in spite of its flaws, including a British promotional tour organized with the help of Peale & Company in Chicago and Baconians overseas. Donnelly's supporters celebrated the impending trip as a chance to secure long-overdue international prestige, while his detractors saw his sojourn as a prime opportunity to undo the fragile yet potentially powerful labor-farmer coalitions he had built at home, and that had recently elected him to the Minnesota statehouse.[57]

On learning that Donnelly would be sailing to Britain in the early winter of 1888 for a lecture and publicity tour, British newspapers moved to defuse, or at least dampen, the coming sensation. In late November, months before the famed Sage of Nininger was due to arrive, the *Daily Telegraph* declared his case all but unwinnable, surmising, "We cannot and will not yet surrender Shakespeare's glorious name and fame to the desperate ingenuity or self-deception of Mr. Donnelly."[58] The *Essex County Standard* in Colchester took a more reasonable approach, insisting that its editors had at least given the extant evidence a fair hearing, and concluding, "We can say to our great relief, and great pleasure that after reading, with an open mind, all that has been vouchsafed to the public about Mr. Donnelly's 'Great Cryptogram' our faith in Shakespeare remains confident up to now."[59] London's *Pall Mall Gazette* appeared to take the seemingly heretical thesis personally, launching an ad hominem attack against the author as an "American crank" while conceding that the points raised in *The Great Cryptogram* were at least "ingenious and interesting" (though not, the newspaper insisted, wholly original).[60]

Like many of their counterparts in the British press, the *Daily Telegraph*, *Standard*, and *Pall Mall Gazette* acted preemptively out of what was presumed to be their shared desire to stop Donnelly's sensational claims from gaining momentum. But all three of the publications published their assessments based on published interviews with the author and on the few advance excerpts of *The Great Cryptogram* that had been shared with the American public via Thomas Davidson's assessment in the *New York World* earlier that summer. The *Pall Mall Gazette* admitted as much, conceding that Davidson's analysis was "of far too elaborate a character to be summarized here" and, further, that the newspaper's editors would be "waiting patiently for the full revelation which this forthcoming work promises." Still, their article, damningly subtitled "An American 'Crank' and his Cryptogram," prematurely declared "that the Shakespearean faith of most men will, we suppose, remain unshaken."[61]

By late March 1888, Donnelly had arrived in London, writing letters to Kate back home in the United States that he expected vociferous criticism from the British for his impertinence. Still, he dared to hope his resistant audience would yield to the light of reason. He commenced his British tour with a trip to Francis Bacon's home in St. Albans, where he believed the great statesman had conceived of the cipher, followed by a trip to Westminster Abbey. He felt humbled standing before the graves of Samuel Johnson and Charles Dickens, but beyond the writers and poets interred there, he remarked mostly on the effects of class and money, writing to Kate that wealth ruled the Abbey, with merit triumphing only in Poets' Corner.[62]

Two weeks after soaking in the inspiration of Poets' Corner, Donnelly argued his case to an audience of nearly nine hundred luminaries at Westminster Hall said to include the Irish playwright Oscar Wilde.[63] He spoke for more than two hours to a sympathetic crowd made up primarily of members of the Bacon Society who were eager to laugh at his jokes and cheer his obstreperousness. According to *The Times*, he told the friendly gathering that he was aware that "he spoke in the face of a mighty prejudice," one that amounted to a "wall of national superstition." Nearing the publication date for the British edition of *The Great Cryptogram*, he risked including in his lecture "an elaborate dissertation on the very complex cipher," replete with diagrams and illustrations, before concluding his address with the bold claim that Bacon was "the greatest intellect of the human race." The Baconians in the room rewarded him with lusty cheers.[64]

London newspapers treated the whole affair as a curiosity, avoiding any serious attempt to deconstruct the complicated cipher for their readers.[65] In early May, *The Times* published the most extensive review yet of the British edition published by Sampson Low & Company. Occupying more than two broadsheet columns top to bottom, the unbylined analysis wondered early and often whether the book that took so much of the writer's time and energy would ever find an audience: "We can only hope he may find a single reader to give him fair play and conscientiously examine all his complex calculations." In keeping with the early US reviews, *The Times*' assessment made no serious attempt to explain the math behind the cipher, focusing instead on debunking the author's literary interpretations and his analysis of the circumstantial evidence. Unabashed in its geographic prejudice, the review openly assumed that "a citizen of the United States must be a somewhat incompetent critic on such matters" as Shakespeare. Faced with the prospect of overcoming a resistant British public and centuries of accumulated historical amnesia, Donnelly's great cryptogram project struck London's newspaper of record as "scarcely compatible with sanity." In *The Great Cryptogram*, it declared, the United States had produced "an example of futile research and perverted ingenuity."[66]

Sensing an unfair shake, Donnelly took the fight directly to the most biased of the British media outlets—those that happily accepted gratis review copies of his expensive opus while subsequently refusing to give it space in their pages. The visiting American author directed his prodigious wrath in particular at the editors of London's *Daily News*, who he claimed had committed just such a transgression. "If one cannot intelligently review a work," he opined in a published letter to the editor, "the next best thing is to discover a flaw in it; and if one cannot lift an ox, one must content himself with finding a sore spot on his back." If his metaphor was a bit homespun, its point was clear: the mighty Sage of Nininger resented the necessity of trifling with the lesser intellects of journalists who, because they could not comprehend his tapestry of an argument in its totality, instead relished pulling at its loose threads. He continued his case with all the aplomb of a defense attorney appealing to a dubious jury: "Now I put it to you as fair-minded men—and all Englishmen pride themselves in their love of fair play—whether it was right to refuse to review my book as a whole, and pass by all the multitudinous evidences which I present." It was the "magots" of "their ostentatious learning," Donnelly argued, that allowed the *Daily News* editors to ignore his book's many proofs in favor of a "trifling, little, supposed error." Rising to an indignant crescendo, Donnelly saved his most damning rhetoric for his letter's final paragraph, where he insisted that the English newspapers were doing little more than standing guard "over the rotten carcass of the national delusion."[67]

During late May and early June, Donnelly took the stage again in defense of his theories in two successive debates. At Oxford, students greeted him with wild applause, but by the conclusion of the evening's contest, they voted against his cipher theory by a reported margin of 127 to 30.[68] At Cambridge five days later, he managed something closer to a draw, as he and a Trinity College professor debated the question before a crowd of one thousand. As they left the lecture hall, audience members were asked to vote for either Shakespeare or Bacon, though at least 750 of them were reported to be too "rattled" to cast their lot. Of those that answered the poll, 120 voted for Shakespeare and 108 for Bacon. Donnelly counted it as a victory.[69] While Donnelly's appearances in Britain gave the Baconian theory its most well-publicized airing yet—earning him visits to the House of Lords and the House of Commons—any pomp and circumstance given the visiting American author seemed to spring from customary politeness rather than a spirited endorsement of his anti-Shakespearean theories. Donnelly suspected collusion against his work among the British literati, and though he felt defeated, the rhetorician in him resolved to fight back in the pages of the US press, where he could spin the unfair criticism as anti-American sentiment generally and, more specifically, as an artifact of innate British prejudice against American thinkers.

His revenge came in the form of a lengthy interview given to the *New York World* and reprinted in newspapers back home in the Midwest. In Minneapolis, the *Irish Standard* ran the interview at length under the headline "Donnelly Strikes Back," devoting two full columns to a rebuttal alleging the "abuse" the author and his book had received in England. "But why, in heaven's name, cannot this discussion be conducted without all the virulence that has been imported into it?" Donnelly wondered, quipping that he could imagine such vitriol if Shakespeare were, for example, running for president. Was he not entitled to a fair hearing on a scholarly question that had been under debate for more than thirty years? Citing an unnamed English newspaper that had implied that he should be lynched for his impertinence, he used the interview to reiterate his claim that many of the reviewers passing judgment on the credibility of his work had not yet read it. This had been demonstrably true with several publications whose editors had either admitted as much in print or whose misstatement of his thesis had been so patently erroneous as to lead to no other possible conclusion.[70]

When the interviewer asked why some of the US newspapers had lodged similarly bitter criticisms, Donnelly cited the Eastern geographic bias against writers from the American Midwest. Such ardent sectionalism infected critics in all regions, he claimed, though Midland authors—those from the Midwest, Great Plains, and Rocky Mountain states—bore the brunt of the unfair treatment. He added, "The man living east of the Alleghenies can scarcely believe that the man west of them can perform any intellectual act worth considering . . . while on the other hand the man of Ohio and Illinois has his misgiving as to the man of Minnesota; and the man of Minnesota experiences more or less mistrust of any literary work born in Montana or Oregon." Ethnic prejudice further fueled the disdain, he contended, insisting that Irish American authors were more likely to be associated with shillelaghs than with scholarly inquiry. If he had been a "blue-blooded professor of Yale or Harvard, with a pedigree that stretched back to the Mayflower" rather than an American of Irish ancestry, his reasoned argument against Shakespearean authorship would surely have received more serious consideration. Donnelly felt that the baked-in bias against *The Great Cryptogram* by reviewers and members of the reading public who objected to his politics, coupled with the "weight of prejudice," contributed to the perfect storm of criticism levied in opposition to his work. He complained to his interviewer, in closing, of the unwarranted bitterness of the "fraternity of scribblers" belittling his investigation, including one St. Paul man who expressly regretted that Donnelly had not gone insane in his ill-fated pursuit of the cipher, like fellow Shakespearean skeptic Delia Bacon, whose obsessive efforts to dethrone the Bard landed her in an asylum in Connecticut. The nameless St. Paul critic who wished insanity on the author of *The Great Cryptogram* had also expressed regret that he could "not pick [Donnelly's] bones."

Donnelly understood how the English would be inclined to unleash their hate speech on an interloping American determined to correct a three-hundred-year-old error, but he simply could not understand, or excuse, what he considered to be the savagery of domestic critics allied against him.[71]

While Donnelly grew increasingly despondent during his lengthy stay in Britain, homegrown satirists gloried in the ridicule the Gopher State's great man of letters received while abroad. Some were all too pleased to join the collective criticism; Joseph Gilpin Pyle of the *St. Paul Pioneer Press* published a pamphlet-length parody under the belittling title *The Little Cryptogram*. Pyle, an assistant editor at the *Pioneer Press* and a longtime Donnelly sharpshooter, originally published his parodic editorial in the pages of his newspaper but found the relish of readers sufficient to justify a stand-alone printing of the spoof.

While conceding that *The Great Cryptogram* is a "monumental work" and a product of the author's "infinite labor," Pyle leads off his public lambast with an epigraph from *As You Like It*, one that pegs Donnelly as the "motley foole" that was "deep contemplative."[72] After briefly explicating the author's infamous arithmetical cipher system, Pyle proceeds to apply the math to six pages of *Hamlet*, hoping to demonstrate to the general public the wishful thinking inherent in the fool's errand that Minnesota's greatest statesman had undertaken. In effect, Pyle uses Donnelly's logic against him, explaining how in *Hamlet*,

> there is circumstantial evidence sufficient to show that the remarkable pointing to the word "Donnelly" could not be a mere coincidence. For example, in the same column with "don," and but a few lines further on, occurs the expression "most violent author." Is this an accident? Again, the word "politician," according to the lexicons, occurs not over half a dozen times in all the plays. It is found twice in these six pages, in intimate connection with the word "Donnelly;" once in the far-fetched expression "life-rendering politician," which means nothing. Still again, popular nomenclature has designated Mr. Donnelly as "The Sage of Nininger."[73]

Applying what he claims to be Donnelly's method, Pyle arrives at the decipherment, "Donnelly, the author, politician and mountebanke, will worke out the secret of this play. The Sage is a daysie."[74] Determined to embarrass the author and his fans while at the same time ostensibly honoring his ambition, Pyle concludes that Donnelly's cipher amounts to finding a mathematical justification to "pick out the words you need to say what you desire."[75] He acknowledges Donnelly's years spent in sincere service of wresting a particular meaning from a Folio so thick that lesser men could not even hope to lift it, and concludes, quite cynically, that the Sage of Nininger would "gather a fortune from his audacious and singularly successful advertisement; and neither friend nor generous enemy will grudge him that." He imagines how rich the irony would be if the author were to take the proceeds from the subscription sale of *The Great Cryptogram* and erect a bronze or marble statue of himself reclined in scholarly repose, with a hint of a grin parting his lips, and with an edition of the Shakespeare plays opened to that famous passage in *A Midsummer Night's Dream*, "What fools these mortals be."[76]

To readers unaware of the long-standing enmity between Donnelly and the editors of the *Pioneer Press*, Pyle's *The Little Cryptogram* seemed like so much harmless fun, but the parody was part of a sophisticated effort by the newspaper to discredit the author and the book before it had a chance to gain a foothold. Twin Cities newspapers reported that the *Pioneer Press* had hired a man to peddle *The Little Cryptogram* door to door for twenty-five cents a copy in an attempt to discredit *The Great Cryptogram* and diminish its subscription sale. The *Pioneer Press* was also reported to have sent copies of the parody to England with the same intention. The concerted efforts of the newspaper were believed by many to have done Donnelly's work demonstrable harm, leading thousands to the mistaken belief that the cipher was a "delusion" or a "fraud."[77]

Pyle wasn't the only prominent figure to apply Donnelly's arithmetical rule to suit their own purposes. The rector of St. Albans, Rev. Aldwell Nicholson, took a more serious approach to disproving Donnelly, publishing the transparently titled *No Cipher in Shakespeare: Being a Refutation of the Honorable Ignatius Donnelly's "Great Cryptogram"* in London in 1888. Nicholson begins his book-length rebuttal with a dramatically direct statement: "Mr. Ignatius Donnelly has not been refuted."[78] *The Great Cryptogram* had been parodied, certainly, and rejected out of hand, but it had not been thoroughly rebutted, Nicholson posits, before undertaking a sixty-four-page dismantling of Donnelly's claims, often using the author's method against him. Nicholson proceeds to use the root number 516 to suss out a secret message contrary to the author's, one that reads "Master Will I am Shak'st spurre writ and was engaged at the Curtain."[79] Like Donnelly, Nicholson shows the mathematical operations by which he arrives at each keyword in his decipherment, and then, going the Sage of Nininger one better, he shares five separate instances in the First Folio in which the same core sentence can be deciphered. He concludes that *The Great Cryptogram* fails to overcome "the double disadvantage of promiscuous terminology and looseness of style,"[80] and that Donnelly's work suffers from "an extemporaneous, slip-shod style" that undermines the precision required by his subject. In fact, Nicholson notes, "When he [Donnelly] sets himself . . . to elucidate anything with special pains, things become more confused than usual."[81]

Like nearly all of Donnelly's most vocal critics, Nicholson had his own reasons for aggressive refutation. Ministering in Bacon's hometown, he clearly resented Donnelly's very public recitation of Bacon's long-buried scandals and controversies; Bacon's reputation would now, regrettably, rise and fall with the reputation of Donnelly unless the two names could be forcibly divorced, a separation Nicholson undertook with relish. Donnelly's claims were, he writes, "an insult to the memory of Lord Bacon," and *The Great Cryptogram* was a "fiction."[82] As a patriotic Englishman, Nicholson insists that Shakespeare and Bacon—in that order—are the first- and second-greatest writers in the Western tradition, and his conclusion is proud, defiant, and prejudiced: "William Shakespeare will never be dethroned. Men and women of the English race, whether in England or America, will continue to contemplate the memory with hereditary pride."[83] Taken together, Pyle's and Nicholson's applications of Donnelly's root number to produce diametrically opposite hidden messages reinforced the prevailing notion among the literati that Donnelly had subconsciously produced the results he had been seeking.[84]

In his 1888 book *Shakespeare in Fact and in Criticism*, Appleton Morgan—the scholar with whom Donnelly had first enthusiastically shared his cipher work—joined the crowd of wits and wags lining up to slam *The Great Cryptogram*. Morgan, still president of the New York Shakespeare Society, had softened the position taken in his 1881 book, *The Shakespearean Myth*, in which he had concluded that the plays attributed to William Shakespeare were likely written by more than "one ready-writer" eager to "write anonymously for bread."[85] In *Shakespeare in Fact and in Criticism*, he maintains that the authorship question remains open and that readers must not let the legitimate doubts about the pen behind Shakespeare's plays distract from their overall enjoyment of the plays, or from the delicious mysteries of the Elizabethan era. Scolding Donnelly for treating the greatest works in Western literature as if they were mere multiplication tables, Morgan methodically debunks much of the Baconians' circumstantial evidence, calling into question Donnelly's assumptions about the unorthodox typography of the First Folio, among other alleged misapprehensions. While Donnelly had regarded anomalies such as italics and parentheses as evidence of a cipher, Morgan counters that Elizabethan printers routinely swapped in italic typefaces when running short of regular roman type. Otherwise inexplicable parentheses, he claims, were very likely actors' marks on original scripts mistakenly copied and codified into print editions.[86] Morgan devotes an entire chapter to highlighting the logical fallacies inherent in *The Great Cryptogram*, and while he makes plain that he disbelieves in "every word of it, or in any foundation for a morsel of it," he insists that Donnelly's cryptogram theory is at least as deserving of critical consideration as "the rubbish of the esthetic, the inductive, and the creative critics."[87]

In *The Little Cryptogram*, Pyle imagines Donnelly greatly enriched by what Pyle considers a laughable literary investigation, but speculation about the small fortunes made in marketing *The Great Cryptogram* turned out to be completely unfounded. In May1888, the Utah-based author and editor J. H. Beadle pointed out that the subscription method, more than even the high price and provocative content, may have scared away traditional readers who were accustomed to purchasing their titles at stores rather than from salespeople going door to door. "The intense feeling against Mr. Donnelly and his book," Beadle notes, "has manifested itself in almost every form of opposition imaginable, from the flippant charge of hallucination and crankiness to the sober imputation of willful and deliberate fraud. Not content with condemning the book in advance, some have gone so far as to find matter of criticism in the method by which the book is published and sold." Beadle explains that publishers are presumed to avail themselves of the subscription method only when "undertaking what would otherwise be too hazardous," allowing such books to reach the public which "could not otherwise see the light." Rising to Donnelly's defense in this regard, he points out that many esteemed authors had sold their works via subscription, including Mark Twain and Shakespeare himself. And the door-to-door subscription method was wholly in keeping with the author-politician's populist beliefs, as thousands of people would read *The Great Cryptogram* who would otherwise "rarely see the inside of a library or a book store."[88]

Back in Britain, Donnelly endured slings and arrows of outrageous fortune. In part due to the subscription method and the concerted efforts made by the *Pioneer Press* to limit the appeal of *The Great Cryptogram*, sales of the book on both sides of the Atlantic languished, and its author began to feel trapped among a foreign people who quietly disdained him or else dismissed him entirely. Deeming his book a failure, he worried that, as a poor man trying to accomplish something lasting "among the base & sordid politicians of Minnesota," his future political prospects would be dim. He admitted a painful truth to his diary—"It may seem as if my hopes rose high only to be crushed"[89]—while finding his downcast mood mirrored by the unusually gloomy late spring weather.

Not even the prospect of a trip to his ancestral homeland of Ireland later that July seemed to cheer him from what seemed at times like a congenital sense of fatalism. He would go to Ireland, but he expected to find there only confirmation of his doomed lot: "My ancestors, for generations led lives of savages and peasants, in mud hovels, without comfort, pleasure, or enlightenment; and I shall feel that the curse which overshadowed them has descended upon their representative and that despite profound thoughts and superhuman industry I can make no headway toward fortune."[90] Donnelly insisted that if only his literary efforts had been given a fair and unbiased appraisal instead of being, as he put it, "howled down by a corrupt press," they would have succeeded on their own merits. Viewing himself as poor and powerless, he felt condemned to suffer as if by some cosmic punishment. By August he had been abroad for nearly six months, and though his trip had brought him the pleasure of visiting the home of the Scottish poet Robert Burns as well as reuniting with some of his Irish relatives, he was eager to return home to Minnesota.[91] "Thank God for Columbus and the land of Sunshine,"[92] he confided to Kate, anxious to leave what he described as a "prejudiced, bigoted, class-ridden, semi-aquatic country."[93]

Unfortunately, the darkness Donnelly had experienced in London followed him back to the States, where his publisher reported that US interest in *The Great Cryptogram* had plummeted during the author's long sojourn overseas. According to the publisher R. S. Peale's account, as of September 1888 the book had lost in excess of $8,000, a figure that ballooned to more than $12,000 when Peale factored in the unrecovered advance on royalties paid his star author. Donnelly suspected Peale of inflating his losses and misrepresenting the subscription method by which the book was sold, while Peale recommended selling the book to syndicates to cut his losses.[94]

The resulting breach-of-contract lawsuit did little to lift the author's spirits, as the negative publicity damaged the book's sales potential still further. "There it was in the paper with headlines & caricature—my enemies rejoicing," Donnelly bemoaned, adding, "I cursed the evil spirits that are pursuing me & swore at the damnable subtlety of Francis Bacon . . . which covered me in ignominy."[95] Donnelly agreed to pay back his advance by trading with Peale for multiple city lots in St. Paul, while Donnelly received the plates for the book in return for the real property. The exchange offered the author just one consolation: that he would have the ability to privately print *The Great Cryptogram* at any point in the future. For the time being, however, the loss of property in exchange for ownership of copyright struck him as a raw deal. Of the plates he reflected ruefully in his diary, "I will put them in my garden, and build a little house to cover them. . . . The little building will be a monument of colossal failure." As to his aspirations of convincing the literary public of the validity of his cipher theory, he saw only "wrecked hopes" and "ruined ambitions."[96] In a journal entry he wallowed further in what he called the bitter "waters of humiliation," writing, "I have drained them to the very dregs, I have swallowed them by the quart. . . . I have plunged into an ocean of them . . . until every fiber of my being has shrieked out its protest against injustice and degradation."[97] The legal resolution to his conflict with Peale did not mean that he renounced the truth of the cipher, but simply that the reading public was not ready to receive it.

In the months that followed, Donnelly would attempt to stir up interest, and drum up money, by debating well-known Stratfordians in the literary equivalent of heavyweight bouts staged at neutral sites. In Chicago he would take on J. C. Freeman at the Central Music Hall, finding the large crowds hostile to his arguments. The *Inter Ocean* newspaper in Chicago defended local pro-Shakespeare sentiments, reminding the visiting author that Chicagoans naturally regarded the Bard as a "constant source of wonder and delight." The city, it claimed, could have only "contempt for the petty attempt at grand larceny which would rob the name which is above all names in the world of letters to enrich another."[98] The cumulative effect of biased newspaper coverage and spectators who seemed keen to jeer him for sport badly wounded Donnelly's pride. "To be made the laughing stock of school-girls!" he complained to his diary. "I feel like Falstaff, when he threatened to take his brains out and butter them and feed them to a dog for his breakfast."[99]

Wearied by the abuse he had taken at debates, and no doubt hoping to chase the negative publicity of the Peale case with a resounding win, Donnelly reentered the political arena. While the nearly six-month sojourn in Europe had been a failure from the standpoint of book sales, the international attention helped his political standing back home among readers disinclined to read the more damning reviews of their hero's magnum opus. Upon his return, the Farmer Labor Party nominated Donnelly as their candidate for Minnesota governor. While his youngest son, Stan, cautioned him against further dalliances with upstart third parties, Donnelly's instinct to fight for the political enfranchisement of the working classes prompted him to concede to the "Draft Donnelly" movement and accept the nomination.[100] Fearing that his candidacy would draw Republican voters to the Farm Labor Party, in effect splitting the vote, the Republican National Committee urged him to withdraw, dangling the prospect of a federal appointment or patronage position if he would instead leave home to campaign for the Republican presidential candidate, Benjamin Harrison, in New York. Stubborn and proud, he refused, replying, "I am greatly obliged to you, "[but] I do not feel that I ought to leave Minnesota at this time. My duty is here, defending the people from the robberies of the railroad corporations." The Republican Party, he wrote, was "in the hands of men who would lead it to the devil," and it could only be reformed by someone "from the outside"—someone like Donnelly.[101]

By early October, the Farm Labor Party lacked the resources to support its candidate. Donnelly formally withdrew, endorsing the Republican William R. Merriam for Minnesota governor while agreeing to campaign for Merriam at a fee of one hundred dollars per speech.[102] In the Twin Cities, Donnelly could still draw crowds of thousands of Republicans with whom he had built rapport as a former member of that party. In Minneapolis, cheering throngs apparently saw no conflict in the politician's mercurial party switching, as they appeared to accept the rationale he offered: he hadn't changed or waffled, and the Republican Party had changed for the better. Donnelly campaigned energetically for Merriam because he believed Merriam to be a like-minded servant of the people, but he refused to use his bully pulpit to disparage the Democratic Party, viewing it as not so different from other established political parties made up of, as he put it, "some able patriotic men" and "another portion," bent on corruption and self-interest.[103] Donnelly had an additional reason to go easy on the Minnesota Democrats, as, in yet another example of his political pantheism and prolific party switching, he accepted the nomination of the Democrats in his home county of Dakota for the Minnesota House of Representatives. Though Dakota County was widely seen as Republican territory, Donnelly was known and respected there by many of the Democrats who knew him and appreciated his people-over-party disposition.

Despite his attempt to have it all ways in the November election, Donnelly the Democrat lost in Dakota County, falling short by less than 150 votes. Still, though he had been forced to withdraw his gubernatorial nomination from the Farm Labor Party only to suffer a narrow defeat in his run as a Democrat in Dakota County, the election season of 1888 proved that he was still a force to be reckoned with in Minnesota politics. And though Donnelly himself suspected that *The Great Cryptogram* had been a failure, it had not diminished his fame or notoriety among the farmers and laborers who lacked widespread access to the publications where the book had been panned. At the ballot box, Donnelly's political agnosticism had begun to cost him, but as a public figure his legend had only grown in the farm-country newspapers that published reports of the homegrown Sage of Nininger dining with earls and lords while debating high-and-mighty British intellectuals to a draw in the hallowed halls of Oxford and Cambridge. In the rural Midwest, his reputation as a fighter and intellectual underdog—one who could hold his own in debates against the wealthy and well born—lived on.

CHAPTER 6

Caesar's Column

In January 1889, Donnelly reached yet another of his personal crossroads prompted by the advent of the new year. Having withdrawn from the race for governor, and having been defeated in his Democratic run for the Minnesota House in his home district, he nevertheless held out hope that divided Republicans in the state legislature might reject his old nemesis William D. Washburn and subsequently elect Donnelly to the US Senate on the second or third ballot. And yet despite support from a dozen delegates on the first ballot, Washburn easily secured the win over Donnelly and former Minnesota state senator Dwight Sabin.[1]

Facing the prospect of a year without political office, Donnelly commenced writing a speculative, futuristic novel he hoped might be an outlet for his growing certainty that US democracy was under assault from corporations. As he had with *Atlantis* and *Ragnarok*, he took full advantage of the frigid Minnesota winter to throw himself into his writing, producing his first novel, *Caesar's Column*, in less than five months.[2] Unsurprisingly, the novel emerged dark, antiutopian, and angry, a manifestation, perhaps, of Donnelly's desire for revenge on those who had rejected him at the polls,[3] and of a long-frustrated desire to secure economic justice for disadvantaged workers.

Manuscript in hand, he approached Harper & Brothers in New York, but, just as it had with *Ragnarok*, the publisher rejected the manuscript, as did Scribner's, Houghton Mifflin, O. B. Bunce, D. Appleton, and A. C. McClurg.[4] Established Eastern presses worried that the new novel might be read as advocating class revolution, with one, McClurg, writing a personal letter to Donnelly in which he argued that the upper classes in the United States recognized their obligation to create a more just and equitable society, and that the US was a country where "men of property and influence" were working "earnestly toward the removal of existing evils on society." McClurg felt that Donnelly's dystopian text treated the upper classes unfairly and could serve to agitate those "who already believe in disturbance and Anarchy." But, assuming Donnelly did succeed in finding a publisher for his fictional treatise, McClurg also pleaded for the book to be sold at a price point that would keep it out of the hands of the masses inclined to read it as an incitement to revolution.[5] Donnelly took strong exception to McClurg's insinuations, countering that the contents of his new novel could never equal the accumulated effect of a corrupt court system and "debauched legislatures, our US Senate filled by men who have bought their seats, our demoralized voters, our indifferent newspapers and their increasing degradation of the laboring classes." He hastened to remind McClurg that "to suppress the truth is not to arrest the consequences of evil,"[6] while back home in St. Paul, the *Great West* rushed to his defense, blaming the book's rejections on the powerful plutocrats who controlled Eastern publishing houses.[7]

As Donnelly traded volleys with East Coast editors over the incendiary nature of the dystopian fiction he had penned, he once again waded into wider cultural controversies, reigniting the populist debate over the imprisonment of the outlaw Younger brothers in Stillwater, Minnesota, for their infamous 1876 robbery of the First National Bank in Northfield alongside Frank and Jesse James. The Civil War veteran Warren Carter Bronaugh had taken up the cause for clemency for the Youngers and had asked Donnelly to write a letter on their behalf. Donnelly agreed, producing a letter in which he relayed an anecdote wherein the outlaw Youngers, recognized by a farmer near Mankato, Minnesota, while attempting to escape Northfield, refused to shoot an innocent bystander, or to bind him, on the grounds that both would be cruel. Instead they released the farmer on the promise that he would not divulge his sighting of the outlaws to local authorities. In his letter, Donnelly remarked, "I always thought there was something heroic in this action of these fugitives from justice, at a time when the woods swarmed with their pursuers. They were ready to risk their own lives rather than take the life of a stranger."[8] After making his case for the supposed virtue and nobility of this exceptional band of outlaws, he lodged a culminating appeal on behalf of the youngest of the Younger brothers, Bob, who had been "a mere boy in years" at the time of the incident and who was now "at the point of death" from tuberculosis. Addressing Minnesota governor William Merriam directly, he urged a just remembering of this "act of humanity performed years ago" in the woods of Blue Earth County, Minnesota, so that this "poor criminal" could die peacefully outside the "shadow of the penitentiary, and in the midst of those who love him." Should the governor grant the release, Donnelly promised, "every humane heart in the state" would be behind his executive action.[9]

Beyond the justifications included in the letter, other motives for the Younger brothers clemency movement could be inferred from the separate statements written by Donnelly and others that were subsequently published in Bronaugh's book *The Youngers' Fight for Freedom*. Since his days as a congressman during the Civil War, Donnelly had been a spirited advocate of reconciliation between the North and South, and, as one letter writer put it, the case of the Younger brothers was now "one of the last remaining reminders of the late war between the states."[10] In his letter, Horace W. Pratt, a former probate judge and mayor of Faribault, Minnesota, echoed Donnelly's sentiments, writing, "I desire to add my testimony to what I believe to be the growing sentiment of the people of this state, that in the case of the Younger brothers the law has been vindicated. . .. I think that such a pardon would be received by the people as a just and merciful act."[11] In his activism on behalf of the Youngers, several of Donnelly's political and personal instincts coalesced, including his habitual advocacy of the marginalized and misunderstood, his long-standing support of Civil War veterans, and his willingness to support individuals too hastily dismissed as pariahs by society at large.

As Donnelly waited without satisfaction for positive news on the Youngers' bid for executive pardon, he rededicated himself to the task of finding a publisher for *Caesar's Column*. His quest led him to F. J. Schulte & Company of Chicago, which agreed to publish the controversial text as it was, without even subtle changes to make the manuscript more palatable, and under the pseudonym "Edmund Boisgilbert, M.D." Schulte perceived an audience for the book at the center of Donnelly's political base in the labor and farm movements, as well as among those with socialist sympathies. He assured Donnelly that among such readers, the book would be read and recommended by word of mouth until it built a loyal following. After his disastrous experience with Pearle's subscription method, the author was skeptical, though the publisher's market predictions proved prescient. By June, steady demand for *Caesar's Column* afforded Schulte the luxury of both hardcover and paperback editions. By December 1890—roughly one year after Donnelly conceived the novel—Schulte was selling approximately one thousand copies a week.[12]

In the late spring of 1890, few outside the author's immediate circle knew that Edmund Boisgilbert, MD, and Ignatius Donnelly were one and the same. Instead, Twin Cities newspapers speculated on Boisgilbert's identity and social status. The *Great West* imagined that the medical doctor turned novelist must be a man of great wealth, education, and station. "No such book has ever appeared before in the annals of civilized literature," it declared, adding, "The truth peers from every page."[13] By June, Twin Cities newspapers had begun to hedge on the authorship question, referring to Dr. Boisgilbert as "the presumed author" while simultaneously undertaking a kind of damage control lest the doctor's prescriptions be considered too radical for the public to stomach: Boisgilbert, said one, "is by no means a fiery-eyed anarchist or red revolutionaire"; instead his calling was to "wake the people of America to the awful dangers that threaten them." No longer depicted as a mere medical man with adjacent literary talent, the pseudonymous novelist had morphed into a true "philosopher, philanthropist and prophet" prone to see the world through a lens of "terrible clearness."[14]

By October, newspapers had deduced that Edmund Boisgilbert was a nom de plume for a writer whose real identity would be revealed by the publisher in due time. In addition to Donnelly, prime suspects included T. V. Powderly, the leader of the Knights of Labor; the railroad executive T. B. Blackstone; the Chicago clergyman David Swing; and Judge Albion Tourgee. R. Pritchard, editor of the *Arkansas Traveler*, favored lawyer-novelist Tourgee as the prime suspect; regardless, Pritchard raved about the book, claiming that its impact would far exceed that of its nearest analog, Edward Bellamy's *Looking Backward*. "I am of the opinion that *Caesar's Column* will live," Pritchard declared, "and that it will win undying distinction for its author, whoever he may be."[15]

Even as he continued to withhold the hand behind the revolutionary novel, publisher F. J. Schulte could count on a network of farm- and labor-friendly newspapers across Middle America to advertise the title to exactly the sorts of everyman readers McClurg had feared would revolt once awoken. By the late fall of 1890, publications as small as the *Princeton Union*, in Princeton, Minnesota, population less than one thousand, were stocking the book at their offices, making paperback copies available for a mere fifty cents.[16] The *Union* and others like it helped generate considerable buzz, exhorting their readers with reminders to "read *Caesar's Column*" alongside ads for such staples as potatoes and butter. While *Caesar's Column* rode a wave of free advertising in heartland villages and small towns, coastal literati largely ignored the work for its first six months on the market, anxious about its incendiary message and the identity of its author. For his part, Donnelly made no public claim of authorship early on, likely reasoning that the mystery could serve to deepen the work's appeal.

Still, as the holiday season approached, regional newspaper editors leaked the author's true identity. In Wichita, the *Saturday Evening Kansas Commoner* declared, "It now appears that the wonderful story . . . was written by no less a man than Hon. Ignatius Donnelly, of Minnesota, for years identified with the Farmers' Alliance." The book, the editors observed, had had a "wonderful sale."[17] In Kansas, the *Burrton Graphic* noted that "the mystery of the authorship of *Caesar's Column* has been cleared up." Almost every celebrated author, it added, had been guessed at prior to F. J. Schulte's revelation of Donnelly as the pen behind the Boisgilbert name.[18] In South Dakota, the *Herald* ran a lengthy and laudatory review on the revelation of the Sage of Nininger as the mind behind the visionary treatise. Calling him "learned in the history of nations" and "one of the boldest thinkers of his age," the editors expressed a preference for *Caesar's Column* over the book to which it was most frequently compared: Bellamy's utopian *Looking Backward*. By contrast with Bellamy's fanciful approach, Donnelly's, they said, was a "sensible portraiture of events with their consequences," well suited to the sensibilities of Middle American readers. The newspaper's message to its mostly agrarian readership was clear and emphatic: "We . . . say to everyone, 'read it.'" H. L. Loucks, the Populist candidate for South Dakota governor, echoed the *Herald*'s sentiments, insisting that Donnelly's cautionary tale should be read "by every farmer in the land."[19]

Display ads purchased in newspapers across Minnesota and the rest of the upper Midwest swiftly changed to reflect Schulte's revelation of the book's authorship. As of late October, the *St. Paul Globe* was still advertising the book as written by E. Boisgilbert; a month later the ads read, "Praised the world around, though written under a pseudonym, *Caesar's Column*, written by Hon. Ignatius Donnelly."[20] The book, with its heretofore concealed authorship, had been printed in ten editions since its publication in April. The title page in the latest editions released by Schulte & Co. now walked the fine line between authorship and anonymity, opting for the hybrid credit line "Ignatius Donnelly writing as Edmund Boisgilbert, M.D." and prefacing the work with a lengthy "note to the public" penned by Donnelly. Newspapers reported that Donnelly had resolved never again to publish any work under his own name in the United States, so great had been his mistreatment over *The Great Cryptogram*.[21] Donnelly's theory of biased treatment was all but confirmed when his friends at the *Great West* republished glowing praise for the novel printed by Donnelly's bitter enemies at the *St. Paul Pioneer Press* prior to his unmasking. They gushed that *Caesar's Column* was "powerful in the extreme" and added, "The effect of an honest purpose is felt in every line."[22]

In the preface to *Caesar's Column*, Donnelly responds indirectly to the criticism leveled at him by McClurg and other prospective publishers. "It must not be thought, because I am constrained to describe the overthrow of civilization, that I desire it," he begins. "The prophet is not responsible for the event he foretells. He may contemplate it with profoundest sorrow. Christ wept over the doom of Jerusalem."[23] Fancying himself a modern Jeremiah, he distances himself from the tenets of social Darwinism while simultaneously allowing them to breathe life into his fictional characters.[24] Nor is he an anarchist, the author assures his readers, though he admits to painting "a dreadful picture of the world-wreck which successful anarchism would produce." To those who believed such an incendiary tract should never have seen the light of day, he replies by way of analogy: "What would be thought of the surgeon who, seeing upon his patient's lip the first nodule of the cancer, tells him there is no danger, and laughs him into security while the roots of the monster eat their way toward the great arteries? If my message be true it should be spoken; and the world should hear it. The cancer should be cut out while there is yet time."[25]

What exactly is the cancer Donnelly purports to cut from the American body politic? The preface makes the Marxist diagnosis clear: "Vast combinations depress the price of labor and increase the cost of the necessaries of existence. The rich, as a rule, despise the poor; and the poor are coming to hate the rich. The face of labor grows sullen; the old tender Christian love is gone; standing armies are formed on one side, and great communistic organizations on the other; society divides itself into two hostile camps; no white flags pass from the one to the other. They wait only for the drum-beat and the trumpet to summon them to armed conflict."[26]

Donnelly's epistolary novel opens with the first letter from the young protagonist, Gabriel Welstein, written to his brother Heinrich in Uganda. In the futuristic missive, dated New York, September 10, 1988, Gabriel marvels at the technological wonders of the largest metropolis in the world. Recently arrived in the bustling city of ten million by intercontinental airline from Africa, he takes in the beauty of a city lit up like gleaming jewel. At dinner, a waiter directs Gabe to a giant screen from which, at the touch of a button, he can order any food in the world, and instructs him how to do the same to order news from the most remote corners of the globe. Missing home, Gabe pushes a button to stream the headlines from his home nation of Uganda, and on the screen before him appears "all the doings of the people of that state—its crimes, its accidents, its business, the output of its mines, the markets, the sayings and doings of its prominent men; in fact, the whole life of the community was unrolled . . . like a panorama."[27]

Written more than a half century before George Orwell's *1984*, *Caesar's Column* predicts the technologies and tyrannies of a dystopian future; both Orwell and Donnelly, according to Steven Trimble and Donald E. Winters, were independent political thinkers "disappointed or disillusioned" with the politics of their time while stopping short of becoming wholly "cynical or unpolitical."[28] In Donnelly's futuristic vision of 1988 New York, well-to-do men and women sport health watches that record every change in their bodies' vital signs, and they often live to one hundred years of age in full possession of their faculties. Dirty fuels like wood and coal are virtually obsolete, Gabe learns from an attendant at the Hotel Darwin, with the city heated and cooled by a kind of clean geothermal power. Assisted suicide is commonplace and made available at hospice houses where those who wish to end their life can do so while penning thoughtful farewell letters to loved ones left behind. Gabe observes: "The truth is, that, in this vast, overcrowded city, man is a drug,—a superfluity,—and I think many men and women end their lives out of an overwhelming sense of their own insignificance;—in other words, from a mere weariness of feeling that they are nothing, they become nothing." He concludes his first letter home to Africa by telling his brother that he intends to visit the great lobbies and parlors of the sprawling Hotel Darwin, though he does not expect to find kindred souls there. "The race has grown in power and loveliness," he notes of the beautiful, if not unsympathetic, faces he sees all around him, adding, "I fear it has lost in lovableness."[29]

Outside the protective walls of the Hotel Darwin, Donnelly's protagonist encounters a world diametrically opposite the agrarian peacefulness of his Ugandan home. The city, he learns, is antiutopian, morally bankrupt, and politically corrupt.[30] A stranger in a strange land, Gabe Welstein seems fated to run afoul of the technocratic, plutocratic New York society of 1988, and by the second chapter the inevitable conflict is well underway. As he walks the streets of the teeming city, he comes on a beggar pinned under the wheels of a vehicle driven by a remorseless driver. He reacts instinctively, pulling the whip from the driver's hands before the car can crush the beggar under the wheels. When the driver refuses to move, Gabe turns the whip on him while the victim scrambles to safety. The driver calls for police to arrest Gabe, at which point the beggar intervenes, spiriting Gabe away through the byzantine city to the house where he makes his home with his mother. There, the beggar removes a disguise and introduces himself as Maximilian Petion, a young attorney.

In the days that follow, Max introduces Gabe to the underbelly of an utterly lawless city. Only pretending to be part of a greater democratic republic, the city of New York circa 1988 functions as a kind of aristocratic city-state wherein the true power is held by a single man known as Prince Cabano, the wealthiest and most vindictive in the metropolis. Cabano functions as a symbol of greed and a manifestation of the social Darwinian logic by which the wealthy and well bred come to rule;[31] he is not literally an American prince, but his father is sufficiently wealthy to own a princedom in Italy, conferring the ceremonial title to his son. Cabano is Jewish, conforming to Max's view that "the aristocracy of the world is now almost altogether of Hebrew origin."[32] In Prince Cabano's New York City, sectarianism and ethnic prejudice inflame simmering resentments. As Max explains it, the Jewish people of the Old Testament are a "noble race" who, after centuries of persecution, have survived to consolidate power, becoming "the great money-getters of the world." Refusing to choose sides in the sectarian conflict, the attorney opines, "They were as merciless to the Christian as the Christian has been to them. They said with Shylock, 'The villainy you teach me I will execute.'" It is a tragic state of affairs, Max laments, "a sad world, and to contemplate it is enough to make a man a philosopher."[33]

As misfortune would have it, the driver Gabe whipped in order to save Max from certain death turns out to be an employee of Cabano's, and Gabe is now wanted for robbery and assault. He imagines it impossible that any New York City jury would convict him of acts undertaken in defense of an innocent life, but Max assures him otherwise: "The image of justice has slipped the bandage from one eye, and now uses her scales to weigh the bribes she receives. An ordinary citizen has no more prospect of fair treatment in our courts, contending with a millionaire, than a new-born infant would have of life in the den of a wolf."[34] The newspapers of New York City, the young attorney insists, function as a bullhorn for the rich rather than as an independent and impartial fourth estate. Calling them the "mouthpiece of power," Max cautions that "their influence is always at the service of the highest bidder; it is their duty to suppress or pervert the truth, and they do it thoroughly. They are paid to mislead the people under the guise of defending."[35] Max reveals to his new African friend the existence of a secret underground resistance movement, a brotherhood sworn to restore true democratic rule within and beyond the city limits. Its members, mostly comprising common laborers, signify their allegiance to the clandestine resistance via secret signals, intervening whenever possible to ensure justice for fellow members, which explained why the policeman who had been prepared to arrest Gabe for robbery had suddenly demurred when he learned that Max was a member of the so-called Brotherhood of Destruction. Gabe closes his third letter to his brother back home in Uganda by disclosing that Max has promised to take him, the following day, into the underworld, which is very different from the veneer of well-bred humanity in the Hotel Darwin.[36]

The city's underworld proves every bit as shocking as Max intimates, and it leaves Gabe shaken. Together they visit countless factories, meeting the workers who make up the multitudes of the working-class Brotherhood. Gabe dutifully narrates the most poignant of these visits in his letters, remarking, "It seemed to me that I was witnessing the resurrection of the dead; and that these vast, streaming, endless swarms were the condemned, marching noiselessly as shades to unavoidable and everlasting misery. They seemed to me merely automata, in the hands of some ruthless and unrelenting destiny. They lived and moved, but they were without heart or hope."[37] After a full day of heart-wrenching visits, he concludes, "In the final analysis of reason, the great criminals of the world are not these wild beasts, who break through all laws, whose selfishness takes the form of the bloody knife, the firebrand, or the bludgeon; but those who, equally selfish, corrupt the foundations of government and create laws and conditions by which millions suffer, and out of which these murderers and robbers naturally and unavoidably arise."[38] The moral equivalency Gabe draws signals his acceptance of potential redress if not retribution; if the thoughtless, covetous rich are as criminal as the "wild beasts, who break through all laws," then the rich are perpetrators of a crime against the people and must be held to account.

As class warfare escalates between the Oligarchy, ruled by Prince Cabano, and the clandestine Brotherhood of Destruction, headed by the brutish revolutionary Caesar Lomellini, Gabe and Max find themselves increasingly alienated by the cultural and political extremes on both sides, though they continue to work on behalf of the Brotherhood. As the conflict degenerates into violent anarchy, they prepare themselves for the worst. Max converts his assets into gold, while Gabe, ever the idealist, prepares for the revolution as a scribe might before the coming of the Dark Ages, making plans to escape to the mountains of Africa with his books. Gabe takes solace in the notion of escape to a room full of "literature, science, art, encyclopedias, histories, philosophies, in fact, all the treasures of the world's genius—together with type, printing presses, telescopes, phonographs, photographic instruments, electrical apparatus, eclesions, phemasticons, and all the other great inventions which the last hundred years have given us."[39]

Here and throughout, Gabe Welstein closely resembles Ignatius Donnelly, a man of enlightenment fully invested in the power of literacy and the rule of law. Like Donnelly to his library in Nininger City, Gabe will escape to the mountains of Africa to wait until "exhausted and prostrate mankind is ready to listen . . . and help . . . us reconstruct society upon a wise and just basis."[40] Clearly Gabe is an idealist, a philosopher more than a warrior. Throughout the novel he makes impassioned pleas for peace to all the warring parties—Oligarchy, Brotherhood, and church—only to have his ideas for a peaceable resolution ignored. Max, meanwhile, assumes the role of realist, reminding his newfound ally that even the churchgoers of 1988 will ultimately consent to the violence practiced by Caesar Lomellini. Caesar, Max reminds Gabe, is "a bigger brute than they are." The difference, he insists, is that the churchgoers are "brutes who are in possession of the good things of this world; and Caesar is a brute who wants to get into possession of them." And there is still another difference, Max insists: mainly that "they are polished and cultured brutes, and Caesar is the brute natural—'the unaccommodated man' that Lear spoke of."[41]

The eponymous Caesar reveals his true brutality as the tide of the outright class warfare turns in favor of the Brotherhood. Its generals inform their drunken leader that nearly a quarter of a million of the Oligarchy's soldiers, poisoned by gas, lay dead in the streets of New York, and with the weather warming, something must be done with them before plague and pestilence overwhelm the city. In a moment described by a critic as "one of the truly horrible scenes in American fiction,"[42] Caesar directs his generals to build a column of the bodies—the titular Caesar's Column. "And if there aren't enough dead to build it of," the bloodthirsty leader adds, "we'll kill some more."[43]

Caesar sends an officer to the home where Max and Gabe reside to demand that Gabe write the inscription for his column of the dead. With Max away appealing to the angry mobs in the streets for calm, and as intruders scale the walls of their safe house, Gabe hastily drafts his copy:

> THIS GREAT MONUMENT
> IS
> ERECTED BY
> CAESAR LOMELLINI,
> COMMANDING GENERAL OF
> THE BROTHERHOOD OF DESTRUCTION,
> IN COMMEMORATION OF THE DEATH AND BURIAL OF
> MODERN CIVILIZATION
>
> It is composed of the bodies of a quarter of a million of human beings, who were once the rulers, or the instruments of the rulers, of this mighty, but, alas! this ruined city.
>
> They were dominated by leaders who were altogether evil.
>
> They corrupted the courts, the juries, the newspapers, the legislatures, the congresses, the ballot-boxes and the hearts and souls of the people.

Written at the command of Caesar, Gabe's commemoration offers a litany of grievances against the defeated supporters of the Oligarchy, and in closing it sounds an apocalyptic note: "Should civilization ever revive on earth, let the human race come hither and look upon this towering shaft, and learn to restrain selfishness and live righteously. From this ghastly pile let it derive the great lesson, that no earthly government can endure which is not built on mercy, justice, truth and love."[44]

Ostensibly, Gabe's poetic memorialization of Caesar's bloody revolution serves as an indictment of the oligarchic ruling classes that led New York City to ruin, but the clever author of its sentiments also includes plenty of subversive irony by which he makes his disgust with Caesar's bloody retaliation known. Gabe carefully words the inscription to commemorate the "death and burial of modern civilization." The column itself is described as "ghastly," and the final line of the commemoration-on-command serves as a reminder to both the fallen Oligarchy and the newly triumphant Caesar that only government founded on "mercy, justice, truth and love" can long prosper. Gabe's words imply that Caesar's government, already characterized by brutality and merciless retribution, will meet the same fate as its predecessor unless it cares for the needs of the millions. Under the rule of Caesar Lomellini, New York City circa 1988 appears destined to share the fate of Atlantis, its once mighty dominion undermined by environmental pressures, food shortages, and, ultimately, social upheaval and destruction. By analogy, Max and Gabe are the Atlanteans who escape the island before, in its wickedness, it collapses.

Safely transported by airplane from the United States to Uganda, Gabe and Max resolve to serve as recorders of the violent class revolution from which they have narrowly escaped. Gabe's first self-appointed task is to collect and preserve the personal letters written to his brother Heinrich, a job he undertakes with no small amount of ego, declaring, "I furthermore had them printed on our printing press, believing that every succeeding century would make them more valuable to posterity; and that in time they would be treasured as we now treasure the glimpses of the world before the Deluge, contained in the Book of Genesis."[45] Gabe's next step is to meet with the five thousand members of the Ugandan colony he intends to form with Max's help. Its would-be members are aghast at the tales he tells of bloody revolution in the United States and are determined to take steps to secure their peaceable agrarian society from similar destruction. Fearing that worldwide chaos may soon engulf Africa, Gabe urges his fellow citizens to establish a series of warning beacons and to increase their manufacture of rifles. Having arranged for the protection of their colony from outsiders, they can now begin to arrange for their own internal self-defense. In close consultation with Max, Gabe pens a new constitution—one whose tenets read very much like the pro-labor populist platforms Donnelly ardently supported, including compulsory education aimed at ending an epidemic of ignorance that "scatters death everywhere." Public education, well supported by society, would be the order of the day, the new constitution decrees: "We believe it to be essential to the peace and safety of the commonwealth that the children of all the people, rich and poor, should, during the period of growth, associate together. In this way, race, sectarian and caste prejudices are obliterated, and the whole community grow up together as brethren. Otherwise, in a generation or two, we shall have the people split up into hostile factions, fenced in by doctrinal bigotries, suspicious of one another, and antagonizing one another in politics, business and everything else."[46]

Gabe and Max's new utopia is to be founded on the basis of fair trade with countries whose prosperity is equal to that of the Ugandan colony. And whenever the people of another country are in greater poverty, or working at a lower rate of wages, trade with exploited nations would stop, as the constitution reminds the colony's citizens that "impoverished labor on one side of a line, unless walled out, must inevitably drag down labor on the other side of the line to a like condition."[47] The constitution of the new colony details a society steeped in socialistic principles. But while life in the planned community would be rational and planned, the colony itself would remain small by design and agrarian in character, free of the massive central governments that cripple more communistic states. Housing exemplifies the difference. Affordable and abundant, it would be secured not through price and rent controls or via subsidies from a far-off capital, but via a grassroots model characteristic of home rule. Max and Gabe's breakaway agrarian republic would acquire all undeveloped contiguous land by paying its owners a fair price; the acquired land would then be held in a kind of escrow by the community until settlers willing to build a home found themselves in need of it, at which time it would be sold to them without profit or interest. In this way the opportunity for the poor to secure affordable housing would never be subject to inflationary or exclusionary market forces.

And what of those within the colony who resist reform? Gabe's journal entries describe internal resistance originating mostly from homegrown conservatives, who are invited to leave if they prefer the classist, oligarchic systems of yesteryear. Given time, he observes, such reluctant conservatives often transform into the most vigorous supporters of the new society. "And this," he adds, "is one of the merits of your true conservative: if you can once get him into the right course he will cling to it as tenaciously as he formerly clung to the wrong. They are not naturally bad men; their brains are simply incapable of suddenly adjusting themselves to new conceptions."[48]

The conclusion of *Caesar's Column* serves as a kind of narrative proof for the rightness of Gabe's (read: Donnelly's) worldview and ideology, as our narrator describes a crepuscular hour wherein the citizens of the colony, fresh from a night of enervating theater, stream out into the night, "laughing and chatting, under the stars, down the long, fruit-embowered streets, to their flower-bedecked, humble homes."[49] The only thing missing, Donnelly has Gabriel note, are the wolves—the class of exploiters, opportunists, and miscreants kept in check by this tightly knit society. He concludes, "The government which formerly fed and housed these monsters, under cunning kennels of perverted law, and broke open holes in the palisades of society, that they might crawl through and devastate the community, now shuts up every crevice through which they could enter; stops every hole of opportunity; crushes down every uprising instinct of cruelty and selfishness. And the wolves have disappeared; and our little world is a garden of peace and beauty, musical with laughter."[50]

By its final page, *Caesar's Column* begins to read more like a biblical parable than dystopian speculative fiction. The virtuous present enjoyed by a relative few looks a lot like the Edenic past, only enhanced by the literacy and lawfulness of learned men and women and the stable husbandry and stewardship of farmers and shepherds. As he had in his nonfiction books *Atlantic* and *Ragnarok*, Donnelly inscribes an almost biblical cataclysm into his fictional account of bloody class revolution and widespread hunger, one that wipes the slate clean for renaissance and renewal of the best in the human spirit. The Arcadian phase of history marks a beginning of inexorable historical processes sure to follow: in time, the agricultural society is destined to produce a higher standard of living made possible by innovation and ingenuity; ingenuity and innovation encourage urbanity; and urbanity, in Donnelly's view, leads to degeneracy and division. Conditions for a great natural cataclysm, coupled with violent social upheaval, are thus induced, and "life returns to a simple agrarian way, in ever repeating cycles," as Allan M. Axelrad puts it.[51] In Donnelly's worldview, Gabe's Ugandan colony is merely a new, hopeful beginning in an unerring pattern of doomed human nature.

Despite its hopeful ending, Donnelly's dystopian novel haunted many who read it. In particular, the specter of mass anarchic revolt against established social and theological orders alarmed many in the church. In one of his popular syndicated newspaper sermons, the preacher Frank De Witt Talmage described his first reading of the "strange, weird, horrible story called *Caesar's Column*." Fascinated at first by its sheer daring, Talmage read with fear and wonder as Donnelly "deftly tore the beautiful pattern of modern society into shreds." The trouble with the book, Talmage wrote in retrospect, was precisely the trouble with its author; the preacher could now see how "Ignatius Donnelly might advocate the destruction of society by finding fault with it, yet with his brain he could not construct for us a better utopia." Like the apostle Paul, Talmage insisted, the Sage of Nininger should not find fault with man unless he could provide a thoughtful remedy to the faults he had named.[52]

For many farmers and laborers in the US hinterlands, however, Donnelly did provide a solution to society's ills, in the form of the isolationist, socialist, agrarian colony his protagonists grow and nurture as a kind of societal heirloom. The fictional African utopia with which Donnelly concludes his book draws its substance from the political and social reforms called for by the Grangers, the Farmers' Alliance, and the Knights of Labor, all of whom Donnelly supported at one time or another in his political career.[53] Unsurprisingly, *Caesar's Column* added to Donnelly's political mandate in Minnesota and across the Great Plains. The Farmers' Alliance approximated the camaraderie and common cause of the fictional Brotherhood imagined in the novel, though the alliance saw itself as nonpolitical, nonpartisan, and public rather than violent and clandestine. The Farmers' Alliance would focus on bettering the lives of its member constituents through industrial and rural reform and through an insurance program that would help safeguard farmers' livelihoods against the threat of wind, hail, and other catastrophic forces of nature.[54] In practice it would function much like the agrarian society Gabe and Max form in the mountains of Africa, leveraging the force of many small local chapters toward the greater good. Still, in scapegoating eastern bankers, book publishers, and newspapers in particular—collectively known as the plutocracy—the alliance risked awakening latent ethnic and religious prejudice. Though the populists may have been egalitarian and democratic at root, their use of the "Shylock symbol" as an indicator of plutocratic evils in books like Donnelly's was not "wholly innocent," as one critic later put it, even when the symbol was invoked as a folk rather than religious stereotype.[55]

Approximately one year after the publication of *Caesar's Column*, Donnelly had successfully integrated his existing identity as a populist, down-to-earth politician with the emerging persona of a Jules Verne-esque fantasist capable of envisaging the future in prophetic fiction. The strange genius thumping the podium at populist gatherings across the upper Midwest was now not just a lawyer, scholar, lawmaker, and presumed polymath but also a dreamer-creator of alternate realities running so close to our own that they sometimes seemed like fact. Like the priests at Delphi in ancient Greece, Donnelly's grand pronouncements on the page were considered by his most ardent supporters to be oracular, his words a byzantine puzzle that could be solved to divine deeper meanings applicable to past, present, and future politics and public policy.

What exactly did the Sage of Nininger, Minnesota, foresee? Literary critics would later point to the similarities between the class warfare the author anxiously envisioned and the horrific bloodshed in the streets during the French Revolution; such a cataclysmic clash appeared destined to repeat itself, this time followed by, as the literary critic Nicholas Ruddick puts it, a "global orgy of destruction when the urban masses . . . rebel against their plutocratic oppressors."[56] In Donnelly's day, signs of analogous horrors could already be seen in Chicago's Haymarket labor riots of 1886, where seven policemen were killed and dozens more injured.[57] Surely the futuristic New York City that Donnelly predicted might serve as the epicenter of a similar class conflict, this one large enough to engulf the rest of the world in its all-encompassing hatred and chaos.

What else did Donnelly foretell in his fiction? In the tradition of fin de siècle narratives exemplified by *Strange Case of Dr. Jekyll and Mr. Hyde*, *Caesar's Column* documents decline, decay, and degeneration characteristic of a species reverting to its most base and primal impulses.[58] As Donnelly reentered political discourse in the spring of 1890, the questions society faced in real and fictive worlds appeared to run parallel. Was *Caesar's Column*—and, by extension, Donnelly's—vision of the world utopian, quasi-utopian, anti-utopian, dystopian, or even apocalyptic utopian? Without a doubt, the author-politician's worldview anticipated a better, brighter tomorrow, a small yet steady beacon of light at the end of long darkness, but what should his readers, followers, and supporters do to reach that light in the interim?

Speaking to a crowd of four hundred Farmers' Alliance delegates at their annual convention in St. Paul, Donnelly hinted at answers to the all-important question of the hour: what must voters do now? The imperative appeared to be this: stand up and resist. Whether spurred on by a crowd eager to listen to the stylings of the renowned author-statesman or by the electric setting of the hall and its cheering supporters, he delivered a combative speech. "We are not here to wage war on any political party," he declared, "but we are here to serve notice on all parties that if they do not work for the welfare of all people, they might as well order their coffins and fix the date of their funerals."[59] The metaphor may have been needlessly macabre, especially for a statesman who had recently written a novel questioning violent reform, but Donnelly's point served as a fair and rational summary of the populist discontent with the established order. He hadn't agreed to address the convention as keynote speaker merely to encourage alliance members to stay engaged in the process. Instead he intended to use the occasion to launch an eleventh-hour accusation of alleged misdeeds committed by organization president George W. Sprague, whom he charged with accepting bribes from insurance companies. When R. J. Hall replaced Sprague, Donnelly remained on the offensive, convinced that the members of the alliance were being exploited to fatten the wallets of the organization's executives. Though he, too, was an executive officer, Donnelly took care to distance himself from the alleged bribery schemes affecting the organization, arguing that his position rendered him above such pettiness. "I was a man of eminence and influence before the Alliance was born and I will be when it's dead," he wrote Hall, adding, "I have fought lions in my day and I am ready now to go on the warpath against jackals—or jackasses."[60]

Despite Donnelly's warnings, the Minnesota Farmers' Alliance moved rapidly toward full politicization, holding a nominating convention in July 1890. Donnelly was there, against his better judgment; without him, one observer noted, a Minnesota convention would be "like catfish without waffles in Philadelphia."[61] *The Sun* in New York City joked that Donnelly had more political affiliations than Minnesota had people in Minneapolis, adding, "He is a bee, he is a humming bird. He skips from flower to flower."[62] Understanding that his opponents were attempting to paint him as a closet Republican eager to take the alliance back in the direction of the GOP, Donnelly rose to the podium determined to beat back the accusations that his loyalties lay anywhere but with the farmers. Every man in the state, he roared from the rostrum, had been fattened on the backs of the yeoman class. And every individual who had stolen money from the pockets of good and loyal plowmen was his sworn enemy. He boasted, "I am not purchasable. If I had been it would have been easier to buy me in the quiet of one of those hotel rooms than placarding me as a thief for twenty years." Donnelly paused his speechifying long enough to remind his audience that if he had been paid for his speeches on behalf of the Grangers and the Farmers' Alliance what he made for his literary lectures, he would have been owed $10,000 to $20,000 by the organization. And yet, he claimed, he had not taken a cent for his efforts in kind in support of its mission. He continued, "Now, we must have harmony. . .. I regret as much as anybody any differences that have arisen. I do not think that I have provoked any of these differences. I am so constituted that if any man kicks me on the stern there are responsive thrills in the cranium. The story is told of a politician in New York who had dealt him a hard kick with the foot, which met with no obstruction until it struck the base of the skull. I have got backbone, thank God."[63]

Unfortunately for Donnelly, labor factions within the alliance were determined to form their own political party and to nominate their own slate of candidates for the legislature and for governor. This new splinter group, the Alliance Labor Union, quickly moved to nominate its own candidate for governor, voting for Donnelly on first ballot before settling on Patrick Rahilly as a candidate palatable to both agrarian and labor interests. Angry at the labor factions within the organization that had prevented him from securing the gubernatorial nomination, and newly determined to expose the corruption at the highest levels within the alliance, Donnelly put the secretary of the alliance, John Lathrop, into his crosshairs for misappropriation of funds. The confrontation between the two men turned ugly, with Donnelly purchasing a revolver to defend himself against what he alleged were Lathrop's threats of violence.[64]

Against this backdrop of political volatility, if not skullduggery, Donnelly could take comfort in the growing readership of *Caesar's Column*, particularly among the alliance faithful, though his political efforts to keep the organization free from corruption and influence peddling, as well as focused on a progressive platform, were rapidly eroding.[65] He admitted in his diary that he felt overwhelmed and disheartened, remarking, "The power of the corporation is so great that it seems like insanity for one man, advanced in life and with small means to attempt to fight them." The growing success of *Caesar's Column* had renewed within him the temptation to leave politics altogether in favor of writing, and yet the "foolish desire to help mankind" pulled him away, with the force of someone "tied to wild horses."[66]

Seeking to free the electorate from corporate influence, the author of *Caesar's Column* had cast his lot away from the two-party system he had supported for much of his political life. Now he risked further political marginalization in abandoning establishment politics for an upstart third party. Still, the "throw the rascals out" sentiment prevalent among farmers and laborers in the Midwest, South, and Great Plains proved sufficiently strong to pull off a political revolution in the autumn of 1890. The same populist groundswell that elected Kittel Halvorson to Congress on the Alliance-Labor ticket carried Donnelly to a surprise victory for a seat in the Minnesota State Senate on a third-party ticket. Having bested both establishment Democrats and Republicans in his home district, Donnelly was flush with confidence sufficient to mount a challenge to become president of the Farmers' Alliance. In so doing, he expected to provoke the full fury of the railroads he had vowed to regulate. Since the railroads didn't have enough money to bribe him into abandoning the cause of the people, he warned his supporters that the railroad rings and corrupt corporations would instead infiltrate the alliance convention with paid agents who would "make the air sulphurous with their lies."[67] The preemptive warning worked, and Donnelly, his standing in the alliance buoyed by the reputation of his reform novel *Caesar's Column*, won decisively.

For the moment, the complexity and daring of Donnelly's convictions, coupled with his learnedness and literary prowess, became a political asset rather than a liability. Several months earlier the author had observed in his diary, "A single-minded fool gets ten times as much comfort out of the world as a mind cut with many facets."[68] And yet by December 1890, populists across the Midwest—seeking an alternative to the corporatization and corruption of major party politics populated with insiders—increasingly saw Donnelly and his many-faceted mind as rare and genuine. In the pages of the *Great West*, St. Paul editor Everett Fish reprinted a celebratory commentary from the *Journal of the Knights of Labor* in the Dakotas. Though labor had often been at odds with farmer factions within the fragile alliance, the *Journal* described the two sides of the difficult conundrum as "Donnelly vs. Harmony." On one hand, the Knights knew that Donnelly's resurgence as a politician and his recent election as president of the Minnesota Farmers' Alliance would inevitably mean a tenure of noisy debate and discord. On the other hand, they reasoned, harmony was often synonymous with complacency and was thus the enemy of the worker seeking meaningful reform. In the final analysis, the *Journal*'s editor concluded that he would side with the Sage of Nininger in the "Donnelly vs. Harmony" debate, noting, "One man like Donnelly can do more toward pulling down plutocracy in one short year than an army of ordinary braying political donkeys could do in a lifetime."[69] Plenty of the so-called political donkeys, however, disagreed with this assessment. The *Great West* excerpted the review of an unnamed critic published in a New York newspaper, who claimed that Donnelly was "not a safe man to be trusted with power." The ideas for reform expressed in his novel, the critic warned, could not be implemented without "very serious detriment to the well-being of the people." The *Great West* dismissed the critique out of hand, declaring, "Mr. Donnelly and *Caesar's Column* will survive." Even if Donnelly was a radical, the St. Paul newspaper concluded, "The nation wants that man!"[70]

While some considered *Caesar's Column* a political liability, by the fall of 1891 there was no denying its popular success. In less than a year and a half on the market, the book had been republished by two houses in Britain and issued in translated editions as far away as Sweden, Norway, and Germany. In the United States, Donnelly's gripping speculative fiction helped precipitate a renaissance of utopian and dystopian novels.[71]

Donnelly's brand benefited from the discontented populist zeitgeist of the time, as sympathetic newspapers cast him as a victim of the forces of orthodoxy and ideological suppression. "No better commentary can be made upon the horrible condition of the United States at this time," the *Great West* opined, "than that the statesman, who could write such a book, has been driven into private life and kept there for twenty-three years, living in poverty in the solitude of his farm, while the Congress of the United States has swarmed with ignorant and sordid creatures, whose sole object was to plunder the people."[72] While such a description of the author and his visionary novel reflected a definite spin—Donnelly was not exactly the poor farmer the *Great West* made him out to be—in the United States, *Caesar's Column*, according to Trimble and Winters, became a "household word" that readers associated with a timely warning of "a world perched on the edge of destruction."[73] By extension its author had become, depending on the politics and the optics of the viewer, a creator, cautioner, or corrector of the destructive forces he had successfully animated on the page.

In an impromptu interview given at a train depot in Kansas City on his way to a speaking engagement, Donnelly explained in his own words why he had written the incendiary novel, telling a reporter, "I had witnessed so much rascality that I decided it would be a capital idea to look forward to see what it would all come to." The trouble, he added, was that he had looked forward too far, since the evils predicted in the book seemed to be coming to pass much more rapidly than he had dared imagine. And why, the reporter asked, had Donnelly kept his authorship secret for the first ten or more editions of the book? The author replied that he had feared publishing under his own name would invite an "attack of the Capitalists" bent on injuring sales, much as had happened with *The Great Cryptogram*. Despite its initial authorship under a nom de plume, it was, he declared, his most successful book yet, with sales estimated at three hundred thousand copies. Before boarding the train, he shared his satisfaction with his literary occupation. The legacy of a book, he firmly believed, lived on, and an author's fame was enduring. "A man may be a politician famous for a day," he observed, "but men who become famous in literature generally die famous."[74]

And with that, Donnelly politely ended the interview. He was on his way to Ottawa, Kansas, he explained, to give a talk on "the signs of the times." Was he speaking apocalyptically or politically? The Sage of Nininger wouldn't say, except to confess that he tended to be a "pretty industrious man" while back home in Minnesota, and the trip to Osage City he hoped to take after delivering his lecture would be a pleasurable escape from the confines of his study. He claimed to be writing several new books, one of which was a continuation of his cryptogram theory. "I think I am working that out with considerable success," he said, keeping the exact nature of his findings to himself.[75]

CHAPTER 7

Doctor Huguet

With his election to the state senate in the autumn of 1890 and his ascension to the presidency of the Minnesota Farmers' Alliance, Donnelly once again enjoyed a seat at the center of political power in his home state, and this time he was not beholden to Democratic or Republican masters. Minnesota's newspapers looked on with interest as Donnelly swept into the statehouse riding an unprecedented wave of populist support. The *New Ulm Weekly Review* led its coverage of New Year's news with a single line: "And the band played Ignatius Donnelly!" Donnelly, it noted, was the "master of the hour and of the Alliance." While it waited for its first reports from the new legislative session begun the day before on January 6, 1891, the newspaper whimsically imagined that the session would commence with "a motion from the Sage of Nininger and author of *Caesar's Column* to sing a sad requiem over the wicked that had gone before . . . a prayer for the death of monopolies, a big sale for *Caesar's Column*, and the building up of Donnelly's boom for Senator."[1]

The editors at the *St. Paul Globe*, meanwhile, opted for a football analogy for the new legislative session as they willed their man on from the sidelines. "Kick off, Ignatius Donnelly," the newspaper cheered, "put the ball in play, on with the game. You have a crowd of a million people waiting to see the fun." The elder statesman and sage, the *Globe* claimed, should be allowed to head the all-important railroad committee even if he was not always the most organized chairman. "What we want in this legislature is somebody to stir things up, and give us food for thought and discussion. No one can do this better than Donnelly. Give him a chance. He never harmed anyone in this world but himself," the editors declared. Further animated by a throw-the-rascals-out sentiment, they concluded, "Thank God for the Sage of Nininger. What a dreary waste of millionaires Minnesota would be without him."[2]

What might have been a well-deserved victory lap after a series of bruising electoral defeats, however, quickly turned into a delicate dance between the very labor and farm coalitions Donnelly had helped bring together. Increasingly, the fragile graft he had engineered had begun to come undone, with the Labor Party attempting to divorce itself from the Farmers' Alliance. Leaders of the Alliance Labor Union boasted that they enjoyed legal status under state law while the Minnesota Alliance did not. Donnelly, whose support within the tenuous coalition came mainly from its agrarian members, sensed imminent bifurcation. As usual, the elder statesman was the locus of a brewing fight between the rival factions that had joined the prior autumn to support a shared ticket but had since found their interests divided in the new legislative session. Adding to the pressure, a patchwork quilt of farm, labor, and reform groups across the country had begun organizing for the coming presidential and congressional elections of 1892. As president of the Minnesota Alliance, Donnelly planned to attend the Cincinnati convention of farm, labor, and reform parties. Not to be outdone, the Alliance Labor Union spokesman announced that it would be sending its own delegation, one that featured Donnelly's alliance rival R. J. Hall. A national figure with popularity among farmers in the South, Donnelly prevailed even when Alliance Labor Union delegates challenged his right to represent Minnesota.[3]

Third parties had triumphed in recent state-level elections, and now the Cincinnati convention wanted to take up the prospect of running a national third-party ticket for president in 1892. Mounting a national ticket too soon, detractors said, could result in an embarrassing defeat that would damage the would-be party's future political prospects. On the other hand, failure to draft candidates for national office would mean failure to capitalize on the populist groundswell and might be seen as a cowardly admission of insufficiency relative to established parties.[4]

Donnelly could be counted on for drama at any national convention, and in Cincinnati he did not disappoint. Even before the convention was fully organized and its committees duly determined, he shocked the delegates by suggesting that they dispense with the formalities and form a national committee straight away, an initiative that would ultimately mean choosing a presidential ticket. In so moving, he intended to give voice to the will of the more than five thousand attendees who had, he pointed out, traveled thousands of miles at their own expense and of their own enthusiasm. To come all this way merely to pass a few resolutions and go home would dishonor the depth of their sacrifice. He called instead for the formation of a People's Party with a national committee that would attend the St. Louis gathering slated for February 1892. Donnelly was chosen as the member of the Resolutions Committee best equipped to address the throngs of delegates, and he did, urging those in attendance to put aside petty or parochial interests to support a shared platform.[5] When the dust had settled, Donnelly emerged as the hero of the Cincinnati convention.[6] The *Kansas City Star* praised him for bringing order to an "unorganized mob" and for establishing "order out of chaos" at such time as leadership was thrust upon him.[7] Meanwhile, the *Great West* in St. Paul characterized him as the father of the People's Party, claiming that he had been "the central figure of the convention" and the "big toad in the puddle."[8] Donnelly now had a new party to serve as the political vehicle for the Minnesota Alliance, and he moved quickly to withdraw the organization's endorsement of the Alliance Labor Union Party that had opposed him in Cincinnati.[9]

When he arrived for an extended stay at the Astor House in New York City in June 1891, Donnelly was riding high. Hailed in print as the "Sage of Nininger, discoverer of the alleged Baconian theory, President of the Farmers' Alliance in Minnesota, and Chairman of the committee that drew the platform for the People's Party at the recent convention in Cincinnati," he had long coattails. A reporter from the *New York Times* was there to greet the visiting luminary now rumored to be a third-party candidate for president in the 1892 general election. "He is considered the best advertised man in the party," the *Times* observed, "and as a talker he has few superiors." Describing the author-politician as "a short man with a smoothly shaven face and . . . blue eyes," who did not smoke or drink, the newspaper recited Donnelly's noteworthy political résumé, including his credentials as a former congressman and lieutenant governor and passing references to his prior political dust-ups and revolts: his long-standing vendetta against the Washburn clan,

James J. Hill, and the libelers at the *Pioneer Press*; his notorious history of party switching; and his revolt against the Minnesota Democratic Party, which had "broken up the party seriously for two years." While he spoke enthusiastically of his ongoing work on the Shakespearean cipher and a new novel in the works, Donnelly was mostly in a mood to talk populist politics. "The country is awake on this third party as it has not been on any question since the war," he confided, predicting that a third-party candidate would win the presidency in 1892 while also vigorously denying the rumors that he had accepted an alliance nomination in advance. In Minnesota alone, he pointed out, the alliance voting bloc was fifty thousand strong, with nearly 1,400 individual Farmers' Alliance chapters working toward a shared goal. Asked whether a conscientious citizen could be a member of the alliance and still vote for a Republican or Democrat, Donnelly replied by metaphor, "A man must either fish or cut bait in the Alliance. He cannot be an Alliance man and a Republican or a Democrat at the same time." Donnelly was "just as hopeful as ever," the *Times* observed in its headline, capturing the gist of its interview in a single lighthearted phrase: "Ignatius Donnelly counts Alliance chickens."[10]

Declining to offer himself as a candidate for national office in 1891, Donnelly instead afforded himself the luxury of a new literary project more daring in many ways than *Caesar's Column*, a literary phenomenon that was in its twenty-sixth edition in the summer of that year. Despite rumors that he would be solicited to run for national office on a People's Party ticket in 1892, he used his new social justice novel to attack what was arguably the most divisive subject in the United States: race relations. As he had with *Caesar's Column*, he finished the manuscript in less than six months, selecting F. J. Schulte once again as publisher.[11] Dubbing *Doctor Huguet* his "fifth baby," Donnelly dined with Schulte and *Farmer's Voice* publisher Lester Hubbard on the night of August 18, to celebrate his latest literary accomplishment. Donnelly, Schulte, and Hubbard toasted the success of a book whose original, fantastical thinking they hoped would shock the American public into greater sympathy for Black Americans living in the Deep South.[12]

In the book's opening chapters, the first-person narrator, the eponymous Dr. Anthony Huguet, introduces his background and lineage. He lives in an unnamed city in South Carolina—very likely Charleston—and his Huguenot slaveholding ancestors were among the first to settle the state, making him "an aristocrat of aristocrats."[13] Huguet is a well-educated Democrat, a thirty-five-year-old bachelor and "supporter of the South on all national questions."[14] Like Donnelly, he is a lover of poetry and music, but unlike the author, he is a man of considerable means, and his fortune has allowed him to retire from professional practice. Like Donnelly, he is deeply cynical about the integrity of public officials, though by virtue of his education and natural leadership abilities, he has been recruited to run for public office. The doctor opens the second chapter with an expansive articulation of his views on public service: "I looked upon public life as discredited, if not dishonored, by the kind of men who ruled it. It appeared to me a sordid and debased struggle of little creatures for honors that faded from the memories of men almost as soon as they were won."[15] Huguet tells us he can count on two hands the statesmen, among thousands he has known, whose legacy he believes will endure. Refusing to campaign for public office, the young physician retreats from the "sordid and barren life" of the politician and into the "communion with the mighty souls of the past" in his extensive library.[16]

And yet even the retiring doctor is drawn into inevitable political debate with his love interest, Mary, and her father, a colonel and gentleman planter from a slaveholding tradition. When the question of race comes up on the plantation house verandah, Huguet insists to all in attendance that Blacks are equally entitled to vote as whites. The right to participate in the government in a republic, he argues, "is like the right to breathe the atmosphere. No man feels degraded because the air he inhales has already passed through the lungs of his fellow-man, differing from him in every respect and condition."[17] Huguet confidently declares, "The rights of a man should not depend upon the shade of his complexion."[18] Unfazed, he tries a scientific approach to the suffrage question, reminding his skeptical conversational partners that Europeans themselves were descended from darker-skinned peoples.

A devious Yankee attorney, Buryhill, spreads word of Huguet's radical theories, and soon even Mary must urge her principled lover to moderate his progressive stance on race relations, lest it wreck the ambition she holds for him that he will one day be elected congressman from South Carolina. Mary implores her lover to remember his audience—men and women who, though intelligent, are not philosophers and readers. "And when," she says, "you talk to them about the possibility, as a scientific theorem, of the white race being descended from an aboriginal negro stock living in Europe, they cannot follow you. They take your reasoning, upon scientific probabilities, as a bare statement of fact that whites were originally black."[19] The couple's Southern neighbors, she warns, will regard the doctor's arguments for racial equality as "high treason against . . . Caucasian blood and lineage." Mary worries aloud that her beau has led a life lost amid the higher ideals that populate his personal library, such that he cannot possibly appreciate "the depth and intensity of white prejudice." Eager to be understood, Huguet offers to go public with his views, speaking his truth plainly at podiums instead of merely musing on front porches in hopes of overcoming "the unreasoning bigotry" infecting the nation. But such an approach is even more risky, according to Mary, who predicts that her beloved would be "hated, despised, persecuted"; his utterances would be misrepresented and he would be regarded as a "demagogue or a lunatic."[20]

In sentiments like these, the similarities between the fictional Huguet and his real-life creator, Ignatius Donnelly, are undeniable. Not only do Mary's fears for her lover's reputation closely match those expressed to Donnelly by his wife, Kate, but Huguet's views on racial equality track closely with those Donnelly articulated nearly three decades earlier in Congress. On May 2, 1864, almost a full year before the Civil War ended, Donnelly went to the floor of the House to urge his fellow lawmakers to respect the Black residents of the Southern states. He reminded his colleagues, "Many of them fought under our banners and suffered wounds in our cause. . .. Can we permit their freedom to hang upon a hazard? Can we leave them . . . to the mercy of their late masters? Can we give them the name and semblance of freedom and yet leave them all to the horrors of renewed slavery?" Donnelly answered his own question emphatically in the negative, arguing that the US government must protect them from prejudice and disenfranchisement, carrying out what he called the "promise of liberty" that had been made them. In subsequent sessions of Congress, he challenged his fellow legislators again, asking them, rhetorically, whether newly liberated enslaved people were not also God's children. Any bill that denied the basic fact of their humanity, he proclaimed, merely "legislates injustice into law."[21]

Dr. Huguet voices similar sentiments when he delivers a prescient sermon in which he decries sanctioned bigotry. Racial enmities, he says, could never be solved by "grouping the people into the separations of race-politics."[22] Instead, the good doctor articulates his fervent hope that the days of persecution and cruelty will end when "in every intelligent white man the black man will find a defender; and the reign of peace and love and brotherhood will begin in the South."[23] "Let no race hatreds divide you," he tells the congregation, adding, "Remember that you are the children of one father."[24] In such dialogue, Donnelly clearly intends *Dr. Huguet* to serve as a means to increase awareness of civil rights deprivations experienced by Blacks in the South, and thereby to awaken pro-reform sentiment among readers with an inclination toward social justice.

In the chapter entitled "The Vision," Huguet experiences the ultimate act of transracial empathy, as he awakens from a nocturnal vision to a luminous Christlike figure surrounded by millions of hands clasped in a position of prayer. The doctor is too mystified for words, as the mysterious figure speaks just two sentences before dematerializing: "These, too, are my children. For them, also, I died upon the cross!"[25] Deeply troubled by the vision and wondering at its significance, a fretful Dr. Huguet eventually falls back to sleep. He awakens sometime later to completely unfamiliar surroundings—a primitive cabin and an unforgiving mattress made of straw. The soul of Dr. Huguet has been transformed by the ghostly visitation and placed in the body of a Black man, Sam Johnsing. The soul of Sam Johnsing, meanwhile, enters the white body of Dr. Huguet. In his Black body, the scholar Huguet is instantly viewed as a menace and a threat by the community that once embraced his white self, and his dark skin prevents him from securing the jobs for which he is eminently qualified. Meanwhile, Johnsing's new white skin seems to aid and abet abuses and trespasses. Here Donnelly's speculative narrative makes a bold leap into fantasy, invoking the Faustian device of transfiguration to embody the argument for racial reciprocity.[26]

The novel's views on race should have appealed to the educated, progressive audiences Donnelly hoped to court, but some early reviews of the new work bristled at its moralizing tone. A mere ten days after Donnelly gathered with Schulte and Hubbard to toast his new title and wish it a soft landing, the October edition of *Book News* panned the fantasy, remarking, "There is no objection to a Sunday-school tract on the duty of civilized man to the colored races, but there is no justification for illustrating this duty by the crude device of transforming a South Carolina gentleman and scholar into a negro . . . transferring their souls to each other's bodies, and interspersing this magic with miraculous visions of Christ." A tale like Donnelly's, the reviewer added, "is not likely to be read out of the nursery except under compulsion and even in the nursery it would be demoralizing."[27] Within a week of the scathing review, Schulte wrote a letter of consolation, reminding his star author that eastern metropolitan reviewers were not the intended audience for *Doctor Huguet* in any case. Among independent-minded readers who didn't depend on cosmopolitan literary critics to dictate their tastes, Schulte expected an enthusiastic response. In fact, the publisher wrote, he would be "rather disappointed" if the critics did not "jump on Dr. Huguet."[28] Any East Coast bias against the author and his work could be partly attributed to Donnelly's habitual fictional villains. In *Caesar's Column*, New York City plutocrats serve as convenient scapegoats for larger socioeconomic injustice, and in *Doctor Huguet*, the antagonist is once again a well-to-do Jewish man from the East—in this case a New York attorney named Buryhill bent on taking possession of Mary's plantation by any means necessary. Donnelly directs much of the blame at Buryhill, conceived as emblematic of the self-serving interests of Yankee carpetbaggers. At various times throughout the novel, the lawyer is referred to as a villain, a knave, a scoundrel, a rascal, a thief, and other sundry pejoratives.[29] As critics later pointed out, however, if Donnelly had been less a product of midwestern agrarian populism, he might have made a co-villain of the Southern landowners who perpetuated the plantation system.[30]

In large part Schulte's prediction of pent-up demand from thoughtful readers proved prescient, as he announced a first US edition of some twenty-five thousand copies and a British edition to be brought out simultaneously by Sampson Low, Marston & Co. in London.[31] Prepublication notices praised Donnelly's transfiguration plotline as "the most startling and original conception in literature." Back home in Minnesota, the pro-Donnelly African American newspaper *The Appeal* ran a lengthy review that autumn, comparing the didactic novel favorably to *Uncle Tom's Cabin* while describing it as "a true exposition of the conditions that exist today." More to the point, *The Appeal* stated, the book demonstrated "how a hellish and damnable prejudice in the Southland refuses to recognize and encourage merit possessed by a person with a black skin. *Doctor Huguet*, the review concluded, "should be read by every Afro-American in America."[32] Barton Aylesworth, a professor of literature tapped to be the next president of Drake University in Des Moines, Iowa, wrote Donnelly personally to endorse the message of the book, observing, "Every black man has been something other than he was, since I read *Dr. Huguet* . . . I am not the same myself!"[33] From Little Rock, Arkansas, Donnelly received a letter of support written by the Black physician J. H. Smith, for whom the book had been a definitive testament of the author's good and decent character. "Any white man who can afford to speak out in such unmistakable terms, for a race who have so little with which to reward him," Smith wrote, "is to be praised by every colored man."[34]

If Donnelly was disappointed by the mixed critical reception of a book whose bravery was widely acknowledged, he didn't seem to show it. Instead, when his years-old libel allegations against his enemies at the *St. Paul Pioneer Press* came to jury trial in October 1891, he threw himself into the effort to defend his good name. Donnelly sued for damages from what he claimed were the libelous actions taken by the newspaper when it printed a piece penned by the Minnesota Republican politician William S. King, accusing Donnelly of offering bribes to help elect William Washburn in 1879. On their face, King's charges were nonsensical if not ridiculous, as the *St. Paul Globe* hastened to point out. "It would be difficult to concoct a more silly lie than this was," it remarked, since Donnelly was at the time formally contesting Washburn's election to Congress, and "the absurdity that he should offer a bribe for his own defeat is too apparent to need a response." Urging Donnelly to pursue his libel case, the *Globe* rejoiced that the "champion liar" at the helm of the *Pioneer Press* would "now have an opportunity to be legally recorded as the scoundrel that he is."[35]

The *Pioneer Press* had accused Donnelly of bribery a second time in an 1887 commentary, citing grounds since judged baseless. Donnelly's suit now sought $100,000 in damages and lost income, given that he drew most of his income from books and public lectures that depended on his good name.[36] The attorney for the *Pioneer Press*, Judge Charles Flandrau, argued that Donnelly's reputation was essentially worthless, and that the bribery assertions made by King in the letter published by the *Press* had been substantively true. Donnelly had long ago made a bitter enemy of Flandrau, who had represented William D. Washburn in Washburn's contested election against Donnelly in 1879.[37]

Donnelly's lawyer, the prominent St. Paul attorney Cyrus Wellington, was well known as a spellbinding orator, and he spoke to the jury for nearly three hours. Crowds packed the courtroom to capacity for closing statements in a trial described as possessing the fervor of a heavyweight fight. The *St. Paul Globe* characterized the proceedings as a "battle of intellectual gladiators," remarking on the addition of a sheriff's deputy posted at the door to prevent rowdiness. Flandrau delivered his closing arguments first, arguing that the question before the jury was largely whether they believed the word of Donnelly or of King. Donnelly was a supreme egotist, the defense argued, adding insult to injury by claiming that only those who had not read his books believed him to be a literary genius. Twisting the knife, Flandrau dared to bring up the much-criticized *The Great Cryptogram* as proof that, as he put it,

"Donnelly is a dandy." The plaintiff's whole life, Flandrau told the jury, had been "one long worship of 'I.' "[38]

Wellington's closing arguments called out the *Pioneer Press* and Flandrau for their ad hominem attacks against his client. He reminded the jury of Donnelly's record of distinguished public service, beginning with his tenure as the state's lieutenant governor, and his successful mustering of Minnesota regiments in defense of the Union during the Civil War. His reputation as a tireless fighter against plutocrats and aristocrats rendered him all but incapable of avarice or greed, but it did make him countless enemies among the rich. "There is not a line written in the history of the state of Minnesota," Wellington commented, "that does not record that Ignatius Donnelly is one of the men battling against this gigantic array of moneyed aristocrats." The trial that was to have been a fairly clear-cut case against the allegedly libelous practices of the *Pioneer Press* was now cast as a conspiracy of powerful special interests banded together against a single man. "It is the final struggle," declared the prosecuting attorney, "the Appomattox, and unless Ignatius Donnelly had the strength of manhood and the courage of a lion he must have laid down long ago."[39]

Wellington successfully rebutted the most substantive claims made in the testimony of the defense's principal witness, King, who performed poorly during cross-examination and could offer no tangible evidence of his allegations that Donnelly had received and given bribes. Cross-examination also revealed that King, despite his reputation for philanthropy in Minneapolis, had fled to Canada to avoid testifying in a lawsuit in 1874, and that he had remained there until he could no longer be prosecuted. He had also been previously indicted for perjury and, during his time in Congress, had refused to obey a subpoena issued by a congressional committee, opting not to run for reelection instead.[40]

After closing arguments were given, the judge reminded the jury that the burden of proof rested with the defense to prove that every charge made in the letter by William S. King printed by the *Pioneer Press* was true. If the jury deemed that it had not met this standard of proof, they were obliged to render their verdict in favor of the plaintiff. Given the libel laws in the state of Minnesota, and the evidence brought forth in the trial to date, many legal scholars predicted that Donnelly would win his case and earn between $5,000 and $50,000 in damages. But when the verdict was rendered at nearly ten o'clock that night, the result stunned the state. Donnelly had indeed won his libel suit, but the damages levied on the *Pioneer Press* company would be a mere $1 plus court costs. "So ends the most notable libel suit in the annals of the state," the *St. Paul Globe* reported. "The case of Ignatius Donnelly against the Pioneer Press company to recover $100,000 for malicious defamation of character will go down in history as an event with few parallels in legal litigations."[41]

While found guilty of libel, the *Pioneer Press* reveled in the court's decision: Donnelly's reputation had been found to be worth one dollar by a group of jurors in his home state. In the newspaper's view, the exceptionally modest damages awarded had been a "final decree of public opinion" on a man whose future political aspirations, it presumed, were now all but ruined.[42] The chairman of the People's Party, which was considering Donnelly as a possible candidate for national office, reluctantly agreed, surmising that the one-dollar damage award had all but eliminated his chances of a future third-party presidential nomination.[43] In the mountain West, newspapers that bitterly resented Donnelly for his vigorous pro-labor, antirailroad politics gloried in the paltry award, repurposing it as a punchline. The *Anaconda Standard* in Montana republished a handful of newspaper excerpts from around the region that reframed the pro-Donnelly verdict as an unprecedented slight. The *Journal* in Helena, Montana, wryly observed, "There was not even one cipher on the damages Ignatius Donnelly captured from the St. Paul *Pioneer Press*. He would doubtless give several cryptograms if he had never gotten in to the fight."[44] Meanwhile, the wags at the *Helena Herald* opined that the one dollar awarded to Donnelly would be found to be about ninety cents in excess of the true worth of the plaintiff's character.[45]

Highly sensitive to the slander of his good name, Donnelly initially received the verdict with a modicum of restraint. The jury, after all, had found in his favor, with at least one juror stating after the fact that he had voted for the nominal amount because he believed that vindication in its purest form was what Donnelly most cared about.[46] In fact, Donnelly had written privately to his wife, Kate, that he dared to hope for as much as $50,000,[47] but the perception of the plaintiff as a man of principle over monetary gain very likely reduced his reward in the end. But the minimal award, while disappointing from a financial standpoint, had the positive effect of splashing his name across the front pages of US newspapers for the first time since the publication of *The Great Cryptogram*, reinforcing the plaintiff's reputation as David in a David-and-Goliath struggle against purveyors of injustice. Little more than one month after receiving the jury's decision, Donnelly noted in his diary that he was more determined than ever "not to be suppressed or trampled underfoot." Instead he was doubly resolved to "fight the good fight for truth and right."[48] In public speeches he began to strike back against the *Pioneer Press*, calling the Republican newspaper "the grandfather of all newspaper demons." He insisted that for more than three decades, the newspaper had been the chief agent thwarting legislation for the good of the people. The otherwise good citizen who takes a plutocratic newspaper into his home, he claimed, was guilty of an "unpardonable sin against himself, his family, the republic, and posterity."[49]

Some of Donnelly's former associates who had been unaware of the libel trial offered their support upon reading of the one-dollar verdict in national newspapers. Colonel Blanton Duncan had worked for the Memphis and El Paso Railroad Company, from which the *Pioneer Press* had claimed Donnelly had taken bribes. In December he wrote a personal letter of support to Donnelly, printed publicly in the pages of *The Sun* in New York City. In his missive, Duncan reassured the onetime congressman, "You are one of the clean-handed. You had opportunities, from great influence and the warm friendship entertained for you by many prominent men, to have amassed a million easily by simply turning rascal: but instead of that you have lived as a poor church mouse for twenty years, expressing your fearless independence on all occasions, and, as I understand, making a bare living from your literary efforts."[50]

The favorable verdict rendered in the libel suit energized Donnelly's commitment to populist politics in the late autumn of 1891, as Minnesota's most well-known author-statesman looked forward to the upcoming Industrial Conference in St. Louis, from which some speculated he would emerge on a path to become a vice presidential or presidential nominee for the People's Party. In mid-November, residents of Indianapolis, Indiana, were treated to the arrival of the man described as "the fattest, cheeriest, most sociable People's Party and Allianceman so far throwing himself into the arena." Donnelly had come trumpeting the news that the party had polled fifty-eight thousand votes in its first appearance on the Minnesota ballot. "We are the third party now," Donnelly told reporters in Indianapolis, "but we hope to be the first."[51]

Less than two months later, in January 1892, Donnelly used the occasion of his annual presidential address to the Minnesota Farmers' Alliance to hone his attack against self-serving politicians of the sort who would vote to build themselves a brand new state office building in marble rather than build inexpensive grain elevators for needy farmers. A reinvigorated Sage of Nininger felt the public sentiment inexorably moving in the direction of the free-thinking reform politics he had championed since his first days in Congress decades earlier. "The thinking part of mankind goes forward," he reminded the state alliance in a speech transcribed in full in the *Great West*, "dragging the conservative part along by the heels." Donnelly's colorful language implied that reformists would recognize the rightness of their path by the marks the conservatives left in the mud as they were dragged into the future. The real issue in politics, he insisted in his address, was whether the "dollar or the man" would rule the country. Man wasn't made by the government; rather, the government was made for man, and if the populists in his home region should lose sight of the primacy of individual voters in the larger political machinery, he predicted, the "long arms and talon fingers of the Plutocracy" would eagerly fill the void. True devotees of the Farmers' Alliance understood that government was nothing more, or less, than an aggregation of humanity and a vehicle to serve the larger end of human happiness. As his speech to the state's farm alliance rose to a crescendo, Donnelly became increasingly combative, reminding any retiring or reticent populist agrarians in attendance of the tenor of the political battle in front of them. "We want harmony with all true, earnest men," he reminded his fellow members, "but not the kind of harmony which involves the sacrifice of our principles. We want peace, but not the peace of the corpse." Honesty, he told them, was indeed a force to be reckoned with when given a chance, but villainy more often won the day to such an extent that the lines between heaven and hell and right and wrong had become blurred in the Gilded Age United States. "If you would save yourself, and save the nation," he warned, "you have a terrible battle on your hands."[52]

His comments foreshadowed the party-crossing ethos at the heart of his vision of the nascent People's Party. Because the party drew its strength from marginalized voting blocs that included prohibitionists, suffragists, labor union members, and farmers, it would have to work doubly hard to build acceptable planks in a common platform. In this regard Donnelly, who in a long career had been a radical Republican, reform Democrat, independent, Farmers' Allianceman, and People's Party populist, was the ideal figure to bring disparate camps under the same tent. Many in the movement had read *Caesar's Column* and viewed it as a kind of visionary treatise on the virtues of populism but also as a cautionary tale about the dangers inherent in an oligarchic government removed from the will of the people.[53] Deep-seated distrust of government, elitism, and inherited privilege, reformers believed, had the power to bridge differences in class, ethnicity, religion, and partisanship, and Donnelly had carried this banner into battle on many a prior occasion.

For all these reasons, it made sense to the delegates convening for the four-day Industrial Conference in St. Louis that February that Donnelly, acting president of the Minnesota Farmers' Alliance and a member of the Resolutions Committee at the Cincinnati convention,[54] would play a crucial role. Many, in fact, harbored the sincere hope that he would seize the opportunity to present from the podium a preamble to the platform of a newly formed People's Party. Symbolically, the conference had begun on George Washington's birthday on February 22, and thus it seemed only fitting that the so-called Father of the Populist Party would deliver its shot across the bow, despite the obvious gravitas of the group assembled. Though Donnelly was only one part of what the *Great West* hailed as the "greatest gathering of the representatives of disaffected political elements that the world has ever seen,"[55] his responsibility as author-reader of the preamble to the platform was outsized. As he read the document he had drafted to a crowd of ten thousand gathered in the exposition hall, his carefully chosen words spoke to the United States' revolutionary past and its present perilous decline:

> We meet in the midst of a nation brought to the verge of moral, political and material ruin. Corruption dominates the ballot box, the legislatures, the Congress, and touches even the ermine of the bench. The people are demoralized. Many of the States have been compelled to isolate the voters at the polling places in order to prevent universal intimidation or bribery. The newspapers are subsidized or muzzled; public opinion silenced; business prostrate; our homes covered with mortgages, labor impoverished, and the land concentrated in the hands of capitalists.[56]

The preamble, and the platform that followed, brought thundering applause. Attendees chanted Donnelly's name inside and outside the exposition hall, where crowds cheered for blocks in every direction for a reported ten minutes.[57] Inside, the throngs that had pushed forward into the orchestra pit reached upward by the hundreds to touch him. One reporter inventoried the joyous scene in images of "hats, papers, handkerchiefs, etc. . .. thrown into the air; wraps, umbrellas, and parasols waved, cheer thundered and reverberated."[58]

For a party that prided itself on its lack of demagogic figures, Donnelly's rapid ascent as a charismatic leader of the national movement drew notice. Donnelly was known as a man who had for a generation "fueled the antimonopoly cause with his eloquent if not somewhat eccentric energies," as the historian Michael Kazin later put it,[59] and this latest incarnation of the sixty-one-year-old elder statesman was a dream come true for Donnelly supporters and a nightmare for his detractors. While Minnesotans had long acknowledged his talents as an orator-leader, Donnelly's rhetorical gifts were now plainly evident to the rest of the nation. In its undeniable power, the address at St. Louis had been a game changer. "No Populist candidate, no symbol in the flesh of the reform upsurge of the 1890s had ever or would ever receive such an ovation,"[60] Kazin would later declare of this rare synchronicity between message and messenger. Whether fueled by anger at their economic plight or by enthusiasm for Donnelly as its mouthpiece, the reform activists who exploded with joy at the approval of the new party's platform widely believed that the Civil War had solved few if any of the United States' systemic inequities. The new enemy was armed not with bayonets or muskets but with wealth, privilege, and technology that would be used to enslave them should they fail to resist.[61]

In his convention speech, Donnelly reiterated that the new party was not a cult of victimhood focused on past transgressions and historical slights, as some in the media preferred to characterize it, but a spirited and sympathetic band of forward-looking revolutionaries come together to seek similar outcomes. "This is not the culmination of all the suffering and ignorance of the past," he clarified, adding, "This is the magnificent efflorescence and flowering of the constitution of the United States and the declaration of independence." Deploying his trademark style, Donnelly moved from soaring rhetoric to folksy humor, declaring that the coming years would witness a wedding—a wedding between the Democrats and the Republicans at the "altar of plutocracy," with the devil giving away the bride. Sounding a combative note, Minnesota's elder statesman-sage predicted irreconcilable differences between the people and the monopolies that ruled them, a contest that would ultimately result in an all-out battle wherein the masses would "storm the citadel" inside which the monopolists and plutocrats lay hidden. Breaking down the doors, the people would glory in tearing "the mask from those who have robbed them."[62]

To Donnelly's great satisfaction, the St. Louis convention approved the preamble and the platform, agreeing to set a formal nominating convention for July 4. In the interim, he moved to transform the Minnesota Farmers' Alliance, a group made up primarily of farmers, into the People's Party by asking its members to accept and ratify the platform agreed to in St. Louis,[63] and in so doing lay the groundwork for his potential third-party run for governor on the People's Party ticket. Sounding very much like the attorney Maximilian Petion from *Caesar's Column*, he railed against corruption in the courts, calling them the "last ditch of the plutocracy in the country."[64] Donnelly believed that objective jurisprudence had been supplanted by the monied interests of railroads and other monopolies over the public weal, and he counseled the public to give its respect to the judiciary only when it acted properly in the public interest. "Judicial wigs and gowns are no more to me than so much horse-hair and dry goods," he declared in a letter to the editor of the *Great West*, in which he accused his enemies, including the Minnesota legislator John Hompe, of misrepresenting his views on legislation intended to set the most severe penalties for lenders who exceeded fair interest rates.[65] Donnelly was a lifelong crusader against usury and usurers, including greedy banks, and the deeply aggrieved tone of his letter suggested his gift for literary hyperbole while hinting at a deeper strain of political paranoia. "These bare-faced lies show the character of my assailants, and the extremities to which they are ready to proceed," he bemoaned in the lengthy missive written in defense of his legislative record. "I pray to God that no dead man—whose taking-off cannot be properly accounted for—is found anywhere within ten miles of Nininger. How my enemies would gather around it, from every quarter, like buzzard scenting carrion." As Donnelly moved closer to playing a leading role in the upcoming People's Party convention, he sensed his opponents were more determined than ever to slander his reputation by looking for skeletons in his closet. If no corpse could be found, he quipped, then his shameless opponents would happily "provide one for the occasion."[66]

Despite the unsuccessful challenge from Hompe and others determined to diminish his reputation as a populist leader, on July 4, 1892, Donnelly was once again chosen to read out the preamble and platform for the People's Party, this time at the nominating convention in Omaha. The enthusiasm for the platform Donnelly drafted exceeded the enthusiasm for the individuals nominated for the presidency and vice presidency: James B. Weaver of Iowa and James G. Field of Virginia, respectively. Donnelly's phraseology intentionally echoed the

Declaration of Independence in its stance against tyranny and in favor of democracy:

> We have witnessed for more than a quarter of a century the struggles of the two great political parties for power and plunder, while grievous wrongs have been inflicted upon the suffering people. We charge that the controlling influence dominating both these parties have permitted the existing dreadful conditions to develop without serious effort to prevent or restrain them. Neither do they now promise us any substantial reform. They have agreed together to ignore, in the coming campaign, every issue but one. They propose to drown the outcries of a plundered people with the uproar of a sham battle over the tariff, so that capitalists, corporations, national banks, rings, trusts, watered stock, the demonetization of silver and the oppressions of the usurers may all be lost sight of. They propose to sacrifice our homes, lives, and children on the altar of mammon; to destroy the multitude in order to secure corruption funds from the millionaires.
>
> Assembled on the anniversary of the birthday of the nation, and filled with the spirit of the grand general and chief who established our independence, we seek to restore the government of the Republic to the hands of "the plain people," with which class it originated. We assert our purposes to be identical with the purposes of the National Constitution, to form a more perfect union and establish justice, insure domestic tranquility, provide for the common defense, promote the general welfare, and secure the blessings of liberty for ourselves and our posterity.[67]

Though Donnelly had prefaced his reading by stating that the platform did not intend to insult or affront the rank and file of the two mainstream parties, the revolutionary nature of the ideas it articulated—public ownership of transportation, limited and reasonable government spending, a graduated income tax in support of the common good, prohibition of land monopolies, and government-backed savings accounts, among other planks—caused many in the Republican and Democratic Parties to pigeonhole Donnelly and his People's Party as complainers and cranks. For his part Donnelly wished the platform might go further, extending to populist consumer boycotts of manufacturers who used what amounted to slave labor,[68] and to a call for women's suffrage and the direct election of US senators.[69]

Buoyed by his starring role at the Omaha convention, Donnelly returned to Minnesota to face charges from his detractors that his prominent role in the fledgling party had rendered him, in effect, a party boss of the type he so vigorously condemned. In rebuttal he was quick to point out that the independent-minded People's Party would never suffer a dictator.[70] In late July the People's Party of Minnesota nominated Donnelly for governor. Though the nomination was by acclamation, it was not without controversy, as the Alliance Labor Union continued to be lukewarm on Donnelly and the People's Party more generally. Beyond Minnesota's borders, Donnelly's third-party nomination for governor earned gibes up and down the East Coast, and the *St. Paul Globe* found itself sufficiently amused to collect and publish the eastern blurbs under the headline "The Sage Considered." While midwesterners were forced to reckon with Donnelly as a formidable political force and a legitimate threat to the establishment, many pundits in the East continued to regard him as a distant regional eccentric, a kind of idiot savant or knight errant associated with a failed Shakespearean cipher. In Donnelly's hometown of Philadelphia, the *Ledger* observed, "Ignatius Donnelly, patentee and sole proprietor of a Baconian cipher, has been nominated by the People's Party for the governor of Minnesota." Philadelphia's evening paper, the *Bulletin*, pulled no punches, calling the Sage of Nininger a "conscienceless humbug" and a "slippery demagogue." Any party who would nominate him, the *Evening Bulletin* decreed, must be "made up of the greenest ignoramuses of the backwoods." Meanwhile, the *Boston Herald* called Donnelly a "glib crank" whose presence could only make the gubernatorial race in the Gopher State more picturesque and lively.[71] The metropolitan East painted the headline-grabbing candidacy as a political sideshow more than a serious effort at reform. In large part its dismissal could be attributed to political payback, since Donnelly had made East Coast moneylenders and newspapermen the villains of several of his books and the bogeymen of countless stump speeches.

Back home in Minnesota, Donnelly reveled in his mandate as third-party spoiler, issuing the Republican gubernatorial candidate, Knute Nelson, and the Democrat, Daniel Lawler, an open invitation to debate. When Nelson refused, Donnelly upped the ante by pledging to deliver seventy-five campaign speeches across the state.[72] The week of June 20 to June 26 typified the frenetic campaign appearance schedule to which he had committed. In that six-day stretch, he made seven stops in Minnesota cities ranging from Slayton to Moorhead.[73] At seven stops per week, Donnelly would easily make his goal of seventy-five speeches by the first of November. He believed that to prevail against Nelson on a nascent third-party ticket, he needed a lively campaign, and if the major party candidates wouldn't debate him on the issues, he would need to open up a second front in what figured to be unprecedented political war.

In Pennsylvania and elsewhere across the Rust Belt that summer, the dystopia Donnelly had predicted in *Caesar's Column* showed signs of becoming reality, with twenty men killed and more than one hundred wounded in what the *Great West* billed as "working men at Homestead, Pennsylvania attacked by minions of plutocracy."[74] Donnelly, who had prophesied riot, carnage, and class warfare, had been included among the ranks of so-called "cranks" and "calamity shriekers" two short years earlier. But now, with bloody labor riots flaring up from Pennsylvania to Idaho, Donnelly's dark dream drew ever closer to reality.

Chapter 8

The Golden Bottle

In August 1892, Ignatius Donnelly, People's Party candidate for governor of Minnesota, once again turned literary sage and man of letters, penning a new novel of ideas in the middle of a heated campaign. Like *Caesar's Column*, the new book would encapsulate Donnelly's creed and ideology. This time, however, the book would be written and published during the race for governor, under Donnelly's own name rather than under a literary alias, with proceeds set to fund his upstart campaign. And in another departure from his prior literary efforts, the novel, titled *The Golden Bottle*, would be published by a Minnesota publisher, D. D. Merrill, with offices in St. Paul and New York.

The first edition, appearing in the late summer of 1892, included an author's preface in which Donnelly apologizes to his reader for a manuscript "hurriedly written" in hotel rooms, on rail cars, and between campaign speeches.[1] It is, he tells us humbly, less a "work" and more a "skit," and he identifies its purpose as to "explain and defend, in the thin disguise of a story, some of the new ideas put forth by the People's Party." The objective is not self-glorification; rather, Donnelly seeks to urge the reader to open-minded inquiry in order to make the world a more equitable place. Like *Doctor Huguet*, *The Golden Bottle* is a fantasy, and Donnelly expresses confidence that the intelligent reader will "have sense enough to draw the line where argument ends and romance begins." The author concludes his preface by turning the book's fate over to friendly readers as well as to the "serrated teeth of its critics."[2]

In the first chapter, the author introduces his readers to the story's first-person narrator and the author's proxy, young Ephraim Benezet of rural Butler County, Kansas. A kind of Great Plains existentialist, Ephraim believes in a higher power but questions how such an all-powerful being could possibly ignore the difficulties of a yeoman's life: debt, despair, drought, disease, deluge. He wants a better life for himself, his beleaguered mother and father, and his love interest, Sophie, who has been forced to make her way in an unforgiving city. Plagued with what he believes to be consumption, and unable to be of much use on the family farm, the dutiful son seeks to lessen his Hamlet-like angst via the one thing he can do to ease his pain: sleep.

Ephraim soon awakens to a vision of an old man announcing himself as the Pity of God. As he looks on, wondering if he is dreaming, the ghostly figure pours an amber-colored liquid onto an iron nail, transforming it into what looks like gold. When Ephraim wakes up the following morning after what he presumes to have been a dream, he finds the bottle and the golden nail. He travels into town to see if the artifact can pass a jeweler's test for purity, and when it does, he sells the now-priceless nail to obtain food for his family.

Before long, Ephraim, with the help of his family and the magical golden bottle, is turning slabs of iron into bricks of pure gold, paying off the mortgage in Kansas City and acquiring a few of life's finer things. The young man observes in wonder, "It is a delightful thing to feel rich. The difference between the mind of a wealthy man and that of a poor man is the difference between a room brilliantly lighted and one shrouded in darkness. In the first case every artistic form is revealed in the flood of illumination; in the other, you bump your head against the walls and break your shins over the furniture; you grope, you crawl, you stumble, you swear."[3]

In short order the newfound wealth of the Benezet family is discovered via the sale of the gold ingots they produce. Initially they are suspected as thieves, frauds, or imposters, but when their gold is determined to be pure throughout Omaha, they find themselves sought after. On the train traveling back to Kansas, they are feted as celebrities by crowds that gather along their route, demanding speeches. In short order, Ephraim, now known by the sobriquet "the gold-maker," locates and marries his childhood love, Sophie, in Philadelphia, where she is abused by her employer in the garment industry. Together the newlyweds discuss how they might use their newfound wealth for the greater good. At Sophie's suggestion they begin an uplift program for factory women, ensuring them a fair wage. Sophie is every bit as philanthropic as her new husband and possessed of a shared passion for economic justice of the kind dispensed when the couple form a Women's Cooperative Association and a Women's League of America. Ephraim summarizes their mutual efforts at societal uplift:

> Not charity, but justice. Not stealing from the poor and giving them back part of it, with many airs and flourishes and ostentations; but stopping the stealing, and permitting industry to keep the fruits of its own toil. How beautiful is industry when it means plenty, prosperity, happiness, a clear mind, a serene heart, a comfortable home! How horrible is industry when it means grinding and unrequited toil. . .. Is it any wonder that under such conditions the soul of the laborer becomes bitterer than death and blacker than hell, and he is ready to curse God and die; aye, ready to blow up a world that permits such things without protest?[4]

In the weeks that follow, Ephraim and Sophie's good offices only increase; altruistic ideals previously scoffed at are now readily accepted as a result of the couple's newfound gold wealth. Ephraim advocates for low-interest loans for farmers, and he is invited to address Congress, where reporters ask for and listen closely to his thoughts on the issues of the day. He cannot help but notice how personal wealth influences receptivity, as he muses in consideration of his new fame: "If I had cried, Boo! on the street corners, mankind would have seen some occult, mysterious, and prophetic meaning in that wondrous syllable." In his address to Congress, he implores lawmakers to work by and for the people, ensuring them an equal measure of opportunity. His soaring oratory resolves into a resounding rhetorical question: "What old-world theory, what interest of a class, can stand in the way of the happiness of the people and the preservation of the Republic? The people pay you your salaries; they hire you to make laws for their benefit, not for the benefit of any class that preys upon them."[5]

As the gold maker continues his campaign for a living wage and low-interest credit, he encounters a plutocracy more powerfully entrenched than previously imagined. While the US House of Representatives passes his workers' rights bill, the Senate does not, reinforcing for Ephraim why he prefers a unicameral rather than a bicameral legislature: "It is like a man who, having survived the ministrations of one doctor and recovered, is at once placed in the hands of another and dies."[6] Why, he reasonably wonders, should there be two doctors? Stuck in interminable gridlock, the United States' vaunted system of government boils down to "liberty with despotism in its belly."[7] When his common-sense prescriptions for a healthier nation die in the Senate, Ephraim is angry. In the contest of sixty-five million Americans—whose wishes he believes he represents—versus US elites, the knaves in Congress seem to have prevailed, and he feels betrayed by the very electorate he aspires to advocate for, cynically reflecting that voters would rather be "kicked by a duke than kissed by a genius."[8]

After his rebuke in the Senate, Ephraim the benevolent philanthropist transforms into Ephraim the aggrieved activist. Summoning a cadre of reporters for a makeshift press conference, he announces his intention to bypass the nation's failed institutions in a bid to uplift the people directly. He declares that he will personally underwrite twenty-year mortgages at 2 percent interest. To put more money into circulation and pay for his massive public spending program, he will manufacture and sell gold on an industrial scale, establishing accounts in Philadelphia, Boston, and New York. With more money flowing and interest rates reduced to a minimum, the everyday citizens he is resolved to help can achieve greater self-sufficiency, keeping more of their own money while reducing the usury portion yearly surrendered to the monied capitalist class.

Expanding his campaign from single homes to whole communities, Ephraim erects cities built on a progressive ideal: providing clean energy, affordable housing, transportation, universal public education, and free libraries. Feeling its grip on American families loosening, the money-lending class on Wall Street attempts to have him assassinated for his impertinence and lobbies Congress to remonetize silver as a counterweight to the monetary power Ephraim has achieved via gold. Meanwhile Ephraim, disgusted at the outright bribes offered Congress by Wall Street and resolved to fight fire with fire, provides fence-sitting congressmen a generous stipend intended to make them immune to bribery and to free them to represent the will of the people. Both Democrats and Republicans seek Ephraim as their presidential candidate, but he pledges himself to the People's Party. When neither Democrats nor Republicans succeed in recruiting him, the two established organizations band together to form a single opposition party. Once the electorate sees the two old political foes awkwardly joined at the hip, the strategy backfires, and the long-standing partisan spell cast on the people is broken. Millions defect to the People's Party and the upstart candidacy of one Ephraim Benezet, who succeeds in winning the presidency.

The plutocracy and its allies will not accept defeat, however, and commence a campaign of character defamation until Ephraim and Sophie realize that to empower the truth they must first become majority shareholders in the nation's newspapers of record. As a case in point, Ephraim quotes the diatribe against him in the *New York Thunder* from the day before and the day after his acquisition of the newspaper's majority stock. The day-before version reads in part, "A thousand Judas Iscariots, ten thousand Benedict Arnolds, could not have effected the evil which this Kansas boor has accomplished in a few short years. And now he seeks to take possession of the presidency, and wield the whole power of the national government for the further working out of his terrible plans."[9] The day-after version, by contrast, reads as an example of how completely the views of the so-called free press can be shaped by the dollars of those who underwrite its opinions: "By his powerful genius Ephraim Benezet has solved the problem which has occupied the minds of the greatest of mankind for a thousand years. . .. And instead of using this tremendous power for his own gratification or aggrandizement, he has employed it to make millions happy."[10]

Terrified by the breathtaking scope and momentum of President Benezet's working-class reforms and their imminent threat to traditional aristocratic order, England declares preemptive war on the United States, spurred on by the saber rattling of a *London Times* that warns the British people that "a madman has been elevated to the presidency of the United States."[11] The new US president's egalitarian notions would, the *Times* maintains, mean the end of "the most cherished and venerable institutions of England and Europe." Calling Benezet a "lunatic" and an "insane miscreant,"[12] England prepares to defend itself against what it deems to be an American demagogue fueled by populist fervor, just as it resisted the excesses of the French Revolution. It vows to lead a European resistance, even as Ireland falls rapidly before a US invasion intended to free the citizens of the impoverished island nation. Benezet lists universal education, suffrage, and religious tolerance as the first three guarantees to the Irish people, followed by separation of church and state, free and fair elections, equal justice before the law, a graduated income tax, and a limit to the amount of land any one individual or corporation can own.[13] It is at this point in *The Golden Bottle*, with

England and the United States having mutually declared war and Ireland having succumbed to a US invasion, that the "argument ends and romance begins," as Donnelly puts it in his preface. Pro-labor populist reforms spread throughout Europe, and Benezet calls for the creation of a "Universal Republic" headquartered in the Azores and charged with the preservation of peace in the world.[14] Anticipating a kind of League of Nations, its member states would elect a president, cabinet, and Congress, substituting arbitration for war in order to "ensure unbroken peace for many generations."[15]

After sowing the seeds of reform in Europe, the Benezets return to the United States to find that their vision of a workers' utopia has taken hold there; a Brotherhood of Justice now counts twenty million men and women among its members, and a new spirit of fellowship, literacy, and compassion infuses the citizenry. As Ephraim explains, "If one fell sick, his brethren cared for him; if he died his family were helped out of poverty by an insurance bounty. And if any man lacked strength or energy and tended to fall down into wretchedness or beggary, there were societies to put the hand of friendship under him, and make life easier, and at the same time self-respecting."[16] When Ephraim and Sophie fall asleep contentedly at the Palmer House in Chicago after a day of parades and celebrations in honor of their return, they sense a renewed spirit of humanity enveloping the land.

That night Ephraim sleeps fitfully, awakening to a bed he recognizes as his lumpy mattress back in Kansas. His mother and father hover over him, fearing for the health of their son. The adventures of President Benezet, Sophie, the Brotherhood of Justice, the golden bottle—all have been a dream. He calls out to a higher power, and the ghostly Pity of God reappears, telling him that his consumption can be cured with fresh air and hard work; that Sophie will one day become his wife, but first she must learn to support herself; that his grand dream of the golden bottle and the dignity of humanity must be written down in a book and shared before it disappears forever. Ephraim asks his ghostly visitor for a glimpse of heaven and a life ever after, only to be told, "There is no hereafter. It is one eternal *is*. We create, you create, everything creates."[17] On that pronouncement, the godlike figure disappears, leaving Ephraim with a unequivocal conclusion: "I would write to Sophie. I would go to work. And I would tell my story to the world."[18]

In the final months of his campaign for governor, Donnelly the politician embraced a similar workmanlike spirit. By early November 1892, he felt he had done everything he could, writing in his diary, "I rejoice to think that I am so near the end of my work. . .. I have conversed with 10,000 persons, wrote a novel . . . carried on a large correspondence and supervised the whole campaign. I hope to win, but nothing is certain." Whether it was the fatalist in Donnelly or some *Golden Bottle*-like intuition, his assessment left room for the prospect of political disappointment: "I may have spent all my immense labor for nothing; but I felt it was my duty to make the fight in the interests of country and mankind. . .. I shall have done some good even if I am beaten."[19]

Newspapers across the Great Plains that supported the People's Party worked hard to help the cause by reacquainting the general public with the strange genius that was the Sage of Nininger. In Kansas, the *Western Advocate* introduced the candidate to readers at length, reminding them that the great man had been in "comparative retirement" prior to his return to the Minnesota State Senate on the Farmers' Alliance ticket in 1890. It observed, "Ignatius Donnelly's national reputation depends more perhaps on his literary ability than on his political experience." Donnelly, it added, "is preeminently a writer but he has the gift that few writers are blessed with, that of being a finished speaker and a political orator."[20] In an election cycle distinguished by a swell of third-party sentiment, the *Western Advocate* and other like-minded publications in the Great Plains wanted to deemphasize Donnelly as a career politician who had suffered many prior losses and rebrand him as a man of letters with a concomitant interest in good governance. And in writing and publishing a novel in the heat of the gubernatorial race, Donnelly undertook a parallel campaign of personal and political reinvention. Meanwhile, his base in the more rural parts of the state remained hopeful at his prospects. The *Dakota Ruralist* reported with glee that Donnelly's ally Everett Fish at the *Great West* was making the plutocrats in Minneapolis "squirm" while Donnelly did his part on the stump. "We would like to see Donnelly . . . governor," remarked the *Ruralist*, "and chances are we will."[21]

Exactly how much the publication of *The Golden Bottle* might improve Donnelly's chances at the ballot box remained unclear. On one hand, the book risked alienating potential supporters who feared that Donnelly had become more enamored with his library and his letters than with winning votes. Sales of the election-year volume might be depressed among those partisan readers who, in a nonelection season, might be willing to pay a dollar to entertain Donnelly's literary stylings but would not do so while he was actively campaigning for office.

From his base at the Hotel Richelieu, J. H. Turner, Donnelly ally and former secretary of the National Farmers' Alliance, wrote letters to the editors of a number of populist newspapers in the Midwest and Great Plains, announcing the availability of Donnelly's latest work and describing how proceeds from its sale would help the nascent People's Party raise sustaining funds. Calling *The Golden Bottle* "a romance with a view to helping the People's Party movement" and a story illustrating "the great questions of the day," Turner explained that fully half of the cover cost of the book would be earmarked for campaign funds. Orders would be filled on a first-come-first-served basis, and those eager to support the cause should not delay, he further advised, anticipating "great demand" if the sales of the author's prior novels were any indication. In his letter, Turner eagerly reminded potential purchasers of Donnelly's sacrifice for the cause, intimating that the gentleman politician of Nininger City had agreed to the arrangement to help the cause of reform even "at the risk of lessening the sale of the book in other quarters."[22]

In the fall of 1892, Donnelly waited anxiously for a twin verdict on both his book and his political fate, which he had uniquely intermingled. The judgment wasn't long in coming. While he polled well in Minnesota's rural districts, the urban vote in St. Paul and Minneapolis sunk his chances. Two days after losing the race for governor to both the Democrat, Daniel Lawler, and the Republican, Knute Nelson, Donnelly described the outcome to his diary: "Beaten! Whipped! Smashed! Our followers scattered like dew before the rising sun."[23]

Sales of *The Golden Bottle* slowed dramatically as a result of the failed run. While the book sold an estimated ten thousand copies in its first months on the market, the majority of those sales could be attributed to its synergy with the cause of the People's Party in a heated election season. Now that the polls were closed and Donnelly had once again emerged a loser, his allies in the newspaper world shifted their focus away from the book as a mouthpiece for populist ideas and toward a last-ditch effort to revive its sales. Everett Fish, editor of the *Great West*, reminded readers, "The questions raised in the book are not political; they belong to a higher level of statesmanship, and will force themselves upon the consideration of men of all parties." While Donnelly may have been the loser in his bid for governor, he was a winner in the literary marketplace according to the *Great West*, which began its review with a recitation of the author's impressive bibliographic track record: *Atlantis* had gone through twenty-five editions in the United States and several more in England; *Ragnarok* had reached its eleventh edition; *The Great Cryptogram* had amassed total sales of nearly 10,000 in the United States and abroad; and *Doctor Huguet* had exceeded 12,000. *Caesar's Column* had now reached 150,000 in domestic sales, with nearly as many sold abroad. The *Great West* dared to proclaim *The Golden Bottle* to be the Sage of Nininger's most remarkable work yet, one that would surely "rival *Caesar's Column* in popularity."[24]

Evaluated in terms of units sold, *The Golden Bottle* represented a modest win for Donnelly, exceeding the sales of *The Great Cryptogram* in just its first few months on the market. On the other hand, his populist pro-worker fantasy had generated a fraction of the popularity achieved by *The Great Cryptogram*, whose novel thesis had propelled its author to lectures and readings as far afield as England. On previous occasions Donnelly had written some of his best, most enduring work for skeptical readers, but *The Golden Bottle* shared an ideology with many of those who purchased it. While his target audience clearly received and appreciated his message, the author was, in effect, preaching to the converted, limiting the mass appeal that had driven his earlier works to such phenomenal success.

Praise for *The Golden Bottle* came more easily to critics once Donnelly had ceased to be a political threat. In the Twin Cities, the *St. Paul Dispatch* observed, "Mr. Donnelly's purpose in writing it, like most of his purposes, is carried out apparently without remote thought as to its effect on himself." The book proved of Donnelly that he "loves his kind, and that his ultimate purpose in life is to do them some little measure of good." Classifying the work among "reform books," *The Representative* reprinted for the benefit of Twin Cities readers a litany of positive reviews gathered from across the Midwest and the nation. In Duluth, the *Herald* had called *The Golden Bottle* a "masterpiece of imagination, dotted with philosophy, sprinkled with metaphors, entwined with a vine of romance and yet so firmly welded with serious meaning." Who in America, it wondered, was better "to tell a man's strength or a woman's tenderness, to roll in fury or sing in tune . . . with grave meaning, romance, philosophy, and imagination than Ignatius Donnelly." In Boston, E. O. Flower, editor of the noted reform magazine *The Arena*, expressed the sentiments of many readers in noting an important difference between Donnelly's latest work and its predecessors: *The Golden Bottle*, he wrote, captured "the zenith of humanity's well-being, as *Caesar's Column* painted the nadir." *The Independent* in Deadwood, South Dakota, encapsulated the book's two-pronged appeal, calling it "interesting as a romance . . . and yet a powerful argument for justice for the masses." Perhaps no other newspaper in the United States was as sanguine, and as celebratory, regarding Donnelly's latest work as the *Pittsburgh Times*, whose review opened with the observation that one's dreams spoke volumes about one's moral character. If that was so, the *Times* maintained, *The Golden Bottle* "symbolizes the hopes and aspirations—the daydreams—of thousands in the West and Northwest who have felt the cold hand of want." While the Sage of Nininger had not exactly produced a work of literary art, the *Times* reviewer marveled at how unfailingly the author "gets at the facts of the human heart."[25] Nonpartisan critics who lauded *The Golden Bottle* often praised it for exactly the qualities *Caesar's Column* lacked. As one later put it, the book is a "fantasy of populist manifest destiny" and the "optimistic obverse of *Caesar's Column*."[26]

Donnelly's human heart was ailing after suffering yet another political defeat, but the call of literary endeavors once more proved an abiding consolation. In a diary entry dated November 10, 1892, he noted that the Shakespearean cipher on which he had toiled for the better part of a decade was "worth more than all the governorships in the world."[27] If uttered in public among establishment politicians, such a claim would surely have served as fodder for further attacks on him as an unreliable political player stuffed to the gills with sour grapes. But for a man like Donnelly, the proof of a cipher would offer the ultimate form of vindication: if a lay scholar could prove that the Bard of Avon had been a fraud, the world would have no choice but to stand up and pay attention.

Chapter 9

Donnelliana and *The American People's Money*

Little more than one month removed from a crushing loss in the race for Minnesota governor, Donnelly intimated that he had had his fill of politics, telling the *St. Paul Pioneer Press* exactly what it longed to hear: that he would not be a candidate in the future for public office after his upcoming term in the state legislature ended. The coming session, he suggested, would be a kind of farewell tour in which he hoped to bury the hatchet and leave the Senate on terms of mutual goodwill.[1]

Even on what appeared to be his way out, however, Donnelly refused to go easy on the corporate interests he had fought against his entire political life. In an eleven-month period from January to November, he initiated investigations into the alleged anticompetitive practices of both the coal and lumber industries. In the first month of the session, he introduced a resolution in the Minnesota legislature to be sent to the US Congress, requesting a formal probe into alleged price fixing on the coal used to heat homes and businesses. Subsequent inquiries revealed an alarming fact: that a single man, John J. Rhodes, controlled the distribution pricing of Minnesota hard coal from top to bottom. Rhodes denied any knowledge of price fixing, maintaining that he kept no business records of his transactions. Incredulous, and determined to exact economic justice for the people, Donnelly arranged to have the Minnesota State Senate officer seize Rhodes's books from his office without a court order. While the move was later deemed illegal by the Minnesota attorney general, Donnelly's bold strike yielded evidence that all but proved criminal conspiracy and price fixing.[2]

While Rhodes pursued legal action against the committee investigating him, Donnelly's popularity as a truth teller and trustbuster surged among the people of Minnesota, who could now plainly see that his persistent claims that they were victims of monopolistic "rings" were substantively true. Three thousand people gathered in St. Paul to protest the coal combines, clamoring for an address from Donnelly, who self-effacingly quipped, "I am the most popular man in Minnesota—between elections."[3]

Buoyed by Donnelly's success advocating in the public interest, Donnelly and Senator Henry Keller joined forces to root out corruption in what many regarded as Minnesota's chief industry: lumber. Donnelly was elected chairman of the investigative committee, and his probe once again turned up indisputable evidence of illegal practices—in this case unethical land sales and lumber cutting that, in effect, cheated the people of Minnesota out of the rightful value of their public pine forests. For his efforts Donnelly won still greater public respect, but he received widespread and vitriolic condemnation from the state's lumber barons, who decried the efforts of Donnelly and his "rat-headed gang of reformers that seek notoriety at the expense of gentlemen."[4] While his efforts at economic justice on behalf of Minnesotans were undertaken under the mandate of a legislative subcommittee and, later, under the auspices of a joint House and State Senate commission, entrenched lumber interests called out Donnelly by name.[5]

Spearheading multiple investigations into what amounted to abuses of the public trust, Donnelly once again emerged as a kind of folk hero. In a formal report summarizing his committee's findings against the lumber industry, he invoked a plainspoken tone consistent with his populist campaign, declaring, "Let the rascals find some other victims than the children of the State." In his report he urged the governor to "build an absolutely impassable wall around the state's property" lest it be exploited by the "sharpest set of rascals." Sounding a progressive note, he cautioned the state's public officials, "The present . . . watchfulness, growing out of this investigation, will soon subside; but the greed and rapacity of mankind are undying."[6]

Donnelly sought not only to hold the coal, lumber, and railroad interests to account but also to secure his own reputation as the down-home yet erudite Sage of Nininger. Everett Fish, editor at the *Great West* and a key figure in the Minnesota Farmers' Alliance, led the renewed efforts to codify Donnelly's legacy with the writing of a campaign biography first announced with great fanfare in the pages of the *Great West* in September 1891. The biography would detail the life and times of the "incorruptible ex. Lieut. Gov. of Minnesota" who had "fought greater battles, been subjected to greater infamies, and risen higher from greater depths of abuse and falsehood, than any other American, living or dead!" Fish declared that the revealing book would "withdraw the shadows cast over him [Donnelly] by the putrid agencies of a purchased press and a corrupt plutocracy," allowing readers to see "what elements of infamy have been at work to crush a great life."[7]

The book, aptly titled *Donnelliana* and subtitled *An Appendix to "Caesar's Column,"* followed some months later. Describing his role as more of an editor and compiler than an author, Fish begins his preface with a bold assertion: "There is, perhaps, no man in the United States who is more talked of today than Hon. Ignatius Donnelly, of Minnesota." Praising his friend's diverse talents, the editor observes, "While one may be more prominent in the political arena and another more conspicuous in scientific circles, and still another more talked of in the literary world, no one man, perhaps, has combined so many diverse fames." Fish remarks on his subject's uniquely varied calling cards: thousands of Europeans knew Donnelly primarily as an author and knew very little of him as a politician, while in the United States, the reverse was true. "One man believes in his *Atlantis*," Fish writes, "another swears by his *Ragnarok*, still another is a convert to *The Great Cryptogram*; and there are hundreds of thousands, on both sides of the Atlantic, who think *Caesar's Column* or *Doctor Huguet* the greatest book ever written." Still, Fish points out, there are tens of thousands more who have never read these books and love Donnelly instead for "his quarter of a century's championship of the rights of the common people, against all the crushing power of Corporations, Rings, Trusts, and the Plutocracy generally."[8]

In his preface, Fish explains that F. J. Schulte of Chicago, publisher of *Caesar's Column* and *Doctor Huguet*, had requested of him a sort of campaign biography. Fish admits he hesitated at first, fearing that a biography of such a many-sided man would take several years and hundreds of pages to complete. A compromise plan was soon reached, whereby the book would become less of a monograph and more of a compendium of quotes from Donnelly's books and diaries. Occupied with his newspaper, Fish would defer the task of searching through Donnelly's personal archives at Nininger to a mutual friend, John A. Giltinan, the brother of Donnelly's son-in-law and himself a St. Paul attorney and former probate judge in Stevens County, Minnesota. Giltinan would stay with Donnelly at Nininger City for several weeks while the two sifted through source material together.

The first third of *Donnelliana* consists of a biographical sketch of the former congressman, beginning with his childhood in Philadelphia and ending with his failed campaign for the Minnesota State Senate in 1888. Fish concludes this part of the book with a curious section entitled "The Future," in which he reassures his readers, "We do not believe Governor Donnelly's career is at an end, or even near its close. . .. Even as we write, a new novel, *Doctor Huguet*, is, as we have shown, attracting the attention of the world."[9] The details suggest Fish was putting the finishing touches on part 1 of *Donnelliana* as early as the fall of 1891, during which time *Doctor Huguet* debuted. But the fact that the biographical portion of the book concludes with Donnelly's state senate race suggests that Fish began the volume as a campaign biography for Donnelly's first failed run for governor during the autumn of 1888. His peculiar choice to conclude part 1 of the book with the apologetic admission that the book was written in haste in the midst of the pressing demands of being a newspaper editor implies that the book project was commissioned in the heady days of the Alliance Labor Union fusion earlier that summer, was paused in progress when Donnelly dropped out of the race, and recommenced when Donnelly ran for governor a second time in 1892, this time on the People's Party ticket. The quasi campaign biography of 1892, then, appears to be an amalgam of writing done between the summer of 1888 and the summer of 1892. Fish's work on the project seems to have mostly concluded in 1889, with a lengthy addendum written in 1891 defending Donnelly against the attacks lodged against him during the *Pioneer Press* libel suit of that year. Given its lengthy rebuttal of the charges, this additional section gives every appearance of having been made at Donnelly's direction after a verdict that awarded him only one dollar in damages. For the sake of pride and posterity, Donnelly surely sought to clean up the unsubstantiated rumors circulated by the defense that he had both bribed and been bribed, and he clearly desired the vindication of his good name in advance of his gubernatorial campaign in 1892.

Part 1 concludes with what Fish clearly hopes will be a clincher: a series of rhetorical questions under the subheading "An Appendix to

'Caesar's Column.'" The editor demands, "Can any one doubt that the events detailed in this biography . . . are a fit and proper appendix to *Caesar's Column*?" He asserts a "subtle, wide-spreading, cruel, degrading despotism" reminiscent of Donnelly's fictional villain Prince Cabano sickening and stifling the nation. Fish ends the first part of *Donnelliana* in a crescendo that is at once ominous and hopeful: "Can any one doubt that if the new political revolution is not able to arrest these evils, peacefully, at the ballot-box, the dreadful figure of the *column of corpses* will soon arise, amid flame and ashes, and the destruction of a rotten civilization?"[10]

Occupying the final two-thirds of *Donnelliana*, part 2 consists of nearly two hundred pages of material billed as "extracts from the wit, wisdom, poetry and eloquence of Ignatius Donnelly." Organized into thematic sections renumbered to begin with page 1, and commencing with "The Intellect," part 2 (or "Part Second") serves as a kind of dictionary of published and unpublished Donnelly quotes, aphorisms, diary entries, poems, and whimsies. The earliest entries, dating back to his salad days as a law clerk in Philadelphia under the tutelage of the attorney Benjamin Harris, speak to the subject's proclivity as a poet, as the young Donnelly, circa 1850, describes the end of the day, for example, as "darkly crumbling down, / Heaping the east with gray, worn, twilight ruins."[11] The most recent entries come from Donnelly's personal journal and speak to the humiliation he felt regarding his treatment over *The Great Cryptogram*: "I have drained them [the waters of humiliation] to the very dregs; I have swallowed them by the quart, the gallon, the bucket-full, the barrel-full; I have been plunged into an ocean of them; I have been soaked in them, for years at a time, until every fiber of my being has shrieked out its protest against injustice and degradation."[12] In between are entries on subjects as specific as "Dakota County after an Election" and as broad as "The Power of Time" and "The Power of Man."

Ironically, *Donnelliana*, a book begun years earlier on the wishful thinking that its subject would be elected governor of Minnesota, turned into a political liability shortly after its publication in 1892. In the intervening years, Fish had become increasingly angry at Donnelly for his openness to a possible fusion between the Farmers' Alliance and the major political parties and also, quite likely, over Donnelly's founding of a rival weekly newspaper, *The Representative*, in St. Paul. The decades-old friendship between the two men unraveled explosively, finding the onetime comrades in arms trading public insults and accusations, including Fish's charge that Donnelly had written *Donnelliana* himself and published it under Fish's name.[13] Donnelly vehemently denied the accusation and announced his intention to sue his old friend for libel. Fish responded by filling the front page of the *Great West* with anti-Donnelly invective, including the headlines "Deep, Dark. Donnelly" and "Facts Which Show the Lizard's Trail to be Luminous Compared to his Shadowy Course." At the bottom of the same column, in big, bold type, Fish dared his erstwhile friend, "Publish the facts, you ungrateful demagogue! Publish ONE!" Fish alleged that Donnelly had in fact written *Donnelliana*, attempting to "cover his tracks in a most ridiculous way."[14]

Though neither man initiated the legal action they threatened, both could easily be proven to have participated in the biography. Donnelly and John Giltinan had, by Fish's own admission, selected most of the archived material, and Donnelly had been a signatory to the contract with the publisher F. J. Schulte. Fish's hand in the biography, meanwhile, is attested to in the book's byline and throughout the book's front matter and back matter. *Donnelliana* is almost certainly the work of three men—Fish, Giltinan, and Donnelly himself—though Donnelly's name is not listed as an author or artistic collaborator anywhere in the volume. Kate Donnelly also read the manuscript prior to its publication, suggesting key edits and flagging key omissions.[15] Regardless of its authorship, a core question implicit in the biography is whether or not Donnelly has reached the pinnacle of his political career, or whether, in fact, the seasoned campaigner has energy left to run for public office. The text takes great pains to emphasize its subject's vitality irrespective of chronological age, as it makes special mention of how the sixty-year-old Donnelly "looks like a man of forty-five" and could effortlessly keep a schedule that would no doubt "kill a man of forty."[16] Donnelly works twelve to fourteen hours a day, the biography claims, saying that he is "as fresh at midnight as he is in the morning."[17] Within the first few paragraphs of the introduction, the authors declare that their subject is a "clearly defined genius," a man who, rather than making a final curtain call, is instead near to "lifting the curtain upon another act, wherein the drama approaches the climax of its power." *Donnelliana*, they note, reflects a desire to chronicle the Sage of Nininger while his skies are still "brilliant with promise and the day pregnant with events."[18]

While Donnelly's star still burned bright, the fate of the nation, and the Midwest in particular, darkened considerably in the autumn of

1893, as deepening economic depression brought mass demonstrations and pushed workers to the brink of the violent revolt the author had prophesied in *Caesar's Column*. Addressing an assembly of unemployed workers crowded into Market Hall in St. Paul, Donnelly reminded the protesters that violence would solve nothing and that only a peaceful solution to their problems should be entertained. Using his newspaper, *The Representative*, as his primary mouthpiece, he empathized with the plight of both farmer and laborer, arguing that their shared goal was not financial profit at the expense of corporations, but merely avoidance of starvation. In a time of economic trouble, Donnelly's tireless advocacy for workers and farmers served him well, especially in light of his pro-worker, pro-consumer investigations into the illegal or unethical practices of the coal, lumber, and railroad industries. By the fall convention season of 1894, his name was once again prominent among the possible nominees for governor representing the Minnesota Farmers' Alliance, though Fish at the *Great West* was dead set against him, as were the editors at the *St. Paul Pioneer Press* whom Donnelly had successfully sued for libel.

At the Farmers' Alliance convention in January, Fish spoke for two hours against his ex-friend's potential nomination, calling him a "fat brute" and an "egomaniac" while demanding a formal investigation into his erstwhile ally. Donnelly supporters countered by turning off the lights, in effect adjourning the meeting while retaining Donnelly as president of the alliance. In retaliation at the perceived injustice, Fish dedicated the entirety of his front page to what he called a "culminating outrage" that was "never dared to be enacted in a convention of any party on earth." The convention had been broken up prematurely by "scoundrels," he claimed, in "Donnelly's gang."[19] Fish lodged his accusations not only in the pages of the *Great West* but before a notary public in Ramsey County, Minnesota, where he, the affiant, swore to the notary that Donnelly had in 1892 divulged to Fish plans to fuse the People's Party with the Democratic Party in exchange for both parties' pledged support of his campaign for governor during that year. In the *Great West*, Fish worded his accusations as if they were being lodged in a court of law: "I plainly, distinctly, unequivocally charge that you, Ignatius Donnelly, otherwise known as the 'Sage of Nininger,' while being an alleged anti-monopoly . . . anti-corporationist, reform alliance man, engaged in contesting for the rights of the people, and writing books like 'Caesar's Column,' have, at different times, and especially from 1880 to 1892, while pretending to be a reformer, taken large sums of money, amounting in the aggregate to several thousand dollars, from prominent Republican politicians or the offices of the republican state central committee."[20] Irate as he was, Fish did not specify where the alleged payout of "several thousand dollars" had originated from, though it was possible that the incensed editor was attempting to make new hay of the well-established fact that Donnelly had been awarded $3,500 by the US Congress in 1881 for personal expenses in his contested election against William Washburn.[21]

Fish darkly predicted that his former friend and ally would engineer a forced fusion of the Farmers' Alliance with the Democrats in 1894, a move that would amount to the "butchery of the People's Party by Ignatius Donnelly." Either the perjuries to which Fish attested in his affidavit were true, declared the *Great West*, or "Donnelly is a villain."[22] Donnelly responded the same day in the pages of the rival *Minneapolis Tribune*, which ran a transcription of his speech preceded by the headline "Fish Flayed Alive." The *Tribune* depicted the bitter confrontation between the two erstwhile friends as an "oratorial duel," arguing that Donnelly had gotten the better of it, "putting to rout Fish and his forces." In a front-page piece that included a transcription of the "flaying," Donnelly doubled down, calling the newspaperman a "fabricator and a falsifier."[23] Fish's allegations were never fully tested, however, as pressure from Donnelly's chief rival in the contest to represent the People's Party, Sidney M. Owen, coupled with Donnelly's concern for his wife's rapidly failing health, caused him to cease any early moves toward party fusion, thereby opening the door to the Owen nomination for Minnesota governor on the People's Party ticket.

Despite the turmoil, by the winter of 1894 Donnelly had scored two important victories: he had retained the presidency of the Minnesota Farmers' Alliance and had successfully defended himself against a vicious barrage of accusations made by Fish, who ultimately conceded the fight by relocating his iconoclastic newspaper to South Dakota. Such political victories, however, paled in comparison to the preoccupying pain and worry Donnelly experienced as his wife's health worsened, making it necessary that she move to St. Paul to be cared for by the couple's eldest son, Dr. Ignatius C. Donnelly. In June, Kate succumbed to a fatal stroke after months of smaller episodes that had left her partially paralyzed. Her funeral was a quiet affair, with the *St. Paul Daily Globe* running a brief notice under the headline "Mrs. Donnelly's Funeral." The first of two services would be held at the Twin Cities residence of the couple's daughter, Mary Giltinan, with a second ceremony planned for the St. Paul Cathedral.[24]

Though she had eschewed publicity and pomp, Kate Donnelly had been a remarkable woman. At home in Hastings, the former school principal from Philadelphia had formed a Sunday school and a church choir she led quite credibly with her three-octave vocal range.[25] During the long spells when Ignatius was away from Nininger, she would undertake many of the more routine farming chores, sometimes chastising her husband for his neglect.[26] Throughout his career, she had been ready with keen advice and sound strategy to help her partner navigate the political pitfalls that awaited a man of principle among unscrupulous politicians.

For Donnelly, Kate's passing marked the first in a series of debilitating family crises. Later that summer, Donnelly's eldest son, Ignatius, exhausted from the caregiving he had done for his mother, experienced a near breakdown, prompting his concerned father to pay for an expensive rural retreat. At the same time, a grieving Donnelly fell victim to painful rheumatism. Enemies and friends in the Twin Cities reached out to the struggling widower, offering monetary support that he felt obligated to refuse, though he noted in *The Representative* that the outreach had left him "profoundly touched."[27]

But with his oldest son's health gradually improving and his grief productively channeled into writing a pamphlet-length memoir that he would eventually publish under the title *In Memoriam: Mrs. Katharine Donnelly*, Donnelly began to heal. Slowly, and for his fiscal survival, he began accepting paid invitations to return to the lecture circuit. The economic depression, coupled with the rise of organized labor, had led to the formation of an anti-Catholic, anti-immigrant society euphemistically called the American Protective Association (APA). With its membership concentrated in Minnesota, Michigan, and Ohio, and with an estimated membership of half a million, the organization was said to embrace a conspiracy theory that the pope had purposely flooded the United States with Catholic immigrants from Europe to compete with Protestant laborers for scarce jobs. These immigrants, the APA believed, were agitators keen on destabilizing the US banking system and, in so doing, paving the way for de facto papal control over the nation.[28]

As a Catholic-born, pro-labor, pro-reform public servant living in the heart of APA territory, Donnelly was solicited for his views on the subject. In March the *Irish Standard* in Minneapolis reported that he would address the topic at the Lyceum Theatre, to what was expected to be a packed house. While some of the *Standard*'s readers hoped the Catholic-reared Donnelly would would skewer the APA, the newspaper conceded that "no one knows exactly how the 'Sage of Nininger' will treat the question," since Donnelly characteristically avoided divisive religious rhetoric. "It is superfluous to speak of the brilliancy and eloquence of 'The Sage' as an orator," the newspaper observed, noting that his popularity as a lecturer recommended that seats be reserved well in advance.[29]

In his March speech, and in a two-part debate with the APA supporter Professor Walter Sims later in April, Donnelly disappointed some Catholics who expected his unquestioning loyalty. He refused to attack the APA, opting to appeal to a spirit of brotherhood instead. The *St. Paul Pioneer Press*, no friend of Donnelly's, praised his impartiality in the Sims debate and his unwillingness to succumb to sectarianism, pointing out that at times Donnelly had actually defended his opponent from a hostile and hateful crowd. Donnelly worried that if the United States yielded to religious discrimination and violence, foreign capitalists would take advantage of the strife to manipulate prices for agricultural commodities. He expressed genuine alarm at the growing unrest in the country while arguing that religious intolerance must be rejected to keep the nation from descending into sectarian bitterness and, potentially, civil war.[30] He addressed the controversial organization at length in a May 1894 edition of *The Representative*, in which he called the APA the "most formidable enemy of the People's Party and the cause of reform today." By sowing the seeds of division, the society could only distract the public from the real question—"the economic questions of the hour" rather than the "questions of the next world." Instead, citizens would be far better served by uniting against the common enemy: monied elites, aristocrats, and plutocrats.[31]

Donnelly carried his unifying tone into a keynote speech at a volatile People's Party convention in July 1894. As the convention began in Minneapolis, President Grover Cleveland sent federal troops into neighboring Illinois to quell violent Pullman strikes mere months after thousands of protesters, inspired by the midwestern businessman Jacob Coxey, had marched hundreds of miles to Washington, DC, to protest rising unemployment. While the pro-labor Donnelly liked the populist Coxey personally and sympathized with the cause of the movement itself, he worried deeply about the prospect of violent unrest in the streets. In Minneapolis, Donnelly began his address on a somber note, intimating that the country had not faced such grave danger since the troops of General Robert E. Lee marched within sight of the Capitol in 1861.[32] He appealed for calm and reiterated the People's Party's rejection of violence, declaring, "We do not believe the path of reform is through the torch and the rifle."[33] He was clear, however, that his sympathies lay with disgruntled workers and, further, that he did not believe that members of the striking American Railway Union had instigated the violence and property damage in Chicago. His stock rising as a senior party statesman, Donnelly attended a People's Party rally in Chicago alongside Eugene Debs in October 1894, during which he emphasized that his party was one of activism in lieu of anarchy.[34]

Mostly he blamed a familiar enemy, the press, for inciting the public's and the government's overreaction to the striking railroad workers and economic justice seekers of the Pullman strikes and of Coxey's Army, of whom he wrote, "A vast array of starving men becomes a terrible thing:—once started no one can control them. . .. If they are encountered by government troops the slaughter may be terrible."[35] Already, the march of what Coxey hoped would be five hundred thousand protesters had received more newspaper coverage than any event in the three decades since the Civil War, save for the possible exception of the contested election of 1876.[36] The journalists who covered the event capitalized on the public's fear, earning the sobriquet "the Argus-Eyed Demons of Hell" for their incendiary and sometimes defamatory descriptions of a march that mustered a small fraction of its intended conscripts and remained predominantly peaceful.[37] On one hand, the wall-to-wall coverage of the protest meant that readers in the "newspaper-enslaved East" were getting their first in-depth introduction to the just causes of populist doctrine. On the other hand, the coverage they were receiving was, by necessity, being filtered through the "hireling press," a class of people who would, Donnelly claimed, "ignore the sun, moon, and stars, or lie them out of their orbits, if Wall Street demanded it." The result, he warned, would be a powder keg—the potent prospect of tens of thousands of road-weary, angry marchers, a government on high alert, and a public predisposed by a fearmongering press to view the ragged Coxey crowd as an existential threat. With the small but growing marching column still several weeks away from the National Mall, Donnelly took to the pages of *The Representative* to pose the prescient, practical questions national leaders had thus lacked the temerity to ask: "How will this mob be scattered? And who will feed them? And who can control them? . . . It may be the beginning of terrible events."[38]

By late April, Donnelly doubled down on his disdain for the yellow press, quoting at length the glib, euphemistic, or simply injudicious coverage of many of the nation's most prominent dailies, including the *St. Paul Globe*, whose accounts of the march of late had made a portentous event seem more like a parade or a picnic than a serious, and potentially violent, mass protest. "Our city papers only give the people what they think their weak stomachs will bear," Donnelly complained, adding, "The news is milked through a monopoly sieve and the cream taken out." He groused that if the Coxey march for employment and economic justice had instead been a fistfight or a horse race, the Twin Cities newspapers would have gladly "given . . . the news by the page full." Donnelly's *Representative* would tell the truth of the matter, he promised readers, covering both the hard-to-stomach images (impoverished, half-clad marchers trudging in tatters) and the celebratory ones (the cheering crowds and bicycle brigades of Coxey's Army).[39]

Still, Donnelly refused to endorse the march's ultimate end—the army's gathering on the Capitol steps to present its demand for unemployment insurance. Already, he warned, Congress was "getting ready its gatling guns; summoning its soldiers; and ransacking obsolete laws to see if the unarmed petitioners could be stopped from . . . assembling in the Capitol grounds to present their grievances."[40] In a contest between "bullets or ballots," Donnelly insisted ballots must always be the preferred weapon. When Coxey and the march organizer Carl Brown were arrested in Washington, DC, before Coxey could deliver his speech, but not before US marshals instituted brutal crowd control, Donnelly couldn't help but see the event as a disappointing decrescendo, and he dared to wonder aloud whether far less harm would have been done had Coxey simply been granted his right to peaceful assembly and free speech. In attempting to distance himself and the nascent People's Party from the unrest of the Pullman strike and the march of Coxey's Army, while still supporting the populist calls for the full employment and fair wages such protests represented, Donnelly walked a fine line, particularly back home in conservative Minnesota.

Later that summer, he accepted the People's Party nomination for state senator in Dakota County. But as a sought-after campaigner across Minnesota and the Midwest, he neglected his home base despite warnings from those on the ground. While his furious campaigning for fellow People's Party nominees in southwest Minnesota yielded victories for the ticket in that region, he finished third in his home county, losing to the Democrat Albert Schaller and the Republican J.

P. Caldwell.[41] The *Pioneer Press* wasted little time glorying in the Sage of Nininger's comeuppance, pointing out that he had wrongly believed the county to be in his "breeches pocket" while wondering what he would do now that his political career had "come to a sudden and final ending."[42] Donnelly's selfless campaigning for others had surely been the primary cause of his unexpected defeat at home, but in distancing the People's Party from the tactics of Coxey's march and the Pullman strikes, he may have lost difference-making support from radical populists. In October, he had insisted to dubious reporters that his party stood for "construction" rather than destruction and, further, that its leaders were statesmen and not, as Republicans and Democrats would have them believe, "cranks" or "anarchists."[43] Among diehard populists, such rhetoric risked sounding deferential if not milquetoast, while to moderates worried more about the specter of mass anarchism and violence than about the need for economic justice, it surely sounded unconvincing.

The day after the election, Donnelly expressed his disappointment with the statewide results to readers of *The Representative*, arguing that in choosing the Republicans, the people of Minnesota had all but guaranteed the continued rule of monopolies, higher interest rates, and unchecked government excesses. The cynical sage sounded a defeatist note, portraying his loss in Dakota County as the ultimate rebuke. Though the People's Party vote was the largest ever cast in Minnesota, the Republican Knute Nelson had won the race for governor. Dakota County had voted against Donnelly and for the Democrat Albert Schaller, and Donnelly couldn't help but feel chastened. Under the umbrella of his recurring column "A Word Personal," he wrote, "Well: a discriminating people, in our own county, have said they did not want us to work for them in the state senate for a pittance of compensation. We are thankful to them. They have relieved us from a vast amount of unrequited labor. We can now look after our own affairs." Perhaps the loss had been for the best; with a sixty-seat Republican majority in the legislature, populist reforms would continually be stymied, and rigorous investigations into monopolies would all but cease. Still, Donnelly couldn't help but be disappointed by the voters in his home state, where, for at least two years, he claimed, nothing would be done for the good of the people. And, he added, the people deserved it, and would suffer for it: "It is enough to shake one's faith in republican institutions to witness the antics of such an unreasonable mob, led by the nose by scoundrels." He blamed the Chicago and Milwaukee railroad interests for his defeat.

Referring to himself in the first-person plural, the Sage of Nininger told his readers, "We shall devote ourselves in the future to our lectures and our books; but for the good of man and the love of God we shall do our best for the cause of right and truth."[44] A week later, Donnelly resigned his presidency of the Minnesota Farmers' Alliance, suggesting that younger leadership would be needed to build the organization into a more formidable voting bloc. This sacrifice in turn produced another moment of rueful self-reflection, prompting the defeated politician to lament, "God seems to have decreed that I should never possess any high position, from which I could carry out my ideas for the good of the human family."[45]

As 1894 drew to a close, the pain of the lost election seemed to dim for Donnelly, who hoped to heal any ill will between the Farmers' Alliance and the People's Party. By late December he had begun looking forward to the presidential election of 1896, hoping to clear the air of any lingering resentments between populist factions. *The Representative* would not be autocratic or dictatorial, he promised: "Let us be patient and tolerant with all honest differences of opinion. . .. Do not conclude that, because a man looks at things differently than yourself, that he is necessarily a rogue, or a party to some conspiracy. He may be right and you may be wrong." No person, Donnelly reminded his readers, had a monopoly on wisdom. Instead he suggested that all of his readers throw their ideas into a pot and "boil them with the fires of discussion." Some good would come of it, he promised, pointing out by analogy that it was all but impossible to make flavorful soup out of a single ingredient.[46] On the other hand, he favored a People's Party with a strong sense of identity and purpose. He eschewed the grab-bag approach to political platforms overstuffed with pet causes. As an engine of reform, the People's Party platform, he said, should be "clean cut and definite" and must avoid becoming a "traveling menagerie" of special interests.[47] As a motto signifying a middle ground between the openness implied by a veritable soup of ideas and the built-in caution against a curio shop of mixed and conflicting causes, Donnelly landed on the tagline "Let us be radically right, but in all things reasonable." A political party, he insisted, must not become a "collection of fantastic *isms*."[48]

In addition to penning regular columns on populism and the People's Party for *The Representative*, Donnelly accepted an invitation from the publisher Laird & Lee in Chicago to write a novel of ideas arguing for economic relief via the monetization of silver. The commissioned book would be written using a similar technique to the one he had employed in *Caesar's Column* and *The Golden Bottle*, featuring didactic dialogue between fictional characters thrown together by circumstance. Donnelly's conflicted feelings on the monetization of silver likely explained his initial apathy at the prospect of writing the novel, as he believed that while a silver-gold standard—bimetallism—was better than a gold standard exclusively, neither was as good as an adequate supply of paper money printed and circulated by the US government.

As in his prior novels of ideas, in this latest one, titled *The American People's Money*, he created a plainspoken but strongly opinionated protagonist—in this case Hugh Sanders, a farmer from Shelby County, Illinois—as a mouthpiece for his personal and political convictions. The action opens with Hugh and James Hutchinson, a Chicago banker, sharing a sleeping car on a train bound from Chicago to California. Eager for conversation, and relieved to find that the man sharing his car is a salt-of-the-earth yeoman, Hutchinson asks his seatmate if he finds farming profitable. When Hugh quips that "society rewards the idler and punishes the toiler," the banker labels him a pessimist, and Hugh concedes that he is something of a "crank," if "crank" is taken to mean "a realist who believes that the world is in bad shape, and likely to grow worse."[49] Hutchinson, by contrast, is a capitalist and a cheerful proponent of social Darwinism. In their first encounter, Hugh speaks his populist creed at considerable length, while Hutchinson mostly listens. Agreeing to disagree on their first night together, the two men decide to pause their conversation with the intention of resuming the following morning.

Day two aboard the Chicago-to-Pacific overland finds Hugh Sanders energized by the clear continental air as the train reaches the High Plains. Here is a high-spirted people who are all but indomitable, he insists, and not likely to be enslaved by a future plutocracy that would return the human family to serfdom if it could. Even these self-sufficient yeomen, however, are susceptible to manipulations in currency. Hutchinson, the capitalist, claims that the amount of currency circulating in the United States is sufficient to maintain a middle-class standard of living, though when Hugh asks how he knows this to be true, he can reply only that the newspapers tell him it is so. Hugh bursts Hutchinson's balloon by pointing out that the wealthy who run the newspapers and the stock exchanges conspire to make the people believe that the supply of money is adequate, thereby falsely encouraging the farmers and laborers of the world to believe that their standard of living is as good as it can possibly be. He explains,

> Hence when it comes to establishing a daily newspaper, at a cost of a hundred thousand, or five hundred thousand dollars, the founders must be rich men. And if they go into such an enterprise it is to increase their wealth. And to do this the conditions which gave them their opportunities must be maintained; and hence the paper must oppose all reform measures that would protect the many from the exactions of the few. And the friends of one kind of oppression are compelled, necessarily, to unite with those of all other forms of oppression; and hence we have a gigantic power, undreamed of by our ancestors, which holds possession of all access to the brains and beliefs of the multitude, and is misleading them to their ruin.[50]

Hugh maintains that the reform impulse is consistently quashed by capitalist newspapermen who feed the lower classes only the information that is consistent with a perpetuation of the status quo. The free-thinking American who seeks the truth is left to read between the lines in books and pamphlets and the half-dozen or so weekly newspapers courageous enough to print the facts. After a lengthy diatribe in which Hugh claims that farmers are generally better versed in financial matters than urban dwellers, Hutchinson takes exception. If Hugh is so thoroughly discontented with the American status quo, the banker points out, he can vote and speak his mind in public and in the press. He and other reformers can band together, agitate, and expose the worst of crooked corporations. Hutchinson asserts that the United States is a great country precisely because of the enduring strength of its democratic ideals.

Hugh concedes the right to free speech, but assuming he was able to find space in the columns of capital-driven newspapers, what then? "Every argument I present is met by millions of printed lies so plausible, so ingenious, that only an expert can answer them," the contrarian farmer argues, adding, "and by the time I have swept away one falsehood, a hundred more, like the heads of a hydra, spring up in its place. The ingenuity of falsification is something unparalleled and appalling. The past history of the world, as I have said, furnishes nothing like it. What we call popular ignorance is simply universal newspaper deception."[51] Indeed, deception—the difference between what those in power would have the powerless believe and true reality—is the topic of the hour on the second day, and Hutchinson and Hugh Sanders continue their dialogue on the subject until the porter interrupts to announce that dinner is ready in the dining car.

Hutchinson assumes the farmer will be too tired to talk money and politics the following morning, but to his surprise, Hugh is as hale as ever. This time their conversation is interrupted by a young woman, Miss Bowman, who has been listening in. Her once middle-class family is destitute, and she is on her way to California to seek work as a teacher in order not to burden her mother and father back home in the Midwest. Why is it, she wonders, that the earth continues to produce, and yet those who labor on it, and from it, cannot seem to earn a living from its wealth? This bright young woman, an economic refugee of sorts, wants to know the deeper source of these inequities, and Hugh is glad to enlighten her, explaining that there are two basic forces acting on human nature: a centripetal force of selfishness that draws everything to the individual, and a centrifugal force, which he names as philanthropy, that reaches outward to the masses. And it is by the interaction of these essential forces that human society advances. At present, Hugh explains, there is too much self-centered centripetal force and not enough concern for one's fellow man. Referencing Darwinian theory, the farmer insists that it is the "hog in human nature" that makes them greedy, wanton, and willfully blind to the struggles of their fellow citizens.[52] The plutocrat is the most hoglike of all, because of his penchant for eating everything around him, monopolizing it, and claiming it as his exclusive right and domain. Look around, the contrarian farmer urges, and it's easy to see the hog-nature of greedy humans even on a train. Hugh paints the picture:

> He puts his overcoat and umbrella in two seats across the aisle, and then he will tell the weary travelers who contemplate sitting down, that the two gentlemen who own the coat and umbrella have just stepped out, and will be back in a minute. He gets in early, unlocks one of the seats and turns it over, and spreads himself and bundles over four places, his noble endowment of feet distributed widely over two of them, while he pretends to go to sleep with his head next to the window on a pile of valises, presenting the most difficult part of his person for an interview to those who have paid just as much for their passage as he has. And out of the corner of his eye he enjoys the sight of the crowd in the aisle—the pale woman with a child in her arms, the gray-haired

> old man, and all the rest; their misery is a kind of Worcestershire sauce to the palate of his enjoyment; he tastes it all the way down to his very boots.[53]

The young lady is appalled by the idea of man as beast, though the banker reassures her that Hugh is speaking in metaphors. And as the yeoman continues, comparing society to a rail car and the brakeman to the arbiter of a just social order, it becomes increasingly evident that Hugh's message is allegorical:

> No one passenger has any more rights than another. We are all God's poor children. Each is entitled to a place and a seat at the dining table. We have paid our way by being human. But the vehicle is all in confusion now. The hogs have seized ten times as much space and food as they are entitled to, and thousands are standing and hungry. And the aggressors have hired a multitude of the idle and vicious to defend them with weapons, in their unjust possessions; and they have bribed the brakemen, and they do not see the protruding, offensive corporosity, or the poor, tired passengers. And the earth spins through space, while groans and cries and piteous appeals go up to God; and it is enfolded in misery as in a bloody garment.[54]

By the fourth and final day on the train, Hugh's case crescendos as he grows more convinced of the rightness of his arguments. The contrary farmer makes his case for the monetization of silver to stand alongside gold and for the graduated income tax as the most fair and just method of taxation. Still, for all its attention to economic justice, Miss Bowman observes, the farmer's worldview is essentially gloomy. Hugh concedes that the predicament of the country is indeed dark, and he posits that the republic has never been in greater peril. He offers his fellow travelers a brief history, albeit an impressionistic one:

> In the last hundred years the resources of this land have been turned into colossal fortunes, which have concentrated in the hands of those who did not produce them; and they are laboring with demoniacal industry and ingenuity to destroy our magnificent free institutions and reduce the common people to European conditions. They do not understand that the American citizen is the old world peasant plus generations of training in liberty—he is a new product; nothing just like him has ever been seen before

> on the face of the earth. He is slow to comprehend the trend of affairs; he can be cajoled through his prejudices and party fanaticism, but when at last it becomes plain, even to his unsuspicious mind, that he is being enslaved, and that his children are to be held in bondage forever, there will come an outburst like the breaking forth of wild beasts.[55]

US citizens, Hugh contends, must be given more control over the wealth of the products they produce, must be able to borrow money at a fair rate of interest, and must have access to an adequate supply of money to buy necessary goods at prices that are reasonably stable and affordable. Bringing his days-long lecture to a conclusion, he asserts that he and his newfound friends must stop arguing over the details and dare to choose between two very different paths forward, one leading to a dark night and the other to a brighter day. The farmer outlines the two diverging roads facing the American people: "The one leads us back into the horrors of the past—irresponsible masters—kingship—the rulers brutes—the people serfs—the bayonet of greed at the throat of the thinker—humanity prostrate, degraded, helpless." The other policy, he assures his fellow train travelers, "points toward the dawn of the world's perfect morning—universal prosperity; universal happiness; no violence . . . no intolerance; no darkened minds; no broken hearts; labor no longer starving, and idleness gorging; but peace, plenty, equal opportunity and fair play over all the earth."[56]

Written at the behest of a publisher to meet market demand, *The American People's Money* exhibits Donnelly's trademark eloquence but lacks the depth, literary style, and extensive if not melodramatic plotting of *Caesar's Column*, *Doctor Huguet*, and *The Golden Bottle*. Written in approximately one month, the book is considerably shorter than its more literary predecessors, though its brevity was designed to enhance its appeal. Though the volume was not widely reviewed in the literary press, it was published in an affordable twenty-five-cent edition and at times sold at a rate comparable to other popular treatises on the subject, such as W. H. Harvey's *Coin's Financial School*. Despite the brevity of the book, Donnelly followed a proven formula in its composition. As he had with his entire oeuvre beginning with *Atlantis*, he patterned it after an already successful title well established in the marketplace. For *The American People's Money*, Donnelly could look to *Coin's Financial School* as a precedent for the American public's thirst for populist tracts taking greedy capitalists to task.[57]

Especially in rural areas, the public hungered for literature to help them combat mounting debts, exorbitant interest rates, and the ever-expanding role of trusts and monopolies. "Every crank in the country is loose and nothing less than a stone wall will stop them," a newspaper editor in Kentucky observed, adding that politics had gone mad.[58] In Indiana, the populist fervor was similar, Kennesaw Landis reported, testifying that otherwise sane family members had gone "utterly wild on the money question."[59] By April 1894, *Coin's Financial School* was considered a must read, selling for twenty-five cents at just about every rail depot and cigar store in the nation's hinterlands. By the time Donnelly's book came along in 1895, *Coin's Financial School* had, by its author's conservative accounting, sold in excess of 400,000 copies in its first twelve months on the market and drawn the attention of the populist icon William Jennings Bryan, who claimed that "no book in recent times has produced so great an effect on the economic question."[60] Donnelly's publisher, Laird & Lee, hoped to capitalize on the financial literacy trend while going it one better. Barely into his forties at the time his phenomenal book was published, and with no experience as an elected official, W. H. "Coin" Harvey lacked Donnelly's gravitas, track record as an established author, and years of public service. While Laird & Lee hoped it could reproduce the success Donnelly enjoyed with *Caesar's Column* and *The Golden Bottle* as People's Party campaign literature, it was Harvey's book that, in the end, served as an unlikely campaign accompaniment, with 125,000 copies purchased by the National Silver Party for the election of 1896.

Still, *The American People's Money* helped solidify Donnelly's standing with Bryan, whom the People's Party had nominated as its candidate for president for 1896. Traveling to Lincoln, Nebraska, for the party's celebration of Bryan's nomination, Donnelly earned a personal audience with the candidate, coming away impressed with the Nebraskan's wisdom and stamina. Among the topics of the Donnelly-Bryan conference was the possibility of a cabinet post for Donnelly, who refused to get his hopes up, having heard similar promises before.[61] Two weeks after his conference with Bryan, however, Donnelly's support paid a lesser dividend, as the Democratic Party, which had likewise nominated Bryan, commissioned the Sage of Nininger to make paid speeches for him in midwestern battleground states such as Illinois, Kansas, and Missouri. Sensing a new opportunity for outreach and sales, Donnelly's publisher in Chicago cleverly reissued *The American's People's Money* with a new title, *The Bryan Campaign for the American People's Money*, and a newly added brief campaign biography, written by Donnelly and subtitled "Portrait, Platform, and Famous Speech of William J. Bryan." Despite Bryan's prominence in the title, the election-year edition, published in 1896, dedicated only 25 pages to the candidate's biography and speeches while reserving more than 150 pages for a lightly revised edition of Donnelly's *The American People's Money*.

The new edition of the volume represented an opportunity for Donnelly and his publisher to ride Bryan's considerable coattails. The reissued book also added, however modestly, to Donnelly's personal platform as he campaigned for Bryan outside Minnesota's borders, though he did follow Bryan on the stump at campaign rallies in St. Paul, where he and Bryan spoke to crowds numbering in the tens of thousands.[62] Donnelly accepted joint nominations from the People's Party and the Democratic Party to run for the state legislature in his home district, though this time he made clear to his supporters that he was obligated at Bryan rallies throughout the Midwest and would seldom stump at home in Dakota County.

On Election Day, Donnelly's regional advocacy for the People's Party–Democratic fusion candidates yielded impressive results in Kansas and in other midwestern states where he had campaigned, but in Minnesota they were not sufficient to help Bryan over the hump of entrenched Republicanism. While Donnelly won his race for the Minnesota House as a People's Party candidate, nearly doubling the vote totals of his Republican foe, C. F. Staples, the news of Bryan's defeat in his home state left little to celebrate, as he viewed Bryan's candidacy as a once-in-a-lifetime chance at meaningful social and economic reform. Despite a vigorous campaign and an ongoing recession, "the bankrupt millions," Donnelly complained, had "voted to keep the yoke on their own necks" by voting for the Republican, William McKinley.[63] No doubt alluding to the species-ending cataclysm described in *Ragnarok*, he opined, "It is well that a few specimen Populists should survive, so that the people may know what the breed looked like." As he looked ahead, Donnelly admitted that his fellow Populists in 1896 were, for the time being, becoming dinosaurs, and he conceded that the members of the People's Party were "not reforming the world as much" as they thought they were, since there were still far too many "fools and traitors."[64] Outnumbered by Republicans nearly four to one in the Minnesota statehouse, third-party reformers would no longer pose much of a threat to the political status quo, as they now held "little power." Populists throughout the state had been knocked on their backs, and it remained to be seen whether they would ever "get on [their] feet again." The trusts and monopolies would be emboldened, Donnelly knew, and the cause of reform would be stifled. Still, he assured the loyal readers of *The Representative*, as well as his Dakota County constituents, that some small good would still be possible.[65]

As the new legislative session commenced in January 1897, it seemed to the *Minneapolis Tribune* that a calmer, gentler Donnelly, one who returned fire only when provoked, had entered the chambers in place of the firebrand. But the calm, it reported, broke "in a most unexpected manner, like a cloudburst on the prairie," as he recovered his old fighting form to contest a proposal made by the chair of the Committee of the Elections, the Republican H. G. Hicks, who proposed that his committee be given new powers to determine which duly elected members of the House could be seated and which could not. Donnelly strenuously objected, smelling a rat. "It was a reminder of the days when Donnelly walked about with a perpetual club on his shoulder," the newspaper noted with a hint of nostalgia, "and when his meat and drink was warfare." The aging sage had had the better of the fight, it declared, so much so that even the leading Republicans lined up to shake his hand once the Hicks motion had withered. This time Donnelly had won a political battle not with clever insults and rhetorical flourishes but by deferring to the wisdom with which many seasons had imbued him. "Mr. Donnelly had acted with the modesty and circumspection due to a realization that life is but a fleeting show," the paper surmised, "and that soon he, like all great and good of ages past, must lay him down to his last sleep, leaving posterity to give him his rightful place in history."[66]

The headline generated by the conflict—"Sage and Judge Cross Swords!"—connoted high drama, though Donnelly had entered the fray reluctantly, expressing his regret that "any personal matter had been allowed to creep into the discussion." While he worried aloud that Hicks sought new autocratic powers for the purpose of self-aggrandizement and control, he conceded that he had resolved to play a more modest part in legislative drama. "I have no ambition for the future," he explained to his colleagues from the House floor, "except . . . in connection with literature. I shall try to do what is right and best for the state and its people." The reporter covering the statehouse for the *Tribune* approved of Donnelly's new ethos, remarking that the statesman had been "singularly free from the egotism that has marked his earlier career" and adding that "his conduct has won him a place in the hearts of the opposition which his experience and ability entitle him to."[67]

The state's newspaper editors weighed in gleefully with opinions adamantly for and vehemently against the latest comeback of their lightning-rod lawmaker. In February, the *St. Paul Globe* devoted more than half a broadsheet page to a roundup of Donnelly takes from around the Gopher State. The *Wahpeton Times* cheered his evolution, declaring, "Let 'em [Donnelly detractors] wink and wallow. Ignatius Donnelly is 'getting there' faster and better than any other man in Minnesota to-day. And richly does he deserve his award." The *New Richmond North Star* agreed, singling out the Sage of Nininger as a "leading light" and the "nemesis of the monopolists," while the *St. Peter Herald* called him a "man of genius" and "a giant among small men." Other outlets were not so kind. The *Pine City Pioneer* predicted that the verbose legislator would soon talk himself to the end of his rope, and then, it said, "off goes Donnelly's head." The man in the statehouse, it added, was a mere apparition, while the real thing could be found "still at Nininger, poring over Shakespeare." The *Owatonna Journal and Herald*, meanwhile, called Donnelly a "demagogue," warning readers to beware his mischievous ways; before the session was through, even his allies in the House would, they claimed, find his rule "tyrannical and distasteful." The *Verndale Journal* even attacked his homespun wit, calling out his "senseless humor" and "pointless garrulity" while he posed as a "champion of the people." The *Journal* summed it up thusly: "He seems to believe ceaseless babble will save the state."[68]

The skeptics at the *Janesville Argus*, who had warned readers that Donnelly could never "bridle his tongue," were surely unsurprised when his newfound composure broke not so many weeks into the new session.[69] The pomp surrounding the inauguration of the victorious Republican, William McKinley, couldn't help but raise Donnelly's old ire. When the Minnesota legislature put the people's business aside for a full day for speeches proclaiming the greatness of McKinley, Donnelly the contrarian once again bucked the trend, marking the occasion with a long speech railing against the greed and corruption of McKinley's predecessor in office, Grover Cleveland, who, he said, had come to the presidency a poor man and left a millionaire. Many saw Donnelly's denunciation of Cleveland as utterly tone-deaf—yet another example of his inability to see beyond a man's faults and play nice, at least for a day. Some Twin Cities observers condemned the timing of a speech delivered on what was to have been a day of celebration, but the *St. Paul*

Globe defended Donnelly's character, conceding as it did that it had differed with Donnelly on many measures he had advocated. But, the newspaper pointed out, "that does not prevent us from recognizing Mr. Donnelly's superior intellectual worth. Nor, simply because we differ with a man on public questions, are we justified in attempting to strike him down. . .. There is well-settled popular conviction that on the issues over which the legislature quarreled with Mr. Donnelly he was nearer right than the legislature." Donnelly was more popular than ever, the *Globe* allowed, "a bigger man today in the estimation of the people of Minnesota than he was before the legislature convened. And the people who have been crowing over Donnelly's downfall have really crowed before they got out of the woods." The idea that he was, or soon would be, "a political corpse" was simply an "unwarranted delusion."[70]

Donnelly's longtime foes at the *Pioneer Press* took strong exception to his lack of decorum, calling him a dog while dredging up outdated, discredited charges against him.[71] True to form, Donnelly sued the St. Paul paper a second time for libel, and once more, the paper hired Judge Charles Flandrau to take Donnelly down. This time, Flandrau, representing the defense, sent out five hundred letters soliciting dirt on the plaintiff. But the scheme backfired, and the attorney was able to turn up only the flimsiest of evidence; Donnelly's bitter political enemies, including Michael Doran, were subpoenaed but, according to *The Representative*, refused to implicate Donnelly in any bribes to or from the Democratic Party. Energized by the conflict with an old nemesis, Donnelly took to the pages of *The Representative* with renewed vigor, saying that even a repeat performance of a $1 jury decision in his favor would make him feel vindicated. With the cost of operating his newspaper draining his coffers, Donnelly turned to his son Stan, a Twin Cities attorney, for legal representation, and by all accounts he performed admirably, earning his father $1,000 in damages and court costs. The elder Donnelly couldn't help but gloat a bit in his column of June 30, 1897, quipping that the *Pioneer Press* had had to pay dearly for the "luxury of calling a gentleman a dog."[72]

With his second *Pioneer Press* libel suit successfully won, and with a modest monetary award with which to buttress his shaky finances, Donnelly returned to work on a manuscript with which he had long teased the reading public: a sequel to *The Great Cryptogram*. In this endeavor he now had a new cheerleader and collaborator, Marion Olive Hanson, a stenographer who had worked for Donnelly at *The Representative* in the years after Kate Donnelly's passing. Hanson was a spirited advocate of the Shakespearean cipher and had spent several months in Nininger City helping Donnelly with his manuscripts. Though Donnelly admitted in his diary to missing Kate profoundly, he also expressed reluctance at resigning himself to a lonely widower's life in Nininger City.[73] Still, any union between the aging, Catholic-reared Donnelly and the young Norwegian Methodist Hanson stood to damage Donnelly's good standing with the Irish Catholic community in the Twin Cities, who had supported many of his successful political campaigns. It also threatened to alienate Donnelly from his three adult children, who remained loyal to their deceased mother and viewed Hanson as interested mostly in their father's estate. Further complicating the family dynamics, Donnelly's eldest son, Dr. Ignatius C. Donnelly, long troubled by tax debts, had recently married and relocated to Butte, Montana.

On January 4, the *Superior Times* in Wisconsin joined newspapers across the region in announcing that Donnelly, variously described as the "well-known Populist leader," "famous . . . author of many popular books," and "upholder of the Baconian authorship of the Shakespeare works," would soon remarry.[74] The engagement of the sixty-six-year-old Donnelly and the twenty-one-year-old Hanson generated page-one headlines across the country, including "He Is Old and She Is Young" and "Ignatius Donnelly to Marry His Pretty Stenographer." In Dayton, Ohio, the *Herald* reported that their courtship was the "topic of conversation in social, literary, and political circles of the Twin Cities" and that Donnelly's children were "not at all satisfied with the choice their father has made."[75] In populist-friendly Kansas, the *Free Press* spun the news differently; under a headline describing the "wise wooing of a Sage," the paper reprinted a piece from the *New York World* insisting that the author-politician had married a "true companion" and "helpmeet" when he might instead have made the mistake of hitching himself to a vapid society girl likely to be unhappy with his rural lifestyle. Hanson, the article insisted, aided his work with "intelligent sympathy, suggestion, and criticism." If Donnelly hadn't already earned the title "Sage of Nininger" by virtue of his literary prowess, the *Free Press* added, he would surely have done so with his marital wisdom.[76]

In Utah, the conservative *Salt Lake Tribune* poked fun by curating the national headlines generated by the unlikely union, reprinting them under the punny umbrella title "A Populist Fusion." The *Tribune* led with what it considered an especially choice send-up from the *Council Bluffs Nonpareil* in Iowa, which mused, "Ignatius Donnelly is now ciphering on how 66 plus 21 are to 1." Elsewhere, editors viewed the unlikely coupling as an occasion for bitter irony. The *Chicago Times-Herald* suggested that Donnelly should check his marriage license to see if it contained a cipher revealing its issuer as Francis Bacon. The *New York Press* cautioned that if marriage was a lottery, then Marion Hanson had surely married a cipher of a man. And in perhaps the most ostensibly magnanimous, and at the same time biting, news item published on the impending nuptials, the *Lincoln Journal* in Nebraska observed that if the "young miss" could succeed in convincing the stubborn Ignatius that "an old Pedant like Lord Bacon could not have written the plays of young William Shakespeare," then the newspaper would withdraw any objections to their matrimony.[77]

In Minneapolis–St. Paul, newspapers treated the coming marriage of the famous Sage of Nininger and the hometown girl Hanson with a sincerely celebratory tone. With its four daily editions, the *Minneapolis Tribune* broke the news to Twin Cities readers under the whimsical summary headline "Cupid Sends an Arrow with Unerring Aim at the Heart of the Great Shakespearean Student."[78] It had been the intention of the couple to keep the engagement a secret, the *Tribune* reported, but the news had leaked at a New Year's Eve party, and, when asked for confirmation by the newspapers, neither Donnelly nor Hanson had denied it. News of the nuptials put Donnelly's newspaper, *The Representative*, in a supremely awkward position, one it registered in the sheepish headline "It Must Be True . . . We Read It in All the Newspapers and *The Representative* Blushes Confirmation."[79] The paper's assistant editor, E. A. Twitchell, took charge of the coverage, opting to deal with the obvious challenge to journalistic objectivity by primarily reprinting coverage from other Twin Cities newspapers.

Twitchell turned to the *Minneapolis Journal*, which had secured a quote from the bride-to-be, for the full scoop. "I didn't answer immediately," Hanson replied when asked about the proposal. "I turned the matter over in my mind for some time. My parents offered no objections: in fact, they thought I was chiefly interested and I should be left to make up my own mind." For Donnelly's response, Twitchell turned to the *St. Paul Dispatch*, to which Donnelly had offered his regrets that the marriage announcement had been leaked prematurely, though he was pleased to confirm that the scoop was indeed true. Asked for details about his fiancée, Donnelly told the *Dispatch*, "She is a young woman of the most elevated character, literary in her turn of mind, educated, and comes from a fine old family." He informed the paper that the wedding, which would occur by the end of February, would be modest. Twitchell closed his article on the impending matrimony with his fervent hope that Hanson would be an asset to the populist movement, imagining her as "a queenly populist Joan D' Arc leading our forces to victory" and adding, "We express hope that this union of forces now proposed may be to the best interests of our cause, to the highest welfare of our party, to the credit of Miss Marion Hanson, to the honor of Ignatius Donnelly and to the long and uninterrupted happiness of both."[80]

Donnelly accepted the jokes and jocular congratulations stoically, but to his personal diary he divulged his enduring love for his first wife, Kate, and the persistent loneliness he had felt since her passing. "I revere the memory of my dear dead wife," he confessed, "but life is very lonely for me . . . and I shrink from the loneliness of a companionless existence. I am not moved by sensual considerations but by the hollowness of the heart—the yawning abyss of solitariness."[81]

The joyous wedding that February proved to be only a temporary reprieve from the difficulties that had lately stalked his family. Just a few short weeks after the ceremony, Donnelly's son-in-law, George Giltinan, contracted meningitis, and by July he was dead at forty-six.[82] Giltinan had grown up in Donnelly's hometown of Philadelphia, and his supportive father-in-law had helped him win election as the auditor of Stevens County, Minnesota. The disease had struck almost without warning, and the end had been swift, leaving Donnelly to bury a son-in-law, console his widowed daughter, Mary, and consider anew his own omnipresent mortality.

CHAPTER 10

The Cipher in the Plays, and on the Tombstone

News of the Donnelly-Hanson union made heavenly fodder for newspaper editors, not just for the obvious wordplay and delicious irony the unlikely coupling invoked but because it confirmed that Donnelly's long-awaited sequel to *The Great Cryptogram* would soon become a reality. Indeed, in breaking news of the union, the *Minneapolis Tribune* trumpeted, "The famous cryptogram which had brought him worldwide renown, now brings him a wife—it was while working on a revised edition that the tale of love was first told."[1]

In its edition of November 9, 1899, *The Representative* teased the forthcoming release with the headline "Donnelly's Cipher Again" and the subheadline "Startling Theory of the 'Sage of Nininger.'" A full three columns in length, the article used unusually exuberant language that sounded more like an advertisement for a swashbuckling romance than for a sober investigation of Shakespearean authorship. It wondered whether Donnelly had "read aright the riddle" to "make the sphinx speak, that all who listen may learn."[2]

Sensitive to ridicule and prone to striking back at his critics, Donnelly had never quite recovered from the humiliation he had suffered at the hands of reviewers who panned *The Great Cryptogram*. After the preponderance of scholars and editors dismissed his thousand-page work as presumptuous if not hasty, he resolved to return to the cipher. Off and on for more than a decade, he had labored to find the key to the Baconian message hidden in Shakespeare's work but had fallen short of a complete cracking of the code. His latest effort, the sum of more than an additional decade of fitful literary labors, would focus on a new angle in the centuries-old controversy, one he hoped would be more comprehensible to the general public. Building on a theory proposed by Hugh Black in the *North American Review* in 1887, he hoped to prove that the curious inscription on Shakespeare's tombstone in Stratford could be decoded as further proof of Francis Bacon's authorship. Inspired by Donnelly's original tract in the *North American Review* on the subject of a Baconian cipher, Black, writing from Ontario, had added his own twist to the argument, claiming that Shakespeare's peculiar epitaph was a bilateral cipher in which Bacon revealed his authorship to the world. Donnelly includes the epitaph on the title page of his book, *The Cipher in the Plays, and on the Tombstone*, preserving the original telltale mix of lowercase and capital letters:

> Good friend for Jesus SAKE Forbeare
> To diGG T-E Dust Enclos-Ased HE.Re.
> Blese be T-E Man $\overset{\text{T}}{\text{Y}}$ Spares T-Es Stones
> And curst be He $\overset{\text{T}}{\text{Y}}$ Moves my Bones.

Both Donnelly and Black recognized that the curious comingling of two sets of different kinds of letters—lower- and uppercase mixed with roman and italic type—potentially signified the presence of the bilateral cipher alphabet developed by Bacon in *De Augmentis Scientiarum*. Using Bacon's cipher alphabet, Black had been able to make from the epitaph the word "Shaxpere" and the "suggestive parts" of five additional words, "Fra Ba wrt ear ya," which, if completed, could read "Francis Bacon wrote Shakespeare's Plays."[3]

Dedicating his latest literary effort to his new wife, Marion, Donnelly begins *The Cipher in the Plays, and on the Tombstone* with a spirited defense of Black's scholarly contribution as "the first man, in the space of two hundred and seventy-one years who had perceived a relationship between Bacon's cipher and the inscription on Shakespeare's tombstone at Stratford."[4] Black's article, however, had been immediately and wrongfully discredited, Donnelly informs his reader, because Black's detractors claimed that the Shakespeare tombstone contained no such distinctive combination of letters; therefore there could be no such clandestine meaning. In his book, Donnelly resolves the apparent incongruity by insisting that Black is right, and that the present-day tombstone is a replacement for the original one documented by Charles Knight in his 1842 monograph *A Biography of William Shakespeare* and later by the Shakespeare scholars Edmund Malone and George Stevens. The gravestone originally inscribed after Shakespeare's death, and not the replacement that later amended some of the unorthodox typography, spelling, and syntax, must be regarded as the original source.

As much as Donnelly hoped to build on the case made in the *North American Review* article, he judged Black's otherwise enticing conclusions unsatisfactory in two key areas: first, Black's decoding of the original gravestone inscription did not yield a complete sentence, and, second, the Bard was not known to have spelled his name "Shaxpere."[5] Donnelly thus begins his own investigation with the intention of not only deriving the complete words "Shakespeare" and "Francis Bacon" from the curious text on the original tombstone but also making a complete grammatical sentence of its hidden message. Using the unorthodox dashes and periods in addition to the unique combinations of capital and lowercase letters, as well as cipher rules similar to those deployed in *The Great Cryptogram*, he is able to produce a sentence that names Bacon not only as the author of Shakespeare's plays but also as the real author of the works of Shakespeare's contemporaries Christopher Marlowe and Robert Greene.

In declaring the deciphered words on the original tombstone to read, "FRANCIS BACON WROTE THE GREENE, MARLOWE AND SHAKESPEARE PLAYES,"[6] Donnelly was said to have gone too far, even in the eyes of many of his supporters, who claimed that the Sage of Nininger's long-standing infatuation with Lord Verulam had created a scholarship of wish fulfillment. Potential publishers, including Sampson Low & Company, which had previously produced editions of Donnelly's work in England, balked at associating their name with his latest work in progress,.[7] Having worked on his sequel to *The Great Cryptogram* for close to a decade, Donnelly arranged to have the book published privately under the name Verulam Publishing Company. In his preface, he acknowledges that the arithmetical basis of the Shakespearean cipher likely would not satisfy readers of romance novels, but he insists that the secret stores of history, biography, poetry, and philosophy "buried by Francis Bacon in the thousand pages of the Shakespeare Folio, of 1623, are . . . the greatest treasure in the world, more precious than all the jewels of Aladdin."[8]

While part 1 of the book works out for the reader the complicated mathematical and syntactical machinery by which the cipher on the tombstone is revealed, the final section, in which Donnelly recounts his personal visits to Shakespeare's grave in Stratford and Bacon's tomb in St. Albans, reads more like a literary adventure narrative. In the chapter entitled "The Present Custodians of the Cipher," Donnelly calls for further investigation of Shakespeare's grave for the possibility that it might contain the original manuscripts of the plays and proof of Bacon's authorship sealed within a watertight casket.[9] Why, the author wonders, was a stone placed over the grave that would invoke curses on anyone who might disturb the Bard's bones in the future? He echoes calls he had made on his earlier trip to London to open the grave. "Our reasoning may be fallacious," he concedes, "and there may be nothing in Shakespeare's grave but dust and ashes; but at least it will cost little of time or means to make the investigation."[10]

In the final pages of *The Cipher in the Plays, and on the Tombstone*, he recounts his own on-site investigation of Bacon's tomb in St. Albans. He confesses that he made repeated visits to St. Michael's Church while in England, taking along with him a pocket compass. He puzzles over the curious results he achieved: the needle had pointed to magnetic north when in the churchyard, but inside the church itself it had mysteriously deviated to point directly at Francis Bacon's monument. He concludes that a large amount of iron must be buried in close proximity to the grave of the great statesman—very likely a metal chest. Next, he talks with the sexton of St. Michael's, who reveals to him that Bacon's statue had been previously toppled by trespassers lacking a clear motive for their ransacking, as the statue was far too large and too well known to be removed and sold. From this Donnelly infers that the burglars had cause to look for something they could carry away, some priceless artifact near or in the monument itself—perhaps a written declaration or message hidden deep inside the statue.[11] If anyone possessed the gravitas to solve such a literary mystery, it would be the Sage of Nininger, *The Representative* insisted, a man who in the search for truth had "searched the libraries of the world" and "patiently borne the mockery of the skeptics." Always, the newspaper noted, he had persisted in the face of considerable doubt, devoting his studies to the "hidden, the unseen, the murky details of semi-civilized age."[12]

By late December, however, even *The Representative* had to acknowledge that *The Cipher in the Plays, and on the Tombstone* would have limited commercial appeal, conceding that the country was simply too busy to "accord the new book by Ignatius Donnelly . . . that full recognition which is its just due."[13] In England, Donnelly's latest attempt to knock the Bard from his pedestal was met with dry wit bordering on derision, with *The Era* in London noting, "Busy man, Mr. Bacon, the hardest-worked Chancellor England ever possessed, yet he found time to write about fifty plays. . . . Little did Shakespeare dream that his bones would be such a cause of contention!"[14] While a relatively small number of Shakespeare critics and scholars would buy the book in the United States and in England, the volume's appeal would be lost on the casual reader. In a lengthy interview given the *Tribune* and reprinted in *The Representative*, Donnelly insisted that his latest work was "meeting generally with a kind reception" and "selling rapidly." While he predicted that his findings would "spread all over the country and over the world," he followed his rather grandiose statement with a more modest request that skeptics first read his work before casting judgment.[15]

Indeed, even as Donnelly promulgated his would-be discovery of a cipher on the tombstone, the tide was turning against the Baconian theory, as new methods of analysis turned up additional candidates for Shakespearean authorship. As Donnelly doubled down on Bacon, T. C. Mendenhall worked out what he called "a mechanical solution of a literary problem" for publication in *Popular Science Monthly*. Counting, classifying, and graphing approximately four hundred thousand words from the Shakespeare plays and about two hundred thousand words from various works penned by Bacon, Mendenhall found that, when graphed, the style used—including, for example, word length and frequency—produced a characteristic "curve" for each author.[16] The telltale curves of Shakespeare and Bacon differed sufficiently as to cast doubt on the Baconian theory, while the strikingly similar graphs of Shakespeare's and Marlowe's styles suggested "something akin to a sensation. . .. Here was a man to whom it has always been acknowledged, Shakespeare was deeply indebted; one of whom able critics have declared that he 'might have written the plays of Shakespeare.'" Mendenhall concluded that "Christopher Marlowe agrees with Shakespeare as much as Shakespeare agrees with himself." He left room, however, for the possibility that a writer gifted with a chameleonlike ability for stylistic imitation could alter his style sufficiently to produce the sort of match likely to throw his pursuers off the scent.[17]

When Donnelly darkly joked that his nomination as the People's Party choice for vice president of the United States would at least make for good advertising for his books, he was only partially kidding. By late 1898 the once unified People Party's had split into two rival factions, with Donnelly accepting a nomination to run on the "Mid-Road" People's Party ticket alongside Wharton Barker. If the unthinkable should happen and the Barker-Donnelly ticket should prevail against both the Democrat nominee, William Jennings Bryan, and the incumbent Republican, William McKinley, Donnelly would earn his highest public office to date—a just reward for years of loyal public service. In fact, *The Representative* noted that at the Cincinnati convention, Donnelly had tallied just eleven votes fewer than Wharton Barker in the nominating vote for the presidency, prompting the newspaper to remark, "It would certainly have been an honor for Minnesota if it had secured the presidential nomination."[18] The allure of Donnelly as a potential presidential candidate had persisted for nearly a decade, as the *Great West* and other pro-Donnelly newspapers dutifully reprinted national news articles extolling the Sage of Nininger's unique fitness for the office, including from *The Sun* in New York City, which had declared in 1891, "Ignatius Donnelly may yet be a presidential candidate." The lesser politicians of the Farmers' Alliance had yet to find their national standard-bearer, *The Sun* had duly noted, suggesting that it would not take them long to recognize the genius of Ignatius Donnelly as presidential material.[19]

On paper Barker and Donnelly looked like a complementary team: both men had edited newspapers, both were erstwhile Republicans, both had written books decrying the gold standard, both had made national reputations as writers, and both had been born in Philadelphia. Barker was believed to be in a position to self-fund much of the campaign, while Donnelly brought political skill, persuasive charm, and personal charisma to the stump. No longer a state legislator, Donnelly relied on a modest lecturing income and book royalties to keep food on the table. Like Barker, he had previously parted ways with both major parties. He blamed the Democrats for purposely fracturing the People's Party, and he blamed the Republicans, and McKinley, for costly imperialist wars in Cuba and the Philippines. Moreover, he agreed with the national Populist Party stance that blamed the McKinley administration for its refusal to condemn, in no uncertain terms, alleged US war crimes in the Philippines.[20]

Absent the saber-rattling jingoism that many Americans mistook for pure patriotism, Donnelly and Barker's candidacy lacked mass appeal from the start, and it quickly ran into financial difficulty when Barker's personal wealth turned out to be insufficient to make up the fundraising gap between the Mid-Road Populist ticket and those of the major political parties. In May 1899, the Mid-Road People's Party held yet another gathering, during which it was speculated that the underperforming Barker might lose the party endorsement. Ultimately the rumors proved unfounded, and the delegates chose to retain the Barker-Donnelly ticket in a referendum.[21]

In late April 1900, Donnelly and his wife, Marion, agreed to a lengthy campaign interview with the *Kansas City Star*. Headlined "The Iconoclast's Life Work," with the subheadline "Ignatius Donnelly, Who Would Destroy the Idol of Literature," the full-page write-up promised to focus on Donnelly's decades of work cracking the Shakespearean cipher. Unsurprisingly, however, the conversation ranged widely, touching on his vice presidential nomination and his ongoing editorship of *The Representative*. "Ignatius Donnelly is one of the most remarkable men of the century," declared the *Star*. "He has been ridiculed and reviled, even threatened . . . but Ignatius Donnelly is one of the men who have the courage of their convictions. He is an iconoclast, and doesn't care what the world thinks of it." Politics, the *Star* noted, was only a "side issue" for the versatile and multitalented Sage of Nininger, who, when asked about his future plans, quipped, "I expect to keep working for Bacon."[22]

A mere few weeks after telling the *Star* he would be working for Bacon, an indignant Donnelly, hackles raised, addressed a gathering of what one British newspaper called, with something of a sneer, "a national convention of Irreconcilable Populists." Riling up the party faithful, Donnelly argued for the secession of his Mid-Road party from the fusionists who jointly nominated the Democrat Bryan. "I feel this is the re-birth of the People's Party," he declared, "with the vermin scraped off."[23]

The long campaign season of 1900 was supposed to have been a boon for the People's Party, giving it ample time to fundraise and to consolidate splinter factions under a common banner. But as the presidential race advanced into the summer, interest in Barker, already lukewarm, waned further, while Donnelly—the ageless campaigner—felt his health begin to slip. By July he experienced difficulty walking, and the stump speeches in the summer heat that had once been his bailiwick became fraught with anxiety. To his diary he expressed embarrassment over an Independence Day rally that had gone badly. For the first time in his life, he wrote, he found himself addled and confused on the stage.[24] What was initially diagnosed as a form of heat exhaustion was later determined to be a mild stroke. The diagnosis, confirmed by Donnelly's physician son, meant that the candidate would not be able to make speeches in the final months leading to the November election. Donnelly offered, without success, to withdraw his name from the ticket.

Results of the presidential election on November 6, 1900, disappointed even the most sanguine of populists, as the Barker-Donnelly ticket managed to earn just over fifty thousand votes nationally—less than half a percent of the national vote. Both the Prohibition Party and the Social Democratic Party outpaced the Populists, as the William McKinley–Theodore Roosevelt ticket prevailed. Regretful, Donnelly observed in his diary that only his stroke had prevented him from making "the whole U.S. ring with my appeals for the Mid-Road ticket."[25] Instead he had stayed close to home that autumn, leaving Nininger once a week for a trip into Minneapolis to finalize each forthcoming issue of *The Representative*. Even this weekly sojourn, however, had become too much in the view of the central committee of Mid-Road Populists, who had scheduled a meeting with Donnelly for January 2 in which they hoped to convince him to preserve his health by taking a rest from his editorial duties and political party leadership.[26]

Sadly, the meeting to preserve what remained of Donnelly's good health would be held without him. On January 1, 1901, the indefatigable Sage of Nininger suffered a fatal heart attack, passing away at his in-law's home in Minneapolis. The *Minneapolis Journal* broke the tragic news to the Twin Cities on the front page of its January 2 edition, saying by way of eulogy that "no Minnesota man was better known in the world at large than Ignatius Donnelly, theorist and scholar," while at home in Minnesota, it noted, he was chiefly known for his "life-long connection with politics."[27] In Hastings, the seat of Donnelly's home county, the *Minneapolis Tribune* reported that the death of the Sage of Nininger was regarded as "public calamity."[28] From the Twin Cities newspapers that had opposed Donnelly throughout his career came sincere praise for a man widely regarded as a genius. Though his second marriage to the much younger Marion Hanson in the Methodist Church had alienated him from some Minneapolis Irish Catholics, the *Irish Standard* in Minneapolis declared that Minnesota had lost "one of the greatest of her adopted sons." On the political stump, the newspaper acknowledged, Donnelly was "without an equal in the West," while in literature he enjoyed a truly international reputation. "We regret his demise," the *Standard* noted. "It will be long before Minnesota has his equal in versatility of genius."[29] From Donnelly's sworn enemies at the *St. Paul Pioneer Press*, whom he had twice successfully sued for libel, came the statement, "After fighting him the greater part of his political life in Minnesota, we are not going to fight him now that he is dead. . .. He was and is entitled to be recognized as an eminent man."[30]

In Montana, where Donnelly's son Dr. Ignatius C. Donnelly lived in Butte, the front-page headline in the *Anaconda Standard* blared, "Died at the Dawn of the Century," and the subheadline read, "Death claims Ignatius Donnelly after an eventful life. He was a radical in literature and in politics. Startled world with the novelty of his theories." A reporter from the *Standard*'s Butte office had woken Donnelly's son at twelve thirty in the morning to inform him personally of the sad news. Ironically, Dr. Donnelly had just received a Christmas letter from his father saying his health was improving. He told grieving reporters gathered at his home on North Idaho Street that he would be leaving later that day to join his brother, Stan, and his widowed sister, Mary, in Minnesota.[31]

Among Mid-Road Populists, Donnelly's death elicited both eloquent praise and bitterness over past political betrayals suffered by their candidate. His fellow populist activist C. B. Maben wrote at length to dispel many of the myths surrounding Donnelly the politician. Contrary to rumor, Donnelly had never been an authoritarian party boss, Maben insisted, but was instead known to say, "Gentlemen, do whatever you think is for the best and let me know where I can be of the most service." Maben, who worked with Donnelly for many years on a number of People's Party matters, confided, "For many years it was my good fortune to know Mr. Donnelly intimately, and I believe that no more truly unselfish, whole-souled, generous and most lovable of men ever assumed the leadership of a forlorn hope." And for his efforts, Maben lamented, the great man had been "slandered by enemies and continually undermined, back-bitten, and stabbed to the heart by jealous, short-sighted associates in his own party." The betrayal by members of his own delegation, which had denied him both a People's Party presidential nomination and a role as chairman at the St. Louis convention in 1896, had, Maben intimated, "stung him to the quick" and "was the direct cause of his health beginning to fail." Maben, however, could console himself with the certain knowledge that his friend's name would be remembered long after "his enemies and villifiers [*sic*] have been buried in oblivion."[32] Writing a retrospective for the *Tribune* in Minneapolis, editor Arthur James Pegler opened his remembrance, "Ignatius Donnelly, whose political enmities were innumerable, has no enemies in any party today. The men who fought with him and those who fought most strenuously against him, unite in recognition of his genius, his goodness of heart, and his unquestioned personal honesty." Donnelly's death, the *Tribune* noted, was decidedly not a local affair, as his passing would be mourned by many around the United States and the world.[33]

While the majority deeply and sincerely mourned the loss of the formidable author-statesman, there were some who celebrated his demise. In London the *Guardian* breathed a sigh of relief that the "best known of the little band of enthusiasts" who believed the "mad hypothesis" that Bacon wrote the plays and poems of Shakespeare would no longer have to be answered.[34] Nearer to home in Topeka, Kansas, the *Daily Capital* reprinted reactions from newspapers around the region, including the sentiments of the *Ottawa Herald* in Illinois. Donnelly's death had been unfortunate, the *Herald* claimed, because he would not be forced to live into the twentieth century to see "what an unadulterated fool book his *Caesar's Column* was." Donnelly's version of the truth in that book was as unrealistic, avowed the newspaper, as his chances of being elected vice president on the Populist ticket.[35]

In Wilmar, Minnesota, the *Tribune* followed a similar line, though it granted that the deceased was "one of the most picturesque figures in Minnesota politics" and that the "great genius of the man" would live on in his books even after he was forgotten for his politics. Pleasantries aside, the *Tribune* risked speaking poorly of the dead in insisting that, for all his talents, Donnelly's intense egotism had held him back from greater political fame. "Seated in his library and dreaming those dreams," the *Tribune* noted, "there was no more altruistic person than Donnelly. But in all these reforms there was to be one central figure—Donnelly." If one wanted to know him at his best—as an "altruist, an advocate of justice, equity, a champion of the lowly, and an elegant and powerful orator," the eulogist advised, one should read *Doctor Huguet* and not the transcripts of Donnelly's retaliatory and vindictive speeches in Congress. And those who sought a testament to the logic, erudition, and virtuoso intellect of the Sage of Nininger should read *Ragnarok*, *Atlantis*, and *The Great Cryptogram*. In these ambitious works, the writer argued, Donnelly forgot himself, leaving his "brilliant genius" unfettered.[36]

In the days and weeks immediately following his death, previously untold stories emerged honoring Donnelly's razor-sharp wit on the stump, lecture circuit, and campaign trail. Over the course of many decades traveling as a prominent politician and bestselling author, he spoke to hundreds of thousands, and many never forgot their encounters with him. From as far away as Arizona came tales of memorable interactions with the charismatic author-politician, including a lengthy tribute from George Smalley, a recent transplant from northern Minnesota who had taken over editorial duties at the *Arizona Daily Citizen* in Tucson. Smalley recalled Donnelly's run for governor on the People's Party ticket in 1892, at which time Smalley was a cub editor at a newspaper in a politically important county seat in the northern part of the state. The editor's job was to dutifully attend a campaign event and then to "roast the Sage" in that evening's newspaper column. Arriving late to an opera house packed "pit to dome" with cheering supporters, Smalley pushed his way through the populist throng to a table near the front to transcribe the speech by which he hoped to reduce Donnelly to a fool. Looking sardonically in Smalley's direction, Donnelly quipped, "I would not be surprised to read in the papers tomorrow that I spoke here to a small crowd who listened for a few minutes and then went home."[37]

"As he spoke," Smalley recalled, "he pointed his little dimpled hand at me, pressing a crown of sarcasm on my youthful brow and driving into my sensitive nature the sting of ridicule. The 'subsidized press' never received a more bitter roast, and no man ever lived who could punish an enemy with words of tongue like Ignatius Donnelly." The sarcastic twist of the knife delighted the crowd, while Smalley, duly chastened, sheepishly soldiered on. Amid the "cheers and jeers of the disciples of populism who packed the hall," the young editor shouldered "the burden of every newspaper in the country for every wrong that had come before the observing eye of the sage of Nininger."[38]

Other stories came to light that showed the more self-effacing, even fatalist quality of the man's trademark sense of humor. One such memory recalled Donnelly at the West Hotel in St. Paul the day after he had lost his bid to become Minnesota's first People's Party governor. Seeing the great man arriving tardily to the hotel lobby the morning after his defeat, the hotel clerk casually remarked, "Late, Mr. Donnelly?"

"Yes," Donnelly darkly punned, "the Late Mr. Donnelly."[39]

Five days after Donnelly's death, the *Minneapolis Tribune* ran a half-page spread celebrating the character of the man. The editors recounted Donnelly's habit of traveling to Minneapolis from Nininger each Tuesday to proof the pages of *The Representative* prior to its weekly press date. After a day of painstaking editorial work, Donnelly would pause at the door, hat in hand, to indulge the staff with some lighthearted, humorous story from his years on the road. His last story, the *Tribune* revealed, featured a man who had died suddenly in a town where practically no one knew him. When it came time for the preacher to ask if anyone had anything to say as last words, the room was silent, and all hope for a comment was abandoned until, as Donnelly told it, a diehard populist in the back of the room piped up and said, "Well, if nobody else don't want to talk, I'd like to say a few words on free silver." And with that Donnelly had grinned, put his hat atop his head, pulled open the door, and walked out. It would be the last funny story, the newspaper ruefully noted, that Donnelly would ever tell.[40]

Preparing his final edition of the *Fergus Globe* in Fergus Falls, Minnesota, Haldor Boen, Donnelly's fellow populist newspaper editor and a former congressman, poignantly summarized the timing of the Sage of Nininger's death, writing, "He was permitted to see the first day of the Twentieth Century, and at midnight, at the end of that day, his earthly career ended. Ignatius Donnelly was a mental meteor, who, as he swept over the intellectual heavens, held the attention of all observers."[41]

That summer, with the new century well begun and the blooms returned to the woodlands of the upper Mississippi River valley, the *St. Paul Globe* visited the famed library at Nininger, opening it like a shuttered vault. A grieving Marion Donnelly ushered the newspapermen in, confessing that her husband had felt the sting of every satirical or abusive thing ever written about him and had saved all the slings and arrows, in addition to more complimentary clippings, in large scrapbooks in his study. "When he was surrounded by his books he seemed to forget the world," she recalled. "There was a look of content on his face that he never carried with him outside the library."[42]

Permitted to linger, the *Globe* found Donnelly's book collection evenly split between politics and literature, as if two men had collected and curated the tomes therein: "One a fighter, glorying in battle, giving blow for blow; the other a scholar, happy only when delving in the musty chronicles of the past, living the shadowy life of a faraway period." Which side of Donnelly's riven nature was stronger? Did the eminent scholar merely play with politics, or did the consummate politician toy with books? Sitting in the library, "fingering the well-thumbed volumes, tracing the lines of the restless pen that printed Donnelly's own individuality on every margin, one is forced to believe that his heart was with his books," the *Globe* concluded.[43]

Having published hundreds of thousands of words across his uniquely productive life as an author-politician, the sage did not leave behind a flowery farewell letter or deathbed prophesy for his constituents to ponder long after he was gone. In the final accounting, what did he make of his career as a public servant? Several years before his death, as he began what would be his final term in the Minnesota legislature, Donnelly found himself fighting a committee chair whose tenure, he feared, would be marked by despotic rule. Feeling attacked, Donnelly told the power-hungry chair that he was ashamed of nothing in his long record, adding, "I am getting to be an old man, and I shall not live a great while longer, but when the history of the Northwest will be written I think the verdict of posterity will be that I have never failed to work for the people."[44]

In the corner of the library, atop a desk, the *Globe* found a copy of *Doctor Huguet* open for inspection. Had Marion staged the room for their visit, or had the library simply been left exactly as it was when Donnelly had last occupied it? Whatever the truth, the book was opened to a passage that read as a fitting end to the endlessly inimitable chronicle of Ignatius Donnelly:

> How little a thing is glory? It consists simply of thoughts of you in the minds of others; and in a short time those others will be dust, and their very names have perished. . . . Fame? Fame is nothing. We leave nothing behind us on this earth that is permanent, except our influence for good or ill; that goes on, visible to God, but invisible to men—a force in the affairs of humanity, spreading like a great, undying ripple in the sea of mind. Big or little, eminent or obscure, we each contribute to that intangible net-work of earth-forces, forever renewing themselves with every new brain that is born into the world. Fame! No; let us do our duty.[45]

Notes

Introduction

1. Everett W. Fish, *Donnelliana: An Appendix to "Caesar's Column"* (Chicago: F. J. Schulte, 1892), 5.

2. Mark Rylance, foreword to Barry R. Clarke, *Francis Bacon's Contribution to Shakespeare: A New Attribution Method* (New York: Routledge, 2019), xx.

3. Nicholas Ruddick, introduction to *Caesar's Column: A Story of the Twentieth Century*, by Ignatius Donnelly (Middletown, CT: Wesleyan University Press, 2003), xiii.

4. Michael Kazin, *The Populist Persuasion: An American History*, rev. ed. (Ithaca, NY: Cornell University Press, 2017), xii, xiii.

5. Ruddick, *Caesar's Column*, xvi.

1. The Making of a Midwestern Sage

1. Ignatius Donnelly, diary entry, November 3, 1881, Donnelly MSS, Minnesota Historical Society, St. Paul.

2. Martin Ridge, *Ignatius Donnelly: The Portrait of a Politician* (Chicago: University of Chicago Press, 1962), 201.

3. Ignatius Donnelly, diary entry, April 14, 1882.

4. William Watts Folwell, *A History of Minnesota*, vol. 2 (St. Paul: Minnesota Historical Society, 1924), 102.

5. Zac Farber, "Ignatius Donnelly, Paranoid Progressive of the Gilded Age," Minnesota Lawyer, May 30, 2018, https://minnlawyer.com/2018/05/30/ignatius-donnelly-paranoid-progressive-in-the-gilded-age/.

6. James P. Boyd, ed., *Men and Issues of 1900* (n.p.: P. W. Ziegler, 1900), 672.

7. Ridge, *Ignatius Donnelly*, 201.

8. Ridge, *Ignatius Donnelly*, 110.

9. Ignatius Donnelly, diary entry, April 3, 1868, quoted in Ridge, *Ignatius Donnelly*, 111.

10. D. Basset to Ignatius Donnelly, April 15, 1868, Donnelly MSS.

11. US Congress, *Congressional Globe*, vol. 3 (Washington, DC: Blair & Rives, 1868), 2351.

12. US Congress, *Congressional Globe*, 2353.

13. George Washington Julian, *Political Recollections, 1840–1872* (Chicago: Jansen, McClurg, 1884), 366–67.

14. *St. Paul Pioneer*, May 6, 1868, quoted in Ridge, *Ignatius Donnelly*, 113.

15. Harlan Page Hall, *H.P. Hall's Observations: Being More or Less a History of Political Contests in Minnesota, from 1849 to 1904* (St. Paul: n.p., 1904), 77.

16. A. Brower to Ignatius Donnelly, May 21, 1868, Donnelly MSS.
17. *St. Paul Pioneer*, August 2, 1868, quoted in Ridge, *Ignatius Donnelly*, 117.
18. Ignatius Donnelly to Kate Donnelly, August 13, 1868, Donnelly MSS.
19. *St. Paul Press*, April 28, 1869, quoted in Ridge, *Ignatius Donnelly*, 124.
20. *St. Paul Pioneer*, April 28, 1869, quoted in Ridge, *Ignatius Donnelly*, 125.
21. *St. Paul Dispatch*, February 14, 1870, quoted in Ridge, *Ignatius Donnelly*, 129.
22. Ridge, *Ignatius Donnelly*, 133.
23. Ridge, *Ignatius Donnelly*, 134.
24. Norman K. Risjord, *A Popular History of Minnesota* (St. Paul: Minnesota Historical Society Press, 2005), 149.
25. Ridge, *Ignatius Donnelly*, 137.
26. W. Mayo to Ignatius Donnelly, July 22, 1871, Donnelly MSS.
27. "A Humble Apology," *Duluth Minnesotan*, June 24, 1871, 1.
28. "Farmer Donnelly," *Grange Advance*, December 10, 1873, 6.
29. "Editor's Drawe," *Harper's New Monthly Magazine*, December 1871, 156.
30. John D. Hicks, "The Political Career of Ignatius Donnelly," *Mississippi Valley Historical Review* 8, no. 1/2 (June–September 1921): 90.
31. "An Honest Confession," *Donaldsonville (LA) Chief*, 1.
32. *Minneapolis News*, September 30, 1871, quoted in Ridge, *Ignatius Donnelly*, 140.
33. Manuscript copy of speech, n.d., Donnelly MSS.
34. *St. Paul Pioneer*, January 5, 1872, quoted in Ridge, *Ignatius Donnelly*, 141.
35. T. Foster to Ignatius Donnelly, June 13, 1872, Donnelly MSS.
36. *St. Paul Dispatch*, June 28, 1872, quoted in Ridge, *Ignatius Donnelly*, 144.
37. "Emigrant Aid Journal of Minnesota," Minnesota Historical Society, accessed July 1, 2020, https://www.mnhs.org/newspapers/hub/emigrant-aid-journal.
38. Ignatius Donnelly and Phillip Rohr, "Our Prospectus," *Emigrant Aid Journal*, December 1, 1856, 1.
39. *Northfield Standard*, July 20, 1872, quoted in Ridge, *Ignatius Donnelly*, 145.
40. *Hastings Gazette*, July 20, 1872, quoted in Ridge, *Ignatius Donnelly*, 145.
41. *Milwaukee News*, October 6, 1872, quoted in Ridge, *Ignatius Donnelly*, 134.
42. Ignatius Donnelly to Kate Donnelly, October 24, 1872, Donnelly MSS.
43. "Frank Daggett's Opinion of the *Anti-monopolist*," *St. Paul Anti-monopolist*, September 17, 1874, 11.
44. Ben Wilde, "Pugnacious Explains," *Minneapolis Daily Tribune*, February 7, 1875, 3.
45. Farber, "Ignatius Donnelly."
46. James W. Cook, *The Arts of Deception: Playing with Fraud in the Age of Barnum* (Cambridge, MA: Harvard University Press, 2001), 210.
47. "Our Position," *St. Paul Anti-monopolist*, July 13, 1876, 1.
48. "Ourselves," *St. Paul Anti-monopolist*, May 10, 1877, 1.
49. "Our Position," 1.
50. Herbert Y. Weber, "The Story of the *St. Paul Globe*," *Minnesota History*, Winter 1965, 329.
51. Weber, "*St. Paul Globe*," 187.

52. Ignatius Donnelly, diary entry, June 10, 1886, Donnelly MSS.

53. "A Minnesota Village," *St. Paul Sunday Globe*, August 14, 1881, 4.

54. Ridge, *Ignatius Donnelly*, 197.

55. David D. Anderson, *Ignatius Donnelly* (Boston: G. K. Hall, 1980), 33.

2. *Atlantis: The Antediluvian World*

1. *St. Paul Pioneer Press*, February 26, 1882, quoted in Ridge, *Ignatius Donnelly*, 201.

2. Ignatius Donnelly, diary entry, September 15, 1881, Donnelly MSS, Minnesota Historical Society, St. Paul.

3. "Ignatius Donnelly as an Author," *St. Paul Daily Globe*, March 20, 1882, 4.

4. "Ignatius Donnelly as an Author," 4.

5. "New Books," *Janesville (WI) Daily Gazette*, March 27, 1882, 1.

6. Ignatius Donnelly, *Atlantis: The Antediluvian World* (New York: Harper & Brothers, 1882), 1–2.

7. "New Publications," *New York Times*, December 15, 1874, 2.

8. Jules Verne, *Twenty Thousand Leagues under the Sea* (New York: Butler Brothers, 1887), 240.

9. Verne, *Twenty Thousand Leagues*, 240.

10. Tricia Cusack, ed., *Framing the Ocean, 1700 to the Present: Envisaging the Sea as Social Space* (London: Routledge, 2014), 245.

11. Elizabeth Cary Agassiz, ed., *Louis Agassiz: His Life and Correspondence* (Boston: Houghton, Mifflin, 1885), 708.

12. Agassiz, *Louis Agassiz*, 704.

13. Thomas Henry Huxley, "The Problems of the Deep Sea," *Popular Science Monthly*, May 1873, 459.

14. *Report on the Scientific Results of the Voyage of H.M.S. Challenger during the Years 1873–76 under the Command of Captain George S. Nares . . . and the Late Captain Frank Tourle Thomson, R.N.* (Edinburgh: Neill, 1895), 12.

15. Donnelly, *Atlantis*, frontispiece, "The Profile of Atlantis."

16. Charles Wyville Thomson, *The Voyage of the* Challenger: *The Atlantic; A Preliminary Account of the General Results of the Exploring Voyage of HMS* Challenger *during the Year 1873 and the Early Part of the Year 1876*, vol. 2 (Cambridge: Cambridge University Press 2014), 24.

17. William Henry Oliphant Smeaton, "The Mystery of the Pacific," *Westminster Review* 144 (1895): 33.

18. Donnelly, *Atlantis*, 46.

19. Donnelly, *Atlantis*, 468.

20. Donnelly, *Atlantis*, 74.

21. Donnelly, *Atlantis*, 24.

22. "New Publications," *New York Times*, February 18, 1882, 5.

23. "New Publications," *Cincinnati Commercial*, February 26, 1882, 2.

24. "New Publications," *Boston Post*, February 27, 1882, 2.

25. Ignatius Donnelly, diary entry, December 31, 1881, Donnelly MSS.

26. Ridge, *Ignatius Donnelly*, 201.

27. Ignatius Donnelly, diary entry, March 26, 1882, Donnelly MSS.

28. Ignatius Donnelly, diary entry, March 26, 1882, Donnelly MSS.

29. Gretchen Kreuter, "Kate Donnelly versus the Cult of True Womanhood," in *Women of Minnesota: Selected Biographical Essays*, rev. ed., ed. Barbara Stuhler and Gretchen Kreuter (St. Paul: Minnesota Historical Society Press, 1998), 20.

30. "The Times Catalogue of New Books and New Editions," *New York Times*, February 28, 1882, 5.

31. "City Globules," *St. Paul Daily Globe*, March 15, 1882, 4.

32. "Notes of New Books," *Times* (Philadelphia), March 9, 1882, 3.

33. "The Lost Atlantis," *St. Albans (VT) Daily Messenger*, November 4, 1882, 2.

34. "Atlantis," *Warrenton (NC) Gazette*, March 24, 1882.

35. "A Curious and Interesting Work," *Deseret News* (Salt Lake City), June 7, 1882, 16.

36. *Central Presbyterian* (Richmond, VA), July 15, 1882, 4.

37. "Another Crank," *St. Louis Post Dispatch*, June 27, 1882, 3.

38. "Literature," *Chicago Daily Tribune*, March 25, 1882, 9.

39. Kate Donnelly to Ignatius Donnelly, March 4, 1882, Donnelly MSS.

40. Ridge, *Ignatius Donnelly*, 204.

41. Ignatius Donnelly, diary entry, November 23, 1881, Donnelly MSS.

42. Ridge, *Ignatius Donnelly*, 202.

43. "Glimpses of Atlantis," *Democratic Advocate* (Westminster, MD), September 1, 1877.

44. "Glimpses of Atlantis."

45. Charles Étienne Brasseur de Bourbourg, *Quatre letters sur e Mexique* (Paris: Auguste Durand et Pedone, 1868), 45.

46. Edward H. Thompson, "Atlantis Not a Myth," *Popular Science* 15 (1879): 761.

47. Thompson, "Atlantis," 761.

48. Daniel Tredwell, "Atlantis," *Brooklyn Daily Eagle*, June 18, 1882, 1.

49. Tredwell, "Atlantis," 1.

50. Tredwell, "Atlantis," 1.

51. "Editor's Literary Record," *Harper's Monthly*, May 1882, 955.

52. Jean Sylvain Bailly, *Lettres sur l'Atlantide de Platon et sur l'ancienne histoire de l'Asie* (Paris: Frères Debure, 1779), 6.

53. Bailly, *Lettres*, 34.

54. Bailly, *Lettres*, 12.

55. Bailly, *Lettres*, 12.

56. Pierre Beaudry, "Bailly's Method of Discovery by Epistemological Hypothesis: An 'Analysis Situs' Approach to the History of Ancient Astronomy," Pierre Beaudry's Galactic Parking Lot, September 9, 2009, https://amatterofmind.org/Pierres_PDFs/ANCIENT_ASTRONOMY_I/BOOK_I/2._BAILLY'S_ANCIENT_ASTRONOMY.pdf.

57. Donnelly, *Atlantis*, 349.

58. Augustus Le Plongeon, *Queen Moo and the Egyptian Sphinx* (London: Keegan Paul, Trench, Trubner, 1896), xi.

59. Le Plongeon, *Queen Moo*, xiii.

60. Le Plongeon, *Queen Moo*, xiv.

61. Anderson, *Ignatius Donnelly*, 34.

62. "The Crescent City's Carnival," *Donaldsonville (LA) Chief*, February 10, 1883, 1.

63. "The Oriole Pageant," *Aegis and Intelligencer* (Bel Air, MD), September 31, 1883, 1.

64. Ridge, *Ignatius Donnelly*, 202.

65. Ridge, *Ignatius Donnelly*, 202.

66. Ridge, *Ignatius Donnelly*, 203.

67. J. T. Trowbridge, "Atlantis," *Weekly Kansas Chief*, March 2, 1882, 1.

68. "Atlantis," *Milwaukee Weekly Wisconsin*, September 21, 1881, 2.

69. A. R. Fulton, "Atlantis," *Fairfield (IA) Tribune*, February 23, 1882, 4.

70. Kansas Historical Society, "Solomon Miller," Kansapedia, January 2013, https://www.kshs.org/kansapedia/solomon-miller/12148.

71. Solomon Miller, "Vestiges of Atlantis," *Weekly Kansas Chief*, March 2, 1882, 1.

72. Ignatius Donnelly, diary entry, July 8, 1882.

73. "Personal," *St. Paul Daily Globe*, July 4, 1882, 1.

74. Ridge, *Ignatius Donnelly*, 206.

75. Ridge, *Ignatius Donnelly*, 206.

76. Ridge, *Ignatius Donnelly*, 196.

3. *Ragnarok: The Age of Fire and Gravel*

1. "Ragnarok," *St. Paul Daily Globe*, July 25, 1882, 2.

2. "Ragnarok," *St. Paul Daily Globe*, July 25, 1882, 2.

3. Martin Ridge, *Ignatius Donnelly: The Portrait of a Politician* (Chicago: University of Chicago Press, 1962), 207.

4. Ignatius Donnelly, diary entry, July 31, 1882, Donnelly MSS, Minnesota Historical Society, St. Paul.

5. "Ragnarok," *St. Paul Daily Globe*, July 25, 1882, 2.

6. "Ragnarok," *St. Paul Daily Globe*, July 25, 1882, 2.

7. Ridge, *Ignatius Donnelly*, 207.

8. "Ragnarok," *St. Paul Daily Globe*, December 6, 1882, 11.

9. "Ragnarok: A Book That Is Certain to Attract the Attention of Scientists," *Chicago Daily Tribune*, December 3, 1882, 19.

10. "Ragnarok," December 3, 1882, 19.

11. H. G. B., "Ragnarok: A Correspondent Who Offers Evidence in Support of Mr. Donnelly's Theory," *Chicago Daily Tribune*, December 11, 1882, 5.

12. E. F. Test, "Donnelly's 'Ragnarok'—the Age of Fire and Gravel—When the Comet Struck the Earth," *Chicago Daily Tribune*, January 14, 1883, 9.

13. "Current Literature," *Quad City (IA) Times*, December 23, 1882, 2.

14. Ignatius Donnelly, *Ragnarok: The Age of Fire and Gravel* (New York: D. Appleton, 1883), 2.

15. Donnelly, *Ragnarok*, 106.

16. Donnelly, *Ragnarok*, 107.

17. Donnelly, *Ragnarok*, 94.

18. "Blizzards and Gray Tissue," *Inter Ocean* (Chicago), December 16, 1882, 12.
19. "Blizzards and Gray Tissue," 12.
20. "Mr. Donnelly's Comet," *New York Times*, December 23, 1882, 7.
21. Ridge, *Ignatius Donnelly*, 196.
22. "Mr. Donnelly's Comet," 7.
23. Donnelly, *Ragnarok*, 113.
24. Donnelly, *Ragnarok*, 116.
25. Donnelly, *Ragnarok*, 45.
26. "Mr. Donnelly's Comet," 7.
27. *Evening Journal* (Jersey City, NJ), July 31, 1882, 1.
28. James W. Cook, *The Arts of Deception: Playing with Fraud in the Age of Barnum* (Cambridge, MA: Harvard University Press, 2001), 5.
29. Ridge, *Ignatius Donnelly*, 208.
30. Ridge, *Ignatius Donnelly*, 209.
31. David D. Anderson, *Ignatius Donnelly* (Boston: G. K. Hall, 1980), 53.
32. Ignatius Donnelly to O. B. Bunce, October 4, 1883, Donnelly MSS.
33. O. B. Bunce to Ignatius Donnelly, October 17, 1883, Donnelly MSS.
34. Ignatius Donnelly, diary entry, n.d., 1887–89 diary, Donnelly MSS.
35. Ridge, *Ignatius Donnelly*, 211.
36. Ignatius Donnelly, diary entry, n.d., 1887–89 diary, Donnelly MSS.

4. The Shakespearean Cipher

1. *Sterling (KS) Bulletin*, March 9, 1882, 2.
2. "A Ringing Speech," *St. Paul Daily Globe*, November 6, 1882, 2.
3. "The Eve of the Battle," *St. Paul Daily Globe*, November 7, 1882, 5.
4. Ignatius Donnelly, diary entry, September 23, 1882, Donnelly MSS, Minnesota Historical Society, St. Paul.
5. Ignatius Donnelly, diary entry, December 14, 1883, Donnelly MSS.
6. Ignatius Donnelly, diary entry, September 23, 1882, Donnelly MSS.
7. Ignatius Donnelly, diary entry, December 14, 1883, Donnelly MSS.
8. Appleton Morgan, *The Shakespearean Myth: William Shakespeare and Circumstantial Evidence* (Cincinnati: Robert Clarke, 1881), xvii.
9. "Donnelly's Shakespeare," *Minneapolis Daily Tribune*, September 7, 1884, 6.
10. "Donnelly's Shakespeare," 6.
11. "Donnelly's Shakespeare," 6.
12. "Donnelly Gets There," *St. Paul Daily Globe*, August 21, 1884, 1.
13. "Mr. Donnelly at Shakopee," *St. Paul Daily Globe*, October 8, 1884, 4.
14. "Mr. Donnelly at Shakopee," 4.
15. "Mr. Donnelly at Shakopee," 4.
16. "Donnelly's Campaign," *St. Paul Daily Globe*, October 17, 1884, 4.
17. "Mr. Donnelly Replies," *St. Paul Daily Globe*, October 17, 1884, 4.
18. *St. Paul Pioneer Press*, April 21, 1885, quoted in Martin Ridge, *Ignatius Donnelly: The Portrait of a Politician* (Chicago: University of Chicago Press, 1962), 216.
19. "Our Ignatius Still Gathers Fame," *Minneapolis Tribune*, October 10, 1884, 2.

20. *St. Paul Pioneer Press*, October 24, 1884, quoted in Ridge, *Ignatius Donnelly*, 218.

21. *St. Paul Pioneer Press*, October 15, 1884, quoted in Ridge, *Ignatius Donnelly*, 218.

22. "Libel Suit against a Liar," *St. Paul Daily Globe*, October 17, 1884, 4.

23. "Sketches of Life," *Watertown (NY) Times*, November 3, 1884.

24. Ridge, *Ignatius Donnelly*, 221.

25. Ignatius Donnelly, diary entry, December 30, 1884, Donnelly MSS.

26. Ignatius Donnelly to Grover Cleveland, October 21, 1884, Donnelly MSS.

27. Kate Donnelly to Ignatius Donnelly, November 8, 1884, Donnelly MSS.

28. Ridge, *Ignatius Donnelly*, 219.

29. "Shakespeare's Plays," *St. Paul Daily Globe*, November 20, 1884, 2.

30. "The Shakespeare Cipher," *Washington (DC) Republican*, March 21, 1885, 1.

31. "What Is Due Bacon," *St. Paul Daily Globe*, October 27, 1885, 4.

32. "The Shakespeare Cipher in the First Folio," *The Sun* (New York, NY), June 13, 1886, 8.

33. Percy M. Wallace, "Mr. Donnelly's Shakespeare Cipher," *Nineteenth Century*, May 1886, 706.

34. Wallace, "Mr. Donnelly's Shakespeare Cipher," 706.

35. Wallace, "Mr. Donnelly's Shakespeare Cipher," 708.

36. "Shakespeare and the Circulation of His Blood," *The Sun* (New York, NY), July 4, 1886, 8.

37. "The Sage of Nininger," *St. Paul Daily Globe*, March 7, 1886, 13.

38. "Sage of Nininger," 13.

39. "Donnelly's Delusion," *Wahpeton (ND) Times*, April 22, 1886, 1.

40. "Donnelly's Day," *St. Paul Daily Globe*, July 2, 1886, 1.

41. Ignatius Donnelly to Lars M. Rand, July 20, 1886.

42. George B. Enberg, "The Knights of Labor in Minnesota," *Minnesota History*, December 1941, 386.

43. *St. Paul Pioneer Press*, September 14, 1886, quoted in Ridge, *Ignatius Donnelly*, 250.

44. Ignatius Donnelly, diary entry, September 14, 1886, Donnelly MSS.

45. Ignatius Donnelly, diary entry, November 3, 1886, Donnelly MSS.

46. *St. Paul Pioneer Press*, December 15, 1886, quoted in Ridge, *Ignatius Donnelly*, 253.

47. *St. Paul Daily Globe*, December 15, 1886, quoted in Ridge, *Ignatius Donnelly*, 253.

48. *St. Paul Daily Globe*, December 13, 1886, 4.

49. "Voice of the People," *St. Paul Daily Globe*, February 7, 1887, 4.

50. Robertus Love, *The Rise and Fall of Jesse James* (New York: Blue Ribbon Books, 1940), 404.

51. Love, *Rise and Fall*, 406.

52. Ridge, *Ignatius Donnelly*, 255.

53. John D. Hicks, "The Political Career of Ignatius Donnelly," *Mississippi Valley Historical Review* 8 (1921): 110.

54. "Ignatius Donnelly," *St. Paul Daily Globe*, March 7, 1887, 4.
55. "Ignatius Donnelly," *St. Paul Daily Globe*, March 7, 1887, 4.
56. Ignatius Donnelly, "The Shakespeare Myth," *North American Review* 145 (July 1887): 67.
57. Donnelly, "Shakespeare Myth," 68.

5. *The Great Cryptogram*

1. "Great Cryptogram," *Minneapolis Star Tribune*, August 28, 1887, 2.
2. Martin Ridge, *Ignatius Donnelly: The Portrait of a Politician* (Chicago: University of Chicago Press, 1962), 230.
3. "Ignatius Donnelly," *National Field* (Salina, KS), June 30, 1893, 8.
4. Delia Bacon, "William Shakespeare and His Plays: An Inquiry concerning Them," *Putnam's Monthly Magazine*, January 1856, 6, https://www.bartleby.com/400/prose/1296.html.
5. Ann Thompson and Sasha Roberts, eds. *Women Reading Shakespeare: An Anthology of Criticism* (Manchester: Manchester University Press, 1997), 105.
6. Bacon, "Shakespeare and His Plays," 4.
7. Appleton Morgan, *The Shakespearean Myth: William Shakespeare and Circumstantial Evidence* (Cincinnati: Robert Clarke, 1881), 188.
8. Nathaniel Thomas, *The Authorship of Shakespeare*, 3rd ed. (New York: Hurd & Houghton, 1875), ix.
9. Thomas, *Authorship of Shakespeare*, 7.
10. Thomas, *Authorship of Shakespeare*, 598.
11. Susanna Ashton, "Who Brings Home the Bacon? Shakespeare and Turn-of-the-Century American Authorship," *American Periodicals* 6 (1996): 23.
12. Thomas Davidson to Ignatius Donnelly, August 17, 1887, Donnelly MSS, Minnesota Historical Society, St. Paul.
13. "It Will Be Another Keely Motor," *The Sun* (New York, NY), August 29, 1887, 2.
14. Everett W. Fish, *Donnelliana: An Appendix to Caesar's Column* (Chicago: F. J. Schulte, 1892), 112.
15. Ashton, "Who Brings Home the Bacon?," 23.
16. "It Will Be Another Keely Motor," *The Sun* (New York, NY), August 29, 1887, 2.
17. Ridge, *Ignatius Donnelly*, 232.
18. R. S. Peale to Ignatius Donnelly, November 6, 8, 1887, Donnelly MSS.
19. Ignatius Donnelly, diary entry, December 11, 1887, Donnelly MSS.
20. Ignatius Donnelly, *The Great Cryptogram: Francis Bacon's Cipher in the So-Called Shakespeare Plays* (Chicago: R. S. Peale, 1888), 6.
21. Donnelly, *Great Cryptogram*, 5.
22. Donnelly, *Great Cryptogram*, 31.
23. Donnelly, *Great Cryptogram*, 72.
24. Donnelly, *Great Cryptogram*, 112.
25. Donnelly, *Great Cryptogram*, 627.
26. Donnelly, *Great Cryptogram*, 507.

27. John M. Robertson, ed., *The Philosophical Works of Francis Bacon* (London: George Routledge & Sons, 1905), 527.
28. Robertson, *Philosophical Works*, 529.
29. Robertson, *Philosophical Works*, 235.
30. Donnelly, *Great Cryptogram*, 514.
31. Donnelly, *Great Cryptogram*, 514.
32. Donnelly, *Great Cryptogram*, 515.
33. Donnelly, *Great Cryptogram*, 516.
34. Donnelly, *Great Cryptogram*, 519.
35. Donnelly, *Great Cryptogram*, 528.
36. Donnelly, *Great Cryptogram*, 528.
37. Donnelly, *Great Cryptogram*, 552.
38. Donnelly, *Great Cryptogram*, 554.
39. Donnelly, *Great Cryptogram*, 528.
40. Donnelly, *Great Cryptogram*, 562
41. Donnelly, *Great Cryptogram*, 563.
42. Donnelly, *Great Cryptogram*, 564.
43. Donnelly, *Great Cryptogram*, 577.
44. Donnelly, *Great Cryptogram*, 575.
45. Donnelly, *Great Cryptogram*, 763.
46. Donnelly, *Great Cryptogram*, 583.
47. Donnelly, *Great Cryptogram*, 584.
48. Donnelly, *Great Cryptogram*, 579.
49. Donnelly, *Great Cryptogram*, 581.
50. Donnelly, *Great Cryptogram*, 582.
51. Donnelly, *Great Cryptogram*, 719.
52. Donnelly, *Great Cryptogram*, 844.
53. Donnelly, *Great Cryptogram*, 844.
54. Donnelly, *Great Cryptogram*, 884–88.
55. David D. Anderson, *Ignatius Donnelly* (Boston: G. K. Hall, 1980), 63.
56. Donnelly, *Great Cryptogram*, 889.
57. Ridge, *Ignatius Donnelly*, 258.
58. *London Daily Telegraph*, November 26, 1887, quoted in Ridge, *Ignatius Donnelly*, 233.
59. "The Shakespeare Sensation," *Essex County (England) Standard*, December 3, 1887, 4.
60. "Who Wrote Shakespeare," *Pall Mall Gazette* (London), September 26, 1887, 11.
61. "Who Wrote Shakspeare?: An American 'Crank' and His 'Cryptogram,'" *Pall Mall Gazette* (London), September 26, 1887, 11.
62. Ignatius Donnelly to Kate Donnelly, April 4, 1888, Donnelly MSS.
63. Ridge, *Ignatius Donnelly*, 238.
64. "Shakespeare and Bacon," *The Times* (London), April 18, 1888, 10.
65. "Donnelly in London," *Lincoln (NE) Daily News*, April 19, 1888, 1.
66. "The Great Cryptogram," *The Times* (London), May 2, 1888, 15.
67. "Mr. Donnelly's Book," *Daily News* (London), June 23, 1888, 3.

68. "The 'Great Cryptogram' at the Universities," *Pall Mall Gazette* (London), September 5, 1888, 12.

69. "Just as Hopeful as Ever," *New York Times*, June 14, 1891, 13.

70. "Donnelly Strikes Back," *Irish Standard* (Minneapolis), June 23, 1888, 1.

71. "Donnelly Strikes Back," 1.

72. J. Gilpin Pyle, *The Little Cryptogram: A Literal Application to the Play of "Hamlet" of the Cipher System of Mr. Ignatius Donnelly* (St. Paul: Pioneer Press, 1888), 5.

73. Pyle, *Little Cryptogram*, 21.

74. Pyle, *Little Cryptogram*, 26.

75. Pyle, *Little Cryptogram*, 28.

76. Pyle, *Little Cryptogram*, 29.

77. "Something about Plutocracy and the Author of 'Caesar's Column,'" *Great West* (St. Paul), September 11, 1891, 2.

78. Aldwell Nicholson, *No Cipher in Shakespeare: Being a Refutation of the Honorable Ignatius Donnelly's "Great Cryptogram"* (London: T. F. Unwin, 1888), 5.

79. Nicholson, *No Cipher in Shakespeare*, 35.

80. Nicholson, *No Cipher in Shakespeare*, 11.

81. Nicholson, *No Cipher in Shakespeare*, 10.

82. Nicholson, *No Cipher in Shakespeare*, 60.

83. Nicholson, *No Cipher in Shakespeare*, 64.

84. David Kahn, *The Code Breakers: The Comprehensive History of Secret Communication from Ancient Times to the Internet* (New York: Scribner, 1996), 877. Google Books.

85. Morgan, *Shakespearean Myth*, 38.

86. Appleton Morgan, *Shakespeare in Fact and in Criticism*, 2nd ed. (New York: William Evarts Benjamin, 1888), 302–3.

87. Morgan, *Shakespeare in Fact*, vii.

88. J. H. Beadle, "Ignatius Donnelly's Book Issued at Last," *Daily Republican* (Winona, MN), May 12, 1888, 4.

89. Ignatius Donnelly, diary entry, July 15, 1888, Donnelly MSS.

90. Ignatius Donnelly, diary entry, July 15, 1888, Donnelly MSS.

91. Ridge, *Ignatius Donnelly*, 241.

92. Ignatius Donnelly to Kate Donnelly, May 4, 1888, Donnelly MSS.

93. Ignatius Donnelly to Kate Donnelly, August 2, 1888, Donnelly MSS.

94. Ridge, *Ignatius Donnelly*, 242.

95. Ignatius Donnelly, diary entry, May 18, 1892, Donnelly MSS.

96. Ignatius Donnelly, diary entry, December 22, 1892, Donnelly MSS.

97. Quoted in Fish, *Donnelliana*, 111.

98. "Some Great Men in Chicago," *The Sun* (New York, NY), May 23, 1891, 6.

99. Ignatius Donnelly, diary entry, April 28, 1891, Donnelly MSS.

100. Ridge, *Ignatius Donnelly*, 258.

101. Ignatius Donnelly to John Lind, September 23, 1888, Donnelly MSS.

102. Ridge, *Ignatius Donnelly*, 260.

103. Ridge, *Ignatius Donnelly*, 261.

6. *Caesar's Column*

1. Martin Ridge, *Ignatius Donnelly: The Portrait of a Politician* (Chicago: University of Chicago Press, 1962), 260–61.

2. David D. Anderson, *Ignatius Donnelly* (Boston: G. K. Hall, 1980), 67.

3. Frederic C. Jaher, *Doubters and Dissenters: Cataclysmic Thought in America, 1885–1918* (New York: Free Press of Glencoe, 1964), 116, 119.

4. Anderson, *Ignatius Donnelly*, 69.

5. A. C. McClurg to Ignatius Donnelly, December 30, 1899, Donnelly MSS, Minnesota Historical Society, St. Paul.

6. Ignatius Donnelly to A. C. McClurg, December 31, 1899, Donnelly MSS.

7. "Something about Plutocracy,'" *Great West* (St. Paul), September 11, 1891, 2.

8. W. C. Bronaugh, *The Youngers' Fight for Freedom* (Columbia, MO: E. W. Stephens, 1906), 96.

9. Bronaugh, *Youngers' Fight for Freedom*, 97.

10. Bronaugh, *Youngers' Fight for Freedom*, 105.

11. Bronaugh, *Youngers' Fight for Freedom*, 106.

12. Ridge, *Ignatius Donnelly*, 267.

13. "Caesar's Column," *Great West* (St. Paul), May 8, 1890, 8.

14. "Caesar's Column," *Great West* (St. Paul), June 20, 1890, 2.

15. "Caesar's Column, Who Wrote This Remarkable Book?," *Great West* (St. Paul), October 3, 1890, 5.

16. *Princeton (MN) Union*, December 25, 1890, 5.

17. "Caesar's Column," *Saturday Evening Kansas Commoner* (Wichita), December 11, 1890, 4.

18. *Burrton (KS) Graphic*, January 17, 1891, 4.

19. "Caesar's Column," *Wessington Springs (SD) Herald*, March 13, 1891, 1.

20. "Caesar's Column," *St. Paul Daily Globe*, November 30, 1890, 4.

21. "Something about Plutocracy," 2.

22. "Caesar's Column," *Great West* (St. Paul), December 11, 1890, 3.

23. Ignatius Donnelly, *Caesar's Column: A Story of the Twentieth Century* (Chicago: F. J. Schulte, 1890), 3.

24. Robert Bannister, *Social Darwinism: Science and Myth in Anglo-American Thought* (Philadelphia: Temple University Press, 2010), 215.

25. Donnelly, *Caesar's Column*, 5.

26. Donnelly, *Caesar's Column*, 4.

27. Donnelly, *Caesar's Column*, 16.

28. Steven Trimble and Donald E. Winters, "*Caesar's Column* and *Nineteen Eighty-Four*," *Minnesota History*, Fall 1984, 110.

29. Donnelly, *Caesar's Column*, 22.

30. Allan M. Axelrad, "Ideology and Utopia in the Works of Ignatius Donnelly," *American Studies* 12, no. 2 (Fall 1971): 52.

31. Bannister, *Social Darwinism*, 216.

32. Donnelly, *Caesar's Column*, 37.

33. Donnelly, *Caesar's Column*, 37.

34. Donnelly, *Caesar's Column*, 32.

35. Donnelly, *Caesar's Column*, 32.
36. Donnelly, *Caesar's Column*, 36–41.
37. Donnelly, *Caesar's Column*, 44.
38. Donnelly, *Caesar's Column*, 50.
39. Donnelly, *Caesar's Column*, 285.
40. Donnelly, *Caesar's Column*, 285.
41. Donnelly, *Caesar's Column*, 222.
42. Anderson, *Ignatius Donnelly*, 76.
43. Donnelly, *Caesar's Column*, 319.
44. Donnelly, *Caesar's Column*, 329.
45. Donnelly, *Caesar's Column*, 350.
46. Donnelly, *Caesar's Column*, 355.
47. Donnelly, *Caesar's Column*, 357.
48. Donnelly, *Caesar's Column*, 363.
49. Donnelly, *Caesar's Column*, 366.
50. Donnelly, *Caesar's Column*, 366–67.
51. Axelrad, "Ideology and Utopia," 51.
52. Frank De Witt Talmage, "Talmage Sermon," *Orleans County (VT) Monitor*, May 23, 1904, 6.
53. Ridge, *Ignatius Donnelly*, 265.
54. Ridge, *Ignatius Donnelly*, 269.
55. C. Vann Woodward, "The Populist Heritage and the Intellectual," *American Scholar* 29, no. 1 (Winter 1959–60): 65.
56. Nicholas Ruddick, introduction to *Caesar's Column: A Story of the Twentieth Century*, by Ignatius Donnelly (Middletown, CT: Wesleyan University Press, 2003), xxv.
57. Ruddick, introduction, xxvii.
58. Ruddick, introduction, xxviii.
59. *St. Paul Pioneer Press*, March 5, 1890, quoted in Ridge, *Ignatius Donnelly*, 270.
60. Ignatius Donnelly to R. J. Hall, May 28, 1890, Donnelly MSS.
61. "The Sage and the Tall Pine," *The Sun* (New York, NY), July 22, 1890, 4.
62. "Sage and the Tall Pine," 4.
63. "Sage and the Tall Pine," 4.
64. Ridge, *Ignatius Donnelly*, 274.
65. Ridge, *Ignatius Donnelly*, 275.
66. Ignatius Donnelly, diary entry, September 18, 1890, Donnelly MSS.
67. Ignatius Donnelly, "Circular from Mr. Donnelly," *Great West* (St. Paul), December 5, 1890, 1.
68. Ignatius Donnelly, diary entry, September 18, 1890, Donnelly MSS.
69. "Donnelly vs. Harmony," *Great West* (St. Paul), January 16, 1891, 4.
70. "Not a Safe Man," *Great West* (St. Paul), January 16, 1891, 4.
71. Kenneth M. Roemer, *The Obsolete Necessity: America in Utopian Writings, 1888–1900* (Kent, OH: Kent State University Press, 1976), 3–4.
72. "Something about Plutocracy," 2.
73. Trimble and Winters, "*Caesar's Column*," 109.
74. "Ignatius Donnelly," *National Field* (Salina, KS), 8.
75. "Ignatius Donnelly," *National Field* (Salina, KS), 8.

7. *Doctor Huguet*

1. *New Ulm (MN) Weekly Review*, January 7, 1891, 4.
2. "Donnelly and the Republicans," *St. Paul Globe*, January 10, 1891, 4.
3. Martin Ridge, *Ignatius Donnelly: The Portrait of a Politician* (Chicago: University of Chicago Press, 1962), 285.
4. Ridge, *Ignatius Donnelly*, 285.
5. Ridge, *Ignatius Donnelly*, 286.
6. Ridge, *Ignatius Donnelly*, 287.
7. *Kansas City Star*, May 23, 1891, quoted in Ridge, *Ignatius Donnelly*, 287.
8. "Donnelly and the Cincinnati Meeting," *Great West* (St. Paul), June 5, 1891, 5.
9. Ridge, *Ignatius Donnelly*, 288.
10. "Just as Hopeful as Ever," *New York Times*, June 14, 1891, 13.
11. *Daily American* (Nashville, TN), August 18, 1891, 4.
12. John R. Bovee, "*Doctor Huguet*: Donnelly on Being Black," *Minnesota History*, Summer 1969, 288.
13. Ignatius Donnelly, *Doctor Huguet: A Novel* (Chicago: F. J. Schulte, 1891), 8.
14. Donnelly, *Doctor Huguet*, 9.
15. Donnelly, *Doctor Huguet*, 11.
16. Donnelly, *Doctor Huguet*, 12.
17. Donnelly, *Doctor Huguet*, 61.
18. Donnelly, *Doctor Huguet*, 60.
19. Donnelly, *Doctor Huguet*, 72.
20. Donnelly, *Doctor Huguet*, 73.
21. Bovee, "*Doctor Huguet*," 289.
22. Donnelly, *Doctor Huguet*, 288.
23. Donnelly, *Doctor Huguet*, 289.
24. Donnelly, *Doctor Huguet*, 290.
25. Donnelly, *Doctor Huguet*, 86.
26. Ridge, *Ignatius Donnelly*, 289.
27. *Book News: An Illustrated Magazine of Literature and Books*, October 1891, 86.
28. F. J. Schulte to Ignatius Donnelly, September 8, 1891 Donnelly MSS, Minnesota Historical Society, St. Paul
29. Bovee, "*Doctor Huguet*," 287.
30. Bovee, "*Doctor Huguet*," 290.
31. *Daily American* (Nashville, TN), August 18, 1891, 4.
32. *The Appeal* (St. Paul, MN), October 3, 1891, 2.
33. Barton Aylesworth to Ignatius Donnelly, February 4, 1892, Donnelly MSS.
34. J. H. Smith to Ignatius Donnelly, March 29, 1892, Donnelly MSS.
35. "Libel Suit against a Liar," *St. Paul Daily Globe*, October 17, 1884, 4.
36. Ridge, *Ignatius Donnelly*, 291.
37. Ridge, *Ignatius Donnelly*, 188–89.
38. "1$," *St. Paul Sunday Globe*, October 25, 1891, 1.
39. "1$," 1.

40. Ridge, *Ignatius Donnelly*, 291.

41. "1$," 1.

42. Quoted in "Donnelly's Verdict," *Anaconda (MT) Standard*, October 28, 1891, 2.

43. Ridge, *Ignatius Donnelly*, 292.

44. Quoted in "Donnelly's Verdict," *Anaconda (MT) Standard*, October 28, 1891, 2.

45. Quoted in "Donnelly's Verdict," *Anaconda (MT) Standard*, October 28, 1891, 2.

46. "1$," 1.

47. Ridge, *Ignatius Donnelly*, 292.

48. Ignatius Donnelly, diary entry, November 3, 1891, Donnelly MSS.

49. "Address of Hon. Ignatius Donnelly, President of the State Alliance, before the Annual Meeting," *Great West* (St. Paul), January 8, 1892, 5.

50. "A Card from Ignatius Donnelly," *The Sun* (New York, NY), December 3, 1891, 6.

51. "Ignatius Is Here," *Great West* (St. Paul), December 11, 1891, 2.

52. "Address of Hon. Ignatius Donnelly," 5.

53. Ridge, *Ignatius Donnelly*, 295.

54. Ridge, *Ignatius Donnelly*, 286.

55. "Victory!," *Great West* (St. Paul), February 26, 1892, 1.

56. Quoted in John D. Hicks, *The Populist Revolt: A History of the Farmers' Alliance and the Populist Party* (Minneapolis: University of Minnesota Press, 1931), 439.

57. John D. Hicks, "The Birth of the Populist Party," *Minnesota History*, September 1928, 242.

58. "Great St. Louis Conference," *Southern Mercury*, March 3, 1892, 9.

59. Michael Kazin, *The Populist Persuasion: An American History*, rev. ed. (Ithaca, NY: Cornell University Press, 2017), 28.

60. Kazin, *Populist Persuasion*, 29.

61. Kazin, *Populist Persuasion*, 31.

62. "Alliance Hosts," *The Chilton View* (Clanton, AL), March 3, 1892, 1.

63. Ridge, *Ignatius Donnelly*, 297.

64. "Mr. Donnelly Replies to Mr. Hompe," *Great West* (St. Paul), April 8, 1892, 2.

65. Carl. H. Chrislock, "The Alliance Party and the Minnesota Legislature," *Minnesota History*, September 1957, 306.

66. "Mr. Donnelly Replies to Mr. Hompe," *Great West* (St. Paul), April 8, 1892, 2.

67. American Presidency Project, "Populist Party Platform of 1892," accessed November 2, 2022, https://www.presidency.ucsb.edu/documents/populist-party-platform-1892.

68. Ridge, *Ignatius Donnelly*, 301.

69. "The Reformers," *St. Louis Globe-Democrat*, February 21, 1892, 11.

70. Ridge, *Ignatius Donnelly*, 299.

71. "The Sage Considered," *St. Paul Daily Globe*, July 24, 1892, 4.

72. Ridge, *Ignatius Donnelly*, 303.

73. "Mr. Donnelly Enters the Field," *Great West* (St. Paul), June 17, 1892, 8.

74. "A Bloody Battle," *Great West* (St. Paul), July 15, 1892, 1.

8. *The Golden Bottle*

1. Ignatius Donnelly, *The Golden Bottle* (New York: D. D. Merrill, 1892), 3.
2. Donnelly, *Golden Bottle*, 4.
3. Donnelly, *Golden Bottle*, 29.
4. Donnelly, *Golden Bottle*, 106–7.
5. Donnelly, *Golden Bottle*, 131.
6. Donnelly, *Golden Bottle*, 145.
7. Donnelly, *Golden Bottle*, 146.
8. Donnelly, *Golden Bottle*, 149.
9. Donnelly, *Golden Bottle*, 195.
10. Donnelly, *Golden Bottle*, 196.
11. Donnelly, *Golden Bottle*, 206.
12. Donnelly, *Golden Bottle*, 206.
13. Donnelly, *Golden Bottle*, 217.
14. Donnelly, *Golden Bottle*, 275.
15. Donnelly, *Golden Bottle*, 276.
16. Donnelly, *Golden Bottle*, 292.
17. Donnelly, *Golden Bottle*, 312.
18. Donnelly, *Golden Bottle*, 313.
19. Ignatius Donnelly, diary entry, November 3, 1892, Donnelly MSS, Minnesota Historical Society, St. Paul.
20. *Western Advocate* (Mankato, KS), April 1, 1892, 4.
21. Quoted in *Great West* (St. Paul), November 4, 1892, 7.
22. "The Golden Bottle," *The Citizen* (Howard, KS), October 12, 1892, 6.
23. Ignatius Donnelly, diary entry, November 10, 1892, Donnelly MSS.
24. "The Golden Bottle," *Great West* (St. Paul), January 13, 1893, 8.
25. "The Golden Bottle," *The Representative* (Minnesota), April 19, 1893, 7.
26. Nicholas Ruddick, introduction to *Caesar's Column: A Story of the Twentieth Century*, by Ignatius Donnelly (Middletown, CT: Wesleyan University Press, 2003), xxiv.
27. Ignatius Donnelly, diary entry, November 10, 1892.

9. *Donnelliana* and *The American People's Money*

1. *St. Paul Pioneer Press*, December 16, 1892, quoted in Martin Ridge, *Ignatius Donnelly: The Portrait of a Politician* (Chicago: University of Chicago Press, 1962), 311.
2. Ridge, *Ignatius Donnelly*, 312.
3. *St. Paul Daily Globe*, "After a Combine," March 24, 1893, 1.
4. *Minneapolis Tribune*, April 12, 1893, 2.
5. Ridge, *Ignatius Donnelly*, 316.
6. Ignatius Donnelly, *Report of the Pine Land Investigating Committee to the Governor of Minnesota, Filed with the Governor December 21, 1894* (St. Paul: Pioneer Press Printing, 1895), 86.

7. "Biography of Gov. Donnelly,'" *Great West* (St. Paul), September 11, 1891, 2.

8. Everett W. Fish, *Donnelliana: An Appendix to "Caesar's Column"* (Chicago: F. J. Schulte, 1892), 5.

9. Fish, *Donnelliana*, 134.

10. Fish, *Donnelliana*, 144.

11. Fish, *Donnelliana*, "Part Second," 3.

12. Fish, *Donnelliana*, 137.

13. Ridge, *Ignatius Donnelly*, 319.

14. "Deep, Dark Donnelly," *Great West* (St. Paul), May 26, 1893, 5.

15. Ridge, *Ignatius Donnelly*, 320.

16. Fish, *Donnelliana*, 134.

17. Fish, *Donnelliana*, 134.

18. Fish, *Donnelliana*, 7.

19. "The Culminating Outrage," *Great West* (St. Paul), January 12, 1894, 1.

20. "Deep, Dark Donnelly," 5.

21. "Ignatius Donnelly's Claim," *Times Leader* (Wilkes-Barre, PA), February 18, 1881, 2.

22. "The Attempted Butchery," *Great West* (St. Paul), January 12, 1894, 1.

23. "Fish Flayed Alive," *Minneapolis Tribune*, January 12, 1894, 1.

24. "Mrs. Donnelly's Funeral," *St. Paul Daily Globe*, June 28, 1894, 8.

25. Gretchen Kreuter, "Kate Donnelly versus the Cult of True Womanhood," in *Women of Minnesota: Selected Biographical Essays*, rev. ed., ed. Barbara Stuhler and Gretchen Kreuter (St. Paul: Minnesota Historical Society Press, 1998), 20.

26. Kreuter, "Kate Donnelly," 24.

27. "The Danger of Private Conversations with Men Who Are Not Gentlemen," *The Representative* (Minneapolis), January 26, 1898, 1.

28. Ridge, *Ignatius Donnelly*, 331.

29. "Donnelly at the Lyceum," *Irish Standard* (Minneapolis), March 10, 1894, 5.

30. *St. Paul Pioneer Press*, April 12, 1894, quoted in Ridge, *Ignatius Donnelly*, 331.

31. "A.P.A. Question," *The Representative* (St. Paul), May 9, 1894, 4.

32. Ridge, *Ignatius Donnelly*, 334.

33. "First in the Field," *The Representative* (St. Paul), July 11, 1894, 5.

34. Ridge, *Ignatius Donnelly*, 338.

35. "Danger Ahead," *The Representative* (St. Paul), March 28, 1894.

36. Michael S. Sweeney, "The Desire for the Sensational: Coxey's Army and the Argus-Eyed Demons from Hell," *Journalism History* 23, no. 3 (Autumn 1997): 114.

37. Sweeney, "Desire for the Sensational," 114.

38. "Coxey's Army a Portent," *The Representative* (St. Paul), April 4, 1894, 1.

39. "The March on Washington," *The Representative* (St. Paul), April 18, 1894, 1.

40. "Bullets or Ballots?," *The Representative* (St. Paul), May 9, 1894, 1.

41. "Minnesota Historical Election Archive," accessed November 5, 2022, https://mn.electionarchives.lib.umn.edu/search/.

42. *St. Paul Pioneer Press*, November 8, 1894, quoted in Ridge, *Ignatius Donnelly*, 339.

43. *St. Paul Pioneer Press*, October 2, 1894, quoted in Ridge, *Ignatius Donnelly*, 338.

44. "A Word Personal," *The Representative* (St. Paul), November 7, 1894, 1.

45. *St. Paul Pioneer Press*, November 30, 1894, quoted in Ridge, *Ignatius Donnelly*, 340.

46. "A Word of Advice," *The Representative* (St. Paul), December 19, 1894, 1.

47. "Woman's Suffrage," *The Representative* (St. Paul), February 13, 1895, 1.

48. "Stand Together and Act Wisely," *The Representative* (St. Paul), September 4, 1895, 4.

49. Ignatius Donnelly, *The Bryan Campaign for the American People's Money* (Chicago: Laird & Lee, 1896), 11.

50. Donnelly, *Bryan Campaign*, 37.

51. Donnelly, *Bryan Campaign*, 52.

52. Donnelly, *Bryan Campaign*, 101.

53. Donnelly, *Bryan Campaign*, 102.

54. Donnelly, *Bryan Campaign*, 104.

55. Donnelly, *Bryan Campaign*, 184.

56. Donnelly, *Bryan Campaign*, 186.

57. Ridge, *Ignatius Donnelly*, 346.

58. Quoted in James Anderson Barnes, *John G. Carlisle, Financial Statesman* (New York: Dodd Mead, 1967), 449.

59. Quoted in Barnes, *John G. Carlisle*, 452.

60. Richard Hofstadter, *The Paranoid Style in American Politics* (New York: Vintage Books, 2008), 242.

61. Ridge, *Ignatius Donnelly*, 360.

62. Ridge, *Ignatius Donnelly*, 362.

63. Ignatius Donnelly, diary entry, November 6, 1896, Donnelly MSS, Minnesota Historical Society, St. Paul.

64. "Ourself," *The Representative* (Minneapolis), November 4, 1896, 2.

65. "Many Thanks," *The Representative* (Minneapolis), November 11, 1896, 2.

66. "Sage and Judge Cross Swords!," *Minneapolis Tribune*, January 17, 1897, 5.

67. "Sage and Judge Cross Swords!," 5.

68. All sources quoted in "Opinions of Donnelly," *St. Paul Globe*, February 7, 1887, 4.

69. Quoted in "Opinions of Donnelly," 4.

70. "Ignatius Donnelly," *St. Paul Daily Globe*, March 7, 1887, 4.

71. Ridge, *Ignatius Donnelly*, 371.

72. *The Representative* (Minneapolis), June 30, 1897, 2.

73. Ignatius Donnelly, diary entry, December 18, 1897, Donnelly MSS.

74. "Donnelly to Marry," *Superior (WI) Times*, January 8, 1898, 1.

75. "Sage of Nininger," *Dayton (OH) Herald*, January 28, 1898, 1.

76. "Wise Wooing of a Sage," *Free Press* (Osage City, KS), January 12, 1898, 4.

77. "A Populist Fusion," *Salt Lake (UT) Tribune*, January 12, 1898, 4.

78. "May–December," *Minneapolis Tribune*, January 5, 1898, 2.

79. "It Must Be True," *The Representative* (Minneapolis), January 5, 1898, 2.

80. "It Must Be True," 2.
81. Ignatius Donnelly, diary entry, December 18, 1897, Donnelly MSS.
82. "George Giltinan Dead," *St. Paul Daily Globe*, July 24, 1898, 10.

10. *The Cipher in the Plays, and on the Tombstone*

1. "May–December," *Minneapolis Tribune*, January 5, 1898, 2.
2. "Donnelly's Cipher Again," *The Representative* (Minneapolis), November 9, 1899, 4.
3. Hugh Black, "Bacon's Claim and Shakespeare's 'Aye,'" *North American Review* 145, no. 371 (October 1887): 28.
4. Ignatius Donnelly, *The Cipher in the Plays, and on the Tombstone* (Minneapolis: Verulam, 1899) 11.
5. Donnelly, *Cipher in the Plays*, 11.
6. Donnelly, *Cipher in the Plays*, 83.
7. Martin Ridge, *Ignatius Donnelly: The Portrait of a Politician* (Chicago: University of Chicago Press, 1962), 393.
8. Donnelly, *Cipher in the Plays*, 4.
9. Donnelly, *Cipher in the Plays*, 363.
10. Donnelly, *Cipher in the Plays*, 365.
11. Donnelly, *Cipher in the Plays*, 371.
12. "Donnelly's Cipher Again," 4.
13. "Ignatius Donnelly Discusses His New Book," *The Representative* (Minneapolis), December 28, 1899, 3.
14. *The Era* (London), July 7, 1900, 10.
15. "Ignatius Donnelly Discusses His New Book," 3.
16. T. C. Mendenhall, "A Mechanical Solution of a Literary Problem," *Popular Science Monthly*, December 1901, 102–3.
17. Mendenhall, "Mechanical Solution," 105.
18. "The Result," *The Representative* (Minneapolis), September 14, 1898, 2.
19. "Donnelly and 1892," *The Representative* (Minneapolis), January 16, 1891, 4.
20. Ridge, *Ignatius Donnelly*, 395.
21. Ridge, *Ignatius Donnelly*, 398.
22. "An Iconoclast's Life Work," *Kansas City Star*, April 22, 1900, 24.
23. "The Presidential Campaign," *The Standard* (London), May 11, 1900, 5.
24. Ridge, *Ignatius Donnelly*, 399.
25. Ignatius Donnelly, diary entry, November 3, 1900, Donnelly MSS, Minnesota Historical Society, St. Paul.
26. "Her Life Is in Danger," *Minneapolis Tribune*, January 3, 1901, 2.
27. "A Famous Man Called Home," *Minneapolis Journal*, January 2, 1901, 1.
28. "Ignatius Donnelly Loved and Admired by All," *Minneapolis Tribune*, January 3, 1901, 2.
29. "Ignatius Donnelly Is Dead," *Irish Standard* (Minneapolis), January 5, 1901, 4.
30. Reproduced in "In Memoriam," *The Representative* (Minneapolis), January 17, 1901, 1.

31. "Died at the Dawn of the Century," *Anaconda (MT) Standard*, January 2, 1901, 1.

32. "Gentle Slumber," *The Representative* (Minneapolis), January 17, 1901, 3.

33. Arthur James Pegler, "Some Stories of Ignatius Donnelly," *Minneapolis Tribune*, January 6, 1901, 20.

34. "Books and Bookmen," *The Guardian* (London), January 5, 1901, 4.

35. *Daily Capital* (Topeka), January 5, 1901, 4.

36. "Ignatius Donnelly," *Willmar (MN) Tribune*, January 9, 1901, 4.

37. George Smalley, "Leaves from a Reporter's Notebook," *Arizona Daily Citizen*, January 3, 1901, 4.

38. Smalley, "Leaves," 4.

39. Smalley, "Leaves," 4.

40. Pegler, "Some Stories," 20.

41. "In Memoriam," 1.

42. "In Ignatius Donnelly's Library," *St. Paul Daily Globe*, June 23, 1901, 14.

43. "In Ignatius Donnelly's Library," 14.

44. "Sage and Judge Cross Swords!," *Minneapolis Tribune*, January 17, 1897, 5.

45. Ignatius Donnelly, *Doctor Huguet: A Novel* (Chicago: F. J. Schulte, 1891), 66.

Selected Bibliography

The selected bibliography that follows highlights the book- and article-length sources that proved most instrumental in the construction of this book, including by design many publications from Ignatius Donnelly's dynamic era. Together they suggest the true interdisciplinary breadth of Donnelly's strange genius, which spanned such disparate disciplines as theology, geology, archaeology, anthropology, mythology, populism and politics, cryptography, classical civilizations, speculative and dystopian fictions, literary history, economics and monetary policy, and countless others. To follow the trail of the Sage of Nininger has been a formidable, if not deeply instructive, challenge to my own committed interdisciplinarity. Not included in this selective listing are hundreds of smaller articles and ephemera originally published in newspapers and magazines read in service to this book. Readers will find the vast majority of these animating periodicals cited in the endnotes. Of special note among the many titles that follow is Martin Ridge's *Ignatius Donnelly: The Portrait of a Politician*, a book that has served as the guiding text for Donnelly scholars since its publication in 1962.

Agassiz, Elizabeth Cary, ed. *Louis Agassiz: His Life and Correspondence*. Boston: Houghton, Mifflin, 1885.

Anderson, David D. *Ignatius Donnelly*. Boston: G. K. Hall, 1980.

Ashton, Susanna. "Who Brings Home the Bacon? Shakespeare and Turn-of-the-Century American Authorship." *American Periodicals* 6 (1996): 1–28.

Axelrad, Allan M. "Ideology and Utopia in the Works of Ignatius Donnelly." *American Studies* 12, no. 2 (Fall 1971): 47–65.

Bacon, Delia. "William Shakespeare and His Plays: An Inquiry concerning Them." *Putnam's Monthly Magazine*, January 1856. https://www.bartleby.com/400/prose/1296.html.

Bacon, Francis. *The Works of Francis Bacon*. London: M. Jones, 1815.

Bailly, Jean Sylvain. *Lettres sur l'Atlantide de Platon et sur l'ancienne histoire de l'Asie*. Paris: Frères Debure, 1779.

Bannister, Robert. *Social Darwinism: Science and Myth in Anglo-American Thought*. Philadelphia: Temple University Press, 2010.

Barnes, James Anderson. *John G. Carlisle, Financial Statesman*. New York: Dodd Mead, 1967.

Black, Hugh. "Bacon's Claim and Shakespeare's 'Aye.'" *North American Review* 145, no. 371 (October 1887): 422–34.

Bovee, John R. "*Doctor Huguet*: Donnelly on Being Black." *Minnesota History*, Summer 1969.

Boyd, James P., ed. *Men and Issues of 1900*. N.p.: P. W. Ziegler, 1900.

Brasseur de Bourbourg, Charles Étienne. *Quatre lettres sur le Mexique*. Paris: Auguste Durand et Pedone, 1868.

Bronaugh, W. C. *The Youngers' Fight for Freedom*. Columbia, MO: E. W. Stephens, 1906.

Chrislock, Carl H. "The Alliance Party and the Minnesota Legislature." *Minnesota History*, September 1957.

Clarke, Barry R. *Francis Bacon's Contribution to Shakespeare: A New Attribution Method*. New York: Routledge, 2019.

Clarke, James Freeman. "Did Shakespeare Write Bacon's Work?" *North American Review* 132, no. 291 (February 1881): 163–75.

Cook, James W. *The Arts of Deception: Playing with Fraud in the Age of Barnum*. Cambridge, MA: Harvard University Press, 2001.

Cusack, Tricia, ed. *Framing the Ocean, 1700 to the Present: Envisaging the Sea as Social Space*. London: Routledge, 2014.

Donnelly, Ignatius. *Atlantis: The Antediluvian World*. New York: Harper & Brothers, 1882.

Donnelly, Ignatius. *The Bryan Campaign for the American People's Money*. Chicago: Laird & Lee, 1896.

Donnelly, Ignatius. *Caesar's Column: A Story of the Twentieth Century*. Chicago: F. J. Schulte, 1890.

Donnelly, Ignatius. *The Cipher in the Plays, and on the Tombstone*. Minneapolis: Verulam, 1899.

Donnelly, Ignatius. *Doctor Huguet: A Novel*. Chicago: F. J. Schulte, 1891.

Donnelly, Ignatius. Donnelly Manuscript Collection. Minnesota Historical Society, St. Paul.

Donnelly, Ignatius. *The Golden Bottle*. New York: D. D. Merrill, 1892.

Donnelly, Ignatius. *The Great Cryptogram: Francis Bacon's Cipher in the So-Called Shakespeare Plays*. Chicago: R. S. Peale, 1888.

Donnelly, Ignatius. *Ragnarok: The Age of Fire and Gravel*. New York: D. Appleton, 1883.

Donnelly, Ignatius. *Report of the Pine Land Investigating Committee to the Governor of Minnesota, Filed with the Governor December 21, 1894*. St. Paul, MN: Pioneer Press Printing, 1895.

Donnelly, Ignatius. "The Shakespeare Myth." *North American Review* 145 (July 1887): 57–68.

Durden, Robert F. *The Climax of Populism: The Election of 1896* (Lexington: University Press of Kentucky, 1965.

"Editor's Literary Record." *Harper's Monthly*, May 1882.

Enberg, George B. "The Knights of Labor in Minnesota." *Minnesota History*, December 1941.

Fish, Everett W. *Donnelliana: An Appendix to "Caesar's Column."* Chicago: F. J. Schulte, 1892.

Folwell, William Watts. *A History of Minnesota*. Vol. 2. St. Paul: Minnesota Historical Society, 1924.

Hall, Harlan Page. *H. P. Hall's Observations: Being More or Less a History of Political Contests in Minnesota, from 1849 to 1904*. St. Paul: n.p., 1904.

Harvey, William Hope. *Coin's Financial School*. Chicago: Coin, 1894.

Hicks, John D. "The Birth of the Populist Party." *Minnesota History*, September 1928, 219–47.

Hicks, John D. "The Political Career of Ignatius Donnelly." *Mississippi Valley Historical Review* 8, no. 1/2 (June–September 1921): 80–132.

Hicks, John D. *The Populist Revolt: A History of the Farmers' Alliance and the Populist Party*. Minneapolis: University of Minnesota Press, 1931.

Hofstadter, Richard. *The Paranoid Style in American Politics*. New York: Vintage Books, 2008.

Huxley, Thomas Henry. "The Problems of the Deep Sea." *Popular Science Monthly*, May 1873.

Jaher, Frederic C. *Doubters and Dissenters: Cataclysmic Thought in America, 1885–1918*. New York: Free Press of Glencoe, 1964.

Julian, George Washington. *Political Recollections, 1840–1872*. Chicago: Jansen, McClurg, 1884.

Kahn, David. *The Code Breakers: The Comprehensive History of Secret Communication from Ancient Times to the Internet*. New York: Scribner, 1996. Google Books.

Kazin, Michael. *The Populist Persuasion: An American History*. Rev. ed. Ithaca, NY: Cornell University Press, 2017.

Knight, Charles. *William Shakespeare: A Biography*. Rev. ed. London: Virtue, 1865.

Le Plongeon, Augustus. *Queen Moo and the Egyptian Sphinx*. London: Keegan Paul, Trench, Trubner, 1896.

Love, Robertus. *The Rise and Fall of Jesse James*. New York: Blue Ribbon Books, 1940.

Mendenhall, T. C. "A Mechanical Solution of a Literary Problem." *Popular Science Monthly*, December 1901.

Morgan, Appleton. *Shakespeare in Fact and in Criticism*. 2nd ed. New York: William Evarts Benjamin, 1888.

Morgan, Appleton. *The Shakespearean Myth: William Shakespeare and Circumstantial Evidence*. Cincinnati: Robert Clarke, 1881.

Nicholson, Aldwell. *No Cipher in Shakespeare: Being a Refutation of the Honorable Ignatius Donnelly's "Great Cryptogram."* London: T. F. Unwin, 1888.

Pyle, Joseph Gilpin. *The Little Cryptogram: A Literal Application to the Play of "Hamlet" of the Cipher System of Mr. Ignatius Donnelly*. St. Paul, MN: Pioneer Press, 1888.

Report on the Scientific Results of the Voyage of H.M.S. Challenger during the Years 1873–76 under the Command of Captain George S. Nares . . . and the Late Captain Frank Tourle Thomson, R.N. Edinburgh: Neill, 1895.

Ridge, Martin. *Ignatius Donnelly: The Portrait of a Politician*. Chicago: University of Chicago Press, 1962.

Risjord, Norman K. *A Popular History of Minnesota*. St. Paul: Minnesota Historical Society Press, 2005.

Robertson, John M., ed. *The Philosophical Works of Francis Bacon*. London: George Routledge & Sons, 1905.

Roemer, Kenneth M. *The Obsolete Necessity: America in Utopian Writings, 1888–1900*. Kent, OH: Kent State University Press, 1976.

Ruddick, Nicholas. Introduction to *Caesar's Column: A Story of the Twentieth Century*, by Ignatius Donnelly, xv–xlv. Middletown, CT: Wesleyan University Press, 2003.

Smeaton, William Henry Oliphant. "The Mystery of the Pacific: Easter Island and the Evidences of a Lost Continent." *Westminster Review* 144 (1895): 29–47.

Sweeney, Michael S. "The Desire for the Sensational: Coxey's Army and the Argus-Eyed Demons from Hell." *Journalism History* 23, no. 3 (Autumn 1997): 114–25.

Taylor, Gary, John Jowett, Terri Bourus, and Gabriel Egan, eds. *The New Oxford Shakespeare: Modern Critical Edition*. Oxford: Oxford University Press, 2016.

Thomas, Nathaniel. *The Authorship of Shakespeare*. 3rd ed. New York: Hurd & Houghton, 1875.

Thompson, Ann, and Sasha Roberts, eds. *Women Reading Shakespeare: An Anthology of Criticism*. Manchester: Manchester University Press, 1997.

Thompson, Edward H. "Atlantis Not a Myth." *Popular Science* 15 (1879): 759–64.

Thomson, Charles Wyville. *The Voyage of the* Challenger: *The Atlantic; A Preliminary Account of the General Results of the Exploring Voyage of HMS* Challenger *during the Year 1873 and the Early Part of the Year 1876*. Vol. 2. Cambridge: Cambridge University Press, 2014.

Trimble, Steven, and Donald E. Winters. "*Caesar's Column* and *Nineteen Eighty-Four*." *Minnesota History*, Fall 1984.

US Congress. *Congressional Globe*. Vol. 3. Washington, DC: Blair & Rives, 1868.

Verne, Jules. *Twenty Thousand Leagues under the Sea*. New York: Butler Brothers, 1887.

Wallace, Percy M. "Mr. Donnelly's Shakespeare Cipher." *Nineteenth Century*, May 1886.

Weber, Herbert Y. "The Story of the *St. Paul Globe*." *Minnesota History*, Winter 1965.

Woodward, C. Vann. "The Populist Heritage and the Intellectual." *American Scholar* 29, no. 1 (Winter 1959–60): 55–73.

INDEX

A. C. McClurg publishers, 115, 118–19
Agassiz, Louis, 32, 57, 63
agrarianism, 4, 11, 17, 36, 118, 121, 125–28, 131, 136, 142
Alexandria, Egypt, 46
Alliance Labor Union party, 131–32, 136–37, 152, 167
American People's Money, The, 5, 178, 182–84
Ames, A. A., 65–66, 80
Anti-Monopolist, 21, 23–24
Anti-Monopoly party, 4, 22, 170
antisemitism, 121, 128, 142
APA (American Protective Association), 172–73
Ashton, Susanna, 87–88
Atlantis: The Antediluvian World, 3, 9–10, 26–49, 51–53, 58, 61–65, 67–68, 72, 77, 89–90, 114, 161, 166, 182, 200
Averill, John T., 16
Aylesworth, Burton, 142

Bacon, Delia, 86, 105
Bacon, Francis, 2, 6, 67–69, 74–77, 86–97, 99–100, 102–4, 189–92, 197, 200
Bacon, Nicholas, 94, 96
Baconian authorship theory, 2, 67–69, 74–77, 86–97, 99–100, 102–4, 189–92, 195, 200
Bailly, Jean Sylvain, 43–45
Barker, Wharton, 196–198
Beadle, J. H., 109
Bellamy, Edward, 117–18
bimetalism, 178
Blackstone, T. B., 117
Boen, Haldor, 202
Boisgilbert, Edmund, 5, 116–19
Boston Herald, 152
Brasseur de Bourbourg, Charles Étienne, 39–41
Bronaugh, Warren Carter, 115
Brown, Carl, 175
Bryan Campaign for the American People's Money, 5, 183
Bryan, William Jennings, 183–84, 196–97
Buchanan, John Young, 31
Bunce, O. B., 52, 62, 115

Caesar's Column, 2, 5, 10, 114–135, 138, 142, 147, 150, 153–54, 162–63, 166, 168, 170, 178, 182–83, 200
Caldwell, J. P., 176
Cecil, Robert, 99
Chicago Inter Ocean, 57–58, 111
Chicago Tribune, 37, 53–54, 57, 88
Cincinnati convention, 136–37, 148, 196
Cipher in the Plays and on the Tombstone, The, 3, 10, 191–95
Civil War, 16, 82, 115–16, 140, 144, 149, 174
Clarke, Barry R., 2
Cleveland, Grover, 73, 173, 186
Coin's Financial School, 182–83
Colbert, Elias, 88
comet impact theory, 1, 6, 50–61, 66
Cox, Eugene St. Julien, 79
Coxey, Jacob, 173–75
Coxey's Army, 173–75
Critias, 31, 43

D. Appleton & Company, 52–53, 62, 115
Daggett, Frank, 21
Dakota County, Minnesota, 113, 168, 175–76, 184–85
Darwin, Charles, 38, 63
Darwinism, 119, 178
Davidson, Thomas, 87–88
De Augmentis Scientarium, 68, 92, 192
Debs, Eugene, 174

Declaration of Independence, 149, 151
Democratic-Alliance Labor Union party, 69, 132
Democratic party, 15–17, 20–24, 69, 71–73, 78–80, 112–14, 132, 135, 138, 147, 149, 151, 157, 170–71, 176, 183–84, 187, 196–98.
Diodorus of Sicily, 43
Doctor Huguet, 5, 135–42, 154, 162, 166–67, 182, 200, 203
Donnelliana, 1, 3, 166–69
Donnelly, Ignatius: as Anti-Monopolist 4, 21–24, 69, 79, 132, 151, 164–66, 170; as author of Omaha Platform 3, 150; as candidate for governor of Minnesota 112, 114, 152, 154, 159–61, 164, 167–68, 170–71, 201; as congressman 8, 10–12, 14, 37, 140, 147; as cryptologist 1, 6; death of 198–203; as farmer 14, 16–17, 91, 133; as folk hero 3, 165; as father of Populist party 1, 137, 148; as Greenbacker 22, 24; as humorist 9, 57, 65–66, 149, 186, 201; as lecturer 14, 18, 26, 30, 65, 101, 103–4, 134, 172, 200; as lieutenant governor of Minnesota 1, 7–9, 12, 14, 16, 27–28, 57, 80, 137, 144, 167; marriages of 7–8, 172, 187–92, 197–98, 202; as Mid-Road Populist vice-presidential candidate 1, 3, 9, 146, 195–198; as newspaper editor 4, 19, 167–68, 170, 174–77, 185, 187, 189, 191, 184–95, 197–98, 201; as practicing lawyer 3, 25, 129, 168; as president of Minnesota Farmers' Alliance 132, 135, 146, 148, 150, 171, 177; as pseudonymous novelist 5, 116–19; as public intellectual 9–10, 28; as radical Republican 4, 147; as Shakespeare debunker 1–2, 9, 67–68, 74–78, 86, 91–93, 105, 108, 188, 191–95
Donnelly, Ignatius Carroll, 7, 171, 188, 199
Donnelly, Katharine, 7–8, 13, 20, 37–38, 73, 102, 110, 140, 145, 169 171–72, 188, 190
Donnelly, Marion, 192, 197–98, 202. *See also* Hanson, Marion
Donnelly, Mary, 7, 172, 190, 199
Donnelly, Stanislaus, 7, 112, 187, 199
Doran, Michael, 73, 79–80, 187
dystopian literature, 10, 115, 120, 127, 129, 133

Egyptian civilization, 29, 39, 41, 45–46
Elizabethan Era, 76, 86, 89, 93, 99, 108–9
Emigrant Aid Journal, 19

F. J. Schulte, 116–17, 119, 138, 141–42, 166, 169
fantasy literature, 141, 154, 162–63
Farm Labor party, 112–13
Farmers' Alliance, 69, 79–80, 118, 128–32, 135–38, 146–48, 150, 160–61, 166, 168, 170–71, 177, 196
Field, James. G., 150
First Folio, 67, 69, 74, 84, 94–98, 107–9, 193
Fish, Everett W. 1, 3, 44, 132, 160–61, 166–71
Flandrau, Charles, 143–44, 187
Flower, E. O., 162
Foster, Thomas, 17–19
Freeman, J. C., 111
French Revolution, 129, 158
Fulton, A. R., 47

Garden of Eden, 29, 33–34
Genesis, 28, 34, 55, 125
Gilded Age, 2, 5, 8, 10, 147
Giltinan, George, 7, 167, 169, 190
Gingrich, Newt, 6
glacier theory, 50, 52, 54
Gladstone, William, 35
gold currency, 3, 125, 137, 178, 181, 196
Golden Bottle, The, 5, 154–63, 178, 182–83
Grange, 16, 21
Grant, Ulysses S., 15–16, 18–20
Gray, Asa, 39
Great Cryptogram, The, 3, 10, 85–113, 119, 134, 143, 145, 162, 166, 168, 187, 191, 193, 200
Great West, 115, 117, 119, 132–33, 137, 147–48, 150, 153, 160–62, 166, 169–71, 196
Greeley, Horace, 20–21
Greenback party, 22, 24

Hall, Harlan, 12–14, 24
Hall, R. J. 130, 136
Halvorson, Kittel, 132
Hamlet, 36, 106, 155
Hanson, Marion, 187–91
Harrison, Benjamin, 112
Harper & Brothers, 9, 26, 35–36, 46, 48, 52–53, 115

Harvey, W. H., 182–83
Hastings, Minnesota, 20, 27, 36, 58, 68–69, 80, 172, 198
Hathaway, Anne, 99, 101
Haymarket riot, 129
Henry IV, 69, 74, 84, 90, 95–100
Henry V, 95
Henry VI, 2
Herodotus, 36, 40
Hicks, H. G., 185
Hill, James J., 73, 79–81, 138
Hompe, John, 150
Houghton Mifflin, 115
House of Commons, 104
HMS *Challenger*, 31–32, 34, 39
Huxley, Thomas Henry, 32

India, 42, 44–45
Ireland, 33, 110, 158–59
Irish Standard, 104, 172, 198

James, Frank, 82, 115
James, Jesse, 82, 115
Jefferson, Thomas, 23
Jerusalem, 35, 119
Julian, George W., 12

Kansas City Journal, 65
Kansas City Star, 137, 197
Kazin, Michael, 2–3, 149
Keller, Henry, 165
Kelly, Patrick, 73, 79–80
King James, 94
King, William S., 143–44
Knights of Labor, 79–80, 117, 128, 132

La Follette, Robert M., 6
labor movement, 4, 8, 83, 101, 117–19, 125–26, 129, 131–32, 136, 145, 147–48, 153, 159, 172–73
Laird & Lee publishers, 177, 183
Landis, Kennesaw, 183
Lawler, Daniel, 152, 161
Le Plongeon, Augustus, 45–46
libel suits, 72, 75, 143–46, 167, 169–70, 187, 198
Lincoln, Abraham, 8, 15
Little Cryptogram, The, 106–7, 109
London, 2, 35, 77, 86, 89, 93, 100, 102–3, 107, 110, 142, 194–95, 200
London Daily News, 103–4
London Daily Telegraph, 89, 101–2
London Guardian, 200
London Times, 158
Looking Backward, 117–18
Loucks, H. L., 118
Love, Robertus, 82–83

Maben, C. B., 199
Madeira, 32, 40
Malone, Edmund, 193
Marshall, William R., 82
Marxist literature, 119
Matthew, Tobie, 95
Mayan civilization, 39–41, 45–46
McKinley, William, 184, 186, 196, 198
Medill, Joseph, 88
Merchant of Venice, The, 91
Merrill, D. D., 154
Merry Wives of Windsor, The, 69, 94
Mid-Road Populist party, 4, 196–99
Midsummer Night's Dream, A, 107
Miller, Solomon, 47–48
Minneapolis 17, 36, 65–66, 71, 104, 112, 130, 144, 160–61, 172–73, 189, 198–99, 201
Minneapolis Daily Tribune, 22, 68–69
Minneapolis Journal, 189, 198
Minneapolis Star Tribune, 85
Minneapolis Tribune, 72, 171, 185, 189, 191, 198, 201
Mississippi River, 7, 27–29, 58, 202
Morgan, Appleton, 68, 86, 108
Murray, John, 31
Murray, Matthew Fontaine, 33

Native Americans, 47–48
neanderthal, 60–61
Nelson, Knute, 152–53, 161, 176
New York City, 26, 28, 48–49, 52–53, 58, 75, 88, 115, 120–22, 124–25, 129–30, 137, 142, 146, 154, 157, 196
New York Press, 189
New York Sun, 75, 77, 88–89, 130, 146, 196
New York Times, 30, 34, 58, 137
New York World, 87, 102, 104, 188
Nicholson, Aldwell, 107–8
Nininger City, Minnesota, 1, 7–10, 16–17, 19–20, 25, 27, 36, 38, 48, 58–59, 65, 71–72, 80–81, 85, 87, 123, 150, 161, 167, 172, 186, 188, 198, 201–2
No Cipher in Shakespeare, 107
Norse mythology, 50, 52, 60
North American Review, 84–85, 192–93
Nottidge, Henry Moseley, 31

Omaha convention, 150, 152
Omaha platform, 3
Orwell, George, 120
Owen, Sidney M., 171
Oxford College, 104, 113

Peale, R. S., 85, 88–89, 101, 110–12
People's party, 1, 3, 5, 137–38, 145–48, 150–52, 154, 157–58, 160–61, 167, 170–71, 173–77, 183–84, 195–97, 199, 201
Pegler, Arthur James, 199
Percy, Henry, 100
Philadelphia Evening Bulletin, 152
Philadelphia, 3–4, 7–8, 10, 15, 19, 25–26, 36, 48, 50–51, 59, 130, 152, 155, 157, 167, 168, 172, 190, 196
Philadelphia Press, 50
Phoenician civilization, 29, 34, 41–43, 45
Plato, 29, 31, 33–34, 40–44
Plutarch, 40, 45
Pompeii, 30–31
Popular Science, 32, 40–41, 62, 195
Powderly, T. V., 117
Plutocracy, 3, 128, 133, 147, 149–50, 153, 156, 158, 166, 178
Priest of Sais, 41
Pseudoscience, 9, 41, 51, 61, 63, 65
Pullman strikes, 173–76
Pyle, Joseph Gilpin, 106–7, 109

Queen Elizabeth, 69, 91, 94, 96, 99

race relations, 4, 21, 138–42
Ragnarok, 2, 10, 50–63, 65, 67–68, 77, 89–90, 114–15, 127, 162, 166, 184, 200
Rahilly, Patrick, 131
railroad regulation, 21, 71, 81, 83, 112, 132, 136, 165, 170, 174, 176
Ramsey, Alexander, 8, 11, 14, 16
Rands, Lars M., 79
Reagan, Ronald, 3
Representative, 162, 168, 170, 172–77, 185, 187, 189, 191, 194–98, 201
Republican party, 4, 14–15, 16–23, 66, 71–73, 112, 130, 138, 147, 149, 151, 157, 176, 184
Richard II, 99
Rhodes, John G., 164–65
Ridge, Martin, 3, 225

Sabin, Dwight, 114
Salisbury, Stephen III., 41
Sampson, Low & Co., 103, 142, 193
Schaller, Albert, 175–76
Schulte, F. J., 116–17, 119, 138, 141–42, 166, 169
Scientific American, 38–39
Scribner's, 48, 51
Shakespeare authorship controversy, 1, 9, 67–68, 74–78, 86, 91–93, 105, 108, 188, 191–95
Shakespeare in Fact and in Criticism, 108
Shakespeare, William, 2, 8, 67–68, 74–75, 77–79, 86–111, 186, 189, 192–95, 200
Shylock symbol. 121, 128. *See also* antisemitism
Shakespearean Myth, The, 68, 86, 108
silver currency, 151, 157, 177–78, 181, 202
Sims, Walter, 173
Smalley, George, 201
Smeaton, Henry Oliphant, 32
Social Darwinism, 119, 178
Solon, 39–40, 42, 45
speculative fiction, 1–2, 31, 114, 127, 133, 141, 225
Springer Affair, 25, 72
Springer, William, 25
St. Albans, England, 77, 95, 102, 107, 194
St. Louis convention, 137, 146, 148–50, 199
St. Louis Post Dispatch, 37
St. Paul 13, 17, 22, 26, 28, 36, 48, 58, 66, 71, 73–75, 80, 83, 105, 111, 115, 129, 132–33, 137, 143, 154, 161, 165, 167–68, 170–72, 184, 187, 189, 201
St. Paul Daily Globe, 24, 28, 36, 53, 65, 74–75, 77–78, 171
St. Paul Dispatch, 12, 14, 162, 189
St. Paul Pioneer, 12–14, 18
St. Paul Pioneer Press, 10, 13–14, 22, 27, 63, 72–73, 75, 80, 82, 106–7, 110, 119, 138, 143–46, 164, 167, 170, 173, 176, 187, 198
St. Paul Press, 10, 14
Staples, C. F., 184
Stevens County, Minnesota, 38, 67, 167, 190
Stevens, George, 193
Strait, Horace, 69–71
Stratford-upon-Avon, England, 2, 67, 77, 86–87, 100, 192, 194
Swing, David, 117

Timaeus, 33, 43, 46
Thomas, Francis, 13
Thomas, Nathaniel, 86–87

Thompson, Edward Herbert, 40, 41, 45
Thomson, Charles Wyville, 31–32
Tourgee, Albion, 117
transfiguration, 141–42
Tredwell, Daniel M., 41–42
Trimble, Steven, 120, 133
Trinity College, Cambridge, 104
Troilus and Cressida, 95
Trowbridge, John Townsend, 47
Trump, Donald, 3
Turner, J. H., 161
Twain, Mark, 6, 109
Twenty Thousand Leagues Under the Sea, 30–31

Uganda, 120, 122, 125
U.S.S. *Dolphin*, 32–33, 39
utopian literature, 118, 129, 133

Verne, Jules, 30, 51, 62, 129
Voltaire, 43
voting rights, 3, 20, 112, 139, 151, 158

Washburn, William, D., 11, 23, 25, 65–66, 72, 114, 143, 171
Washburne, Elihu, 10–13, 22–23, 26
Washington, DC, 6, 14, 18, 36, 73–74, 173, 175
Washington Republican, 74
Weaver, James B., 150
Wellington, Cyrus, 143–44
Westminster Abbey, 102
Wilde, Ben, 22
Wilde, Oscar, 102
Willemoes-Suhm, Rudolf von, 31
Wilson, Eugene, 14
Winters, Donald E., 120, 123
women's suffrage, 151, 158. *See also* voting rights

Youmans, E. L., 62
Younger, Bob, 82, 116
Younger, Cole, 82
Youngers' Fight for Freedom, The, 116